Jerusalemites
A Living Memory

Hazem Zaki Nusseibeh

RIMAL PUBLICATIONS

©Hazem Zaki Nusseibeh 2009

The right of Hazem Zaki Nusseibeh to be identified as the author of this work has been asserted by him in accordance with the Copyright, Designs and Patents Act 1988.

All rights reserved

No part of this publication may be reproduced or utilized in any form or by any means electronic or mechanical, including photocopying, recording or any information storage and retrieval system, without permission in writing from publisher.

First published 2009
Rimal Publications
Nicosia
Cyprus

ISBN 978 9963 610 38 9

Rimal Publications, Nicosia
and
Melisende Publishing, London

For information on our publications, visit our website www.rimalbooks.com and for Melisende Publishing, UK, www.melisende.com

Edited by Gerald Butt
Design by Lynn Osman
Printed and bound by Calligraph
Beirut, Lebanon

Table of Contents

	Foreword	5
1	The Beginning	7
2	The Decade of Innocence	17
3	Gathering Storms: A Decade of Turbulence	39
4	The Quiet Before the Storm	49
5	Palestine Vivisected	59
6	A New Start	79
7	The Call of Jerusalem	99
8	Settling Down	115
9	From Economics to Politics	133
10	Moving Around	155

11	Drift Towards a Second Catastrophe: 1967	187
12	From Politics to Diplomacy	239
13	Turkey: Home of Two Great Empires	283
14	Two Sovereign States in One	295
15	From Binational to Multinational: The Game of Nations	321
16	Return	371
17	Contemporary Jerusalem: The Jerusalem I Knew	389
18	Who Am I? A Question of Identity	431
	Index	451

Foreword

This autobiography is yet another contribution to the mountain of books written on the tragic subject of Palestine which I humbly present from the perspective of a Jerusalem person. It is a subject that I have lived through, inside and outside Jerusalem, but with the city as its main focus. Even though this book might seem to some to be 'out of time', the ongoing and seemingly intractable Palestinian-Israeli and Arab-Israeli conflicts render it both timely and timeless, from the perspective of purveying the fundamental facts of the problem from their genesis up to the present day.

But quite apart from its functional utility in the context of the contemporary debate over the issue, the book has its own inherent justification as an historical record of an era when Jerusalem – the whole of Jerusalem – was the prosperous and dynamic capital of Palestine. In this era I was born, reared and educated, before working in the Palestinian civil service. My testimony is a personal one that should not be buried, but rather recorded, remembered and commended.

With the unity of the West and East Banks of Jordan in 1950, much of my life was spent struggling with the many problems of nation building. Jordan felt the pressure at the national and international levels, because the relentless Palestine tragedy affects Jordan and its people more intimately than any other Arab state. My career was rich and varied, encompassing economic development, refugee care and international diplomacy, cresting at the United Nations Security Council.

I wish to acknowledge with gratitude those who helped make possible the publication of this work. Foremost was Nora Shawwa of Rimal Publications, Nicosia, and Melisende Publishing Ltd, London who encouraged its publication when some other publishing houses had demurred for their own good reasons. I also wish to thank editors Leonard Harrow and Gerald Butt for their extremely useful contributions and comments.

I also wish to thank Qadar, my wife, who has shared with me thus far six decades of my life, for her patience and support, and whose store of memories came to my aid when my memory faltered, providing details of names and events which were germane to this work.

The laborious hard work involved in arranging, typing and proof-reading of the text was undertaken by my son Khaled, director of the Ubada Center for Translation work and research, in Amman, Jordan. Thanks are also due to Mohammad Zaid who typed the manuscript in English and Arabic with considerable skill, despite my hardly readable handwriting. This lightened the burden of proof-reading.

Finally, I also wish to express the hope that I will be excused for any inadvertent commissions or omissions, made in good faith, in the course of writing this autobiography. With these words, I launch this book, trusting in the judicious judgement of its readership.

Hazem Nusseibeh
Amman, Jordan
February 2009

CHAPTER 1

THE BEGINNING

I was born in Jerusalem on 6 May 1922. As I begin writing this book of reminiscences in 2005, that day seems like (and is) an age away, and I am daunted, if not thrilled, by the thought of it. My father, Zaki Abdul Rahim Nusseibeh, was a venerable notable of Jerusalem and, for years, a member of its elected municipal council, and head of its Municipal Court. The Jerusalem I am talking about here is the united city in which Palestinian Arabs and Jews, Muslims and Christians lived side-by-side in amity, friendship and peace, in a harmonious community of Jerusalemites under a British League of Nations mandate. My father was already in retirement as I was growing up, having served as director of finance in Jerusalem under the Ottomans, and having made some successful trading deals during World War I. These enabled him to invest in select real estate in the newly emerging and sumptuous residential quarters, just outside the historic walls of the Old City and, primarily, in the Herod's Gate (known in Arabic as *Bab al-Zahira*) and Sheikh Jarrah quarters.

I was the third of seven brothers and three sisters. This was the average size of a Palestinian family, in urban and rural centres alike, and if it had not been for the devastating infant mortality rates, family sizes would have been even greater.

My father was authoritarian yet compassionate, austere yet loving, intimate yet distant and formal, never losing his composure. Even a laugh would be controlled and measured, and no triviality was allowed. Such was the character of those who belonged to what were categorised as the *effendi* class, the upper strata of an entrenched, structured society. I would kiss my father's hand as I said good morning, and my elder brothers, Hassan and Anwar, years older, would leave the room if they wished to smoke a cigarette or a pipe or even sip a cup of coffee, which was regarded as an undue indulgence and unbecoming in his presence. How else, I wonder in retrospect, would a head of such a household maintain an atmosphere of discipline and tranquillity if such a regimen did not exist?

My mother, Fattouma (Fatima) Nashashibi, also belonged to one of those venerable Jerusalem families which prided themselves on their genealogy, linking them to hundreds of years of recorded history. Jerusalem has always been renowned for its cluster of old celebrated families. They earned their status as governors, men of learning, judges, Sufi Sheikhs (mystics), warriors and landlords in the turbulent, sometimes cataclysmic, history of Jerusalem and Palestine, situated astride three continents and a focal point for the world's three great monotheistic religions: Judaism, Christianity and Islam. Their status emanated from centuries of association with monumental spiritual and historic sites, such as the noble sanctuary of the Aqsa Mosque, the inimitable Dome of the Rock, the Holy Sepulchre, and the *Salahiya khanaqah* (seminary for Sufis), to mention but a few.

My mother was very warm and loving, with an abundance of affection to instil in her children. She married young, immediately after graduating from an Italian school for girls in Jerusalem. In fact, the city was blessed with scores of foreign schools – English, French, American, Italian, German, Russian, and Greek, side-by-side with the official Ottoman and Arab schools which had been a hallmark of this holy city, the site of Islam's first *qibla* (the focal point to which the faithful turn their faces for prayer), the birthplace of Christianity and the setting for the Passion of Jesus Christ, and the site of Judaism's ancient City of David.

My mother not only radiated love and affection to her children but also fortified them with pride and self-confidence, which stood them in good stead throughout their lives. In such a close-knit and closed society, it was sometimes constricting, if not stifling, to be so inward-looking, and this tight pattern gradually unravelled with the march of time and changing circumstances. The closed and static society gave way to a mobile, modern and open one, under the influences of British rule, Jewish immigration, foreign tourism, and ever expanding education.

Looking back at that era is like revisiting another age. Things we take for granted today were unheard of. For example, the media at that time consisted of only a few budding but brave newspapers, with around six pages each, gradually finding a readership within a community which had been largely illiterate, a legacy of 400 to 500 years of stagnation and immobility under Ottoman rule. I distinctly remember as a child going to school at Rawdha College, at a spot in the Old City directly overlooking the *Haram al-Sharif* (noble sanctuary) area. Near the entrance to the Old City at the Damascus Gate was a coffee shop, serving usually about 25 customers sitting on low wooden and bamboo chairs, sipping coffee, smoking *narguilas* (hubble-bubble) and, most importantly, listening earnestly and with great adulation to one man sitting on a higher elevation and reading the daily newspaper to them. Most of the crowd were illiterate but could, of course, understand the standard Arabic of the newspapers. Only in 1935 did radio broadcasting emanate from Jerusalem (the Palestine Broadcasting Service) and television was not introduced to Jordan and Palestine until the mid-1960s.

Without access to mass media, acquiring a rounded education and learning about the world at large depended almost entirely on being accepted by the best available schools and colleges. Indeed, it was not by any means easy, after my father's untimely passing away in 1938, to shoulder the burden of bringing up our multitude of brothers and sisters, and ensuring that they received higher education. But the goal was achieved, in the best schools and universities throughout the world.

Members of our family moved on from Rawdha College, the Arab College and St George's School in Jerusalem to Perse School in Cambridge in the United Kingdom and Victoria College in Alexandria, Egypt. From there they went on to university: Cambridge and Sheffield, the American University of Beirut (AUB), the Sorbonne in Paris, the Egyptian University in Cairo and Princeton, New Jersey.

Providing education in this way entailed sacrifice, and required motivation and the determination to achieve success, to which Palestinian families have been committed with spectacular results: Palestinians can boast over 90 percent literacy and one of the highest per capita college education attendance records in the world.

My mother provided much of the inspiration as members of our family pursued their educational goals. Like all other city women, she had had to wear the *milaya* (black silk robe), which covered her from head to foot. It was an aberration, in those early decades of the 20th century, to simply wear a headscarf, which today has become a symbol of conservative Islam, showing how relative morals and mores are. Sixty years ago, the scarf was audacious and revolutionary, worn by the brave and the *avant-garde*; today, it is viewed as ultra-religious, constraining and an impediment to women's liberation. This shows how social norms develop with time and circumstance, rather than being dogmatic and eternal.

At home, our kitchen was truly superb, producing cosmopolitan dishes that had been perfected over the centuries through the influence of the finest Syrian and Turkish cuisine. My mother had learnt the art from her mother, Nuzha, also known as Um Umar, who belonged to the renowned Abu Ghosh clan, whose abode is still astride the Jerusalem-Jaffa-Tel Aviv highway, at Qaryat al-Inab (the village of grapes), also called Qaryat Abu Ghosh.

My parents, like the vast majority of people, had strong religious backgrounds: prayer times were strictly observed, fasting during the month of Ramadhan was adhered to meticulously, and moral behaviour, as transmitted from generation to generation, was expected of all of us.

But beyond religious rituals, which my grandfather on my mother's side ordered us to observe, what did religion really mean to me as a child? I remember some of my earliest questions to my parents, both of whom were profoundly religious and comfortable in their faith: who created this world? Their answer was: 'God the Almighty, the All-Merciful, of course.' Their tolerance was laudable as, to their deep chagrin, I went on to ask: but if God created the universe, then who created God? The answer would be a stern reminder that I was close to blaspheming, and getting into areas which were unanswerable and would merely undermine faith. So I stopped there, realising that my instinctive and childish curiosity had its limitations which, if overstepped, would become improper and unacceptable.

But it is a question which children nonetheless ask, largely to satisfy a passing curiosity. The child, in his incipient years, is eager to learn about himself and the world around him. They are the most impressionistic years of his life and they remain in his store of memories, notwithstanding the advance of years. One such memory is of a big earthquake that jolted Jerusalem in 1927, but did little damage to stoutly built homes. I was five years old at the time. What I remember clearly from the quake is that it caused a dish of stuffed eggplants (known as *Battiri*, from the village of Battir west of Jerusalem) to overturn and drench my clothes with its boiling sauce as I took it impetuously from the maid.

Then I remember standing with hundreds of other students at the Rawdha College plaza in the Old City, watching, thrilled and in amazement, the giant German airship, the Zeppelin, as it flew over to enjoy from above the architecture and beauty of the one square kilometre walled city of Jerusalem. I remember, too, walking to and from school each day along the

Via Dolorosa, playing with other boys, unaware of the sanctity of this particular street which is daily traversed by Christian pilgrims from all corners of the world, as they retrace the last steps of Christ before his Passion. I remember Halloween being celebrated in 1929 in a neighbouring Jewish quarter; but, alas, it coincided with general disturbances in Jerusalem and the whole of Palestine in what came to be known as *Thawrat al-Buraq* (the Buraq rebellion) in which hundreds of Arabs and Jews were killed or wounded. The dispute, which I will come back to later, was over jurisdictional rights in the Buraq Wall area, adjacent to the Aqsa Mosque, where Muslims believe the Prophet Muhammad's mythical creature (Buraq) carried him on his nocturnal journey to heaven. While there were exchanges of stone-throwing, I am sure none of the children, on either side, had the slightest inkling about what had caused the trouble. The Buraq Wall to the Jews is the Wailing Wall, which they believe is a remnant of Solomon's temple, even though archaeology has not proved this thesis. But it appears that to some people what is important is not reality but assumed reality, which is the case here.

I joined the towering YMCA (Young Men's Christian Association), opposite the King David Hotel in West Jerusalem, as one of the 100 founding members of the boys' department. Our photographs were hung at the main entrance, but when I visited the YMCA, in the mid-1970s after Israel's occupation of East Jerusalem and the West Bank, I was astonished to find that the pictures were no longer there. It is a shame that those in charge did not have the historical perspective and the tolerance to allow this historical record to remain, even though the vast majority of members had been Palestinian Arabs, both Christian and Muslim, with a smaller number of Jewish members. But this imbalance reflected the demographic reality of the early years of the 1930s.

One of the most impressive YMCAs in the world, the cost of construction was met through a donation from an American millionaire who, miraculously we were told, escaped the ravages of the stock market crash of 1929. The YMCA building was dedicated in 1933.

What a blessing and precious gift the YMCA was to Jerusalem and its youth. It boasted facilities for tennis, swimming, table tennis, basketball, and football, along with a gymnasium, cafeterias and conference rooms – all possible facilities and amenities for sport and entertainment. During holidays and at weekends, I would walk briskly from my house in Sheikh Jarrah, covering the few kilometres to the YMCA where I would spend several hours. I would then walk home, feeling extremely fit. My diligence and persistence must have served me well, because I won the Palestine Under-18 Junior Tennis Championship in 1940, and eventually won the Open Championship.

The rooftops of many buildings in the vicinity, as well as the balconies of the King David Hotel and the YMCA, were crowded with enthusiastic spectators when championships were under way. This was particularly the case, I remember, when I played doubles with my brother, Mahmoud, against the Peretz brothers who were being prepared to represent the Jewish community at international championships. Tenacity, skill and the cheering crowds helped us to win the cup and the championship. That was sportsmanship at its best, with no thought that a mere few years later it would turn into a duel of blood, resulting in suffering and dispersal.

Let me say a word or two about the book I am writing. The narrative consists of a personal tale, with portraits, glimpses, and memories of the Jerusalem in which I was born and reared, and where I played and was educated. I then recall some scenes from my later life in the worlds of politics and diplomacy. I called Jerusalem my home, until the war of 1948 and, more particularly, the war of 1967 turned it into a forbidden city, one in which I am not permitted to live. On occasions I can visit it, not by virtue of my birthright but by the authority of an Israeli visa, which may be granted or withheld at will, for a period not exceeding one month at a time. It is useless to invoke human rights, for such invocations have been to no avail; it is futile to invoke international law and norms of justice for those have remained ink on paper.

In these portraits I have deliberately refrained, whenever possible, from turning to reference books, and other publications and documents. For as one learned observer once remarked: 'If we were to bind together the material printed on Palestine, it would span the Atlantic Ocean.' While the remark is a gross overstatement there can be little appetite for yet more lengthy and studious publications.

So the following is a genuine and simple narration, with spontaneous impressions and reflections from one who lived through this period of history, and wants to convey it in human terms. Chronological sequences and the constraints of research have not been allowed to circumscribe a free-flowing narrative, which emerges spontaneously and, sometimes, in a haphazard fashion. But impressions and events do not fall into a chronological sequence, because events often overlap, in time and place and in one's own consciousness. It is a tale told by one who lived and saw it firsthand over many decades;

and although the story is recounted from the viewpoint and perspective of an individual, it is in many ways the story of the unparalleled tragedy of the Palestinian people.

CHAPTER 2

THE DECADE OF INNOCENCE

From my early childhood onwards, I was smitten with a deep and tender love for the city. Its unique serenity and magnificence left an inexplicable imprint on me. It is true that every individual is attached to the place of his birth, and the attachment intensifies as the years go by. But as I was to learn later in life, the deep imprint is shared to some extent, by all those who make a pilgrimage to visit, or come to live in Jerusalem. The air is pure, and the climate is seasonably temperate. The seasons run one into the other like clockwork. Even irregularities in the climate can be foretold, the timing of their occurrence having been passed on from generation to generation.

The same sense of rhythm can be observed in the fabric of the city itself: the stone-built houses are a harmonious combination of new and old.

The centre of gravity remains predominantly the walled Old City—dating back, in many instances, a millennium and, in certain cases, a few centuries more than that: the Holy Sepulchre 1,700 years, the Dome of the Rock 1,400 years.

The restoration of buildings worn down by age or ravaged by war has had to conform to the harmonious pattern of the city, established over centuries, rather than years or decades. Silhouetted on the skyline and set against the surrounding landscape can be seen magnificent monuments, painstakingly fashioned by man to the glory of God. The stone structures, often intricately and expertly carved and decorated, reflect the abundance of rock in the hilly regions around the city. The rock is white, pink and pale blue, and enduring as the age of the structures testifies.

The stonemasons and artisans over countless generations perfected the art of stonecutting and trimming, in a variety of styles and shapes. They toiled without the benefit of modern machine tools to lighten their burden or diminish the satisfaction of individual accomplishment.

Palestinian craftsmen, richly endowed with skill and experience, fashioned works that were a match for anything produced in Roman, Byzantine or Arabesque styles. But, after all, was their country not a gem, a single province in those vast empires? And was Palestine not the inheritor of all these traditions, an amalgam of all those grand civilisations and races, supplementing and enriching indigenous talents and the beauty-inspiring habitat?

The houses in the city were for the most part, large, independent entities, to accommodate the extended family system, a hallmark of Palestinian family organisation and solidarity. The small unit apartment was a rarity and considered anathema, because its existence ran counter to the profound sense of family cohesion which characterised the familial relationship. It is impressive that even after decades of dispersal and displacement in every corner of the globe, family solidarity is still widely prevalent, with all the duties and obligations which family cohesion affords and exacts. This is a unique sociological and hereditary phenomenon which I shall have occasion to revert to in another context.

As I resume my recollections, I remember as a child being awakened at the break of dawn by a confluence of Muslim *muadhinns* and resonantly ringing church bells, calling the faithful to early prayers. And living a mere few hundred yards from the Mea Shearim Jewish quarter, the horn would be blown at dusk every Friday, signalling the start of the Sabbath. The close geographic proximity of my family house to the neighbouring Jewish quarter subsequently proved perilous and costly, for the neighbourhood suffered destruction twice within a mere two decades, once in 1948 and again in 1967. I do not blame the residents of Mea Shearim for the destruction caused on these two occasions; for, as I was to learn in due course, those residents were truly religious in the fundamentalist sense. Indeed, many of them regarded, and continue to regard, the creation of Israel as a deviation from the fulfilment of God's purpose. But I have no intention of delving into theology at this point. Besides, I am narrating my early experiences; and, as a child, I possessed neither the knowledge nor the entitlement, or for that matter the interest, to get into such deep waters.

Having been awakened in those lean hours of dawn, I was kept awake by the bustling and singing of Palestinian villagers – men and women – who were bringing the fruits of the earth, grown with their own toil and sweat, to sell in Jerusalem. There they would use the proceeds to buy the merchandise which a city produces or imports and they needed.

Their healthy and happy faces were a reflection of their peace of mind, of their solid anchorage to a home and a homeland, and of an average 16 kilometre daily walk to their destination and back. Some drove mules, while others carried on their heads wicker baskets, filled to the brim with seasonal fruit and vegetables, anything and everything that one would find or not find in the supermarkets of today. The only difference is that the produce then was so much more tasty and delicious than today's. I do not know why, beyond venturing the thought as a later amateur farmer that the fruit and vegetables were allowed to mature on their mother branches, with a sufficiency of sun, air, and dew, moreover were unadulterated by modern chemicals which have undoubted benefits but also cause no less undoubted harm.

To mention the price of produce in those days would be to make present-day consumers gasp. Would anybody believe me if I said that up to the mid-1930s 50 eggs could be bought for a mere shilling or one-twentieth of a Palestine pound (Sterling), roughly the equivalent of 1 cent per egg? Or a 15-22 kilo box of gorgeous figs for the equivalent of a few cents? Salaries and wages were proportionately modest. Nonethless, one is entitled to question with righteous indignation the havoc that spiralling inflation has brought in its wake.

I am not oblivious to the dynamism and imperatives of phenomenal economic and social growth. Nor is it plausible to make invidious comparisons between those days and the subsequent six decades. But the point I am trying to stress is that money, as a unit of value and a source of prosperity, is all but meaningless unless it is related to real value in terms of the abundance and quality of life. This is probably an irrelevant historical observation, but one which I thought might be of interest to newer generations concerning an era irrevocably past, never to return again.

Many changes have occurred in daily life. In those days, for example, automobiles were still a rarity. I still remember the British high commissioner's bulky and towering Rolls Royce as I walked to the YMCA. Even buses were only starting to be introduced. The entire setting would have been heaven for modern-day environmentalists and return-to-nature adherents. There was no smoke or smog to foul the air and people adapted to living happily with the minimum of amenities and gadgets of modern civilisation. I, like almost everyone else, had to walk to school, in thunder and lightning, in rain, or in heavy snow for that matter. We did not mind a bit, and the exercise of walking must have made us stouter and healthier. I do not remember that we had any heating at school (Rawdha College in the Old City). But we accepted that as a fact of life, and naturally we were adequately protected in winter clothing.

I have still to see a happier or more contented people, with reasonably nourishing food, and exquisitely embroidered self-made clothing which women, especially those from the villages, wore. The thick walls of the stone houses provided protection against deluges of rain, and insulation from the severity of cold in winter, particularly in the hilly regions of the West Bank and Galilee. The rural people had their village dances (the *dabka*), seasonal festivities, and wedding celebrations in which poetic and rhythmic folk songs, largely improvised and spontaneous, were a joy to hear. I am still puzzled about how simple, mostly illiterate village people in those days, could reach such heights of creativity. Their achievement, I suppose, stemmed from ages-old traditions that seemed to be in their blood and in the hallowed soil that gave them their livelihoods.

It is interesting to record how easy it was to identify which village or area the rural folk belonged to: it was discernible in the patterns of the hand-woven embroidery with which women's dresses were adorned. The Jerusalem countryside patterns could be differentiated from those of Bethlehem, Ramallah, Gaza, or Galilee. And if any doubts should arise pertaining to identification, the accents and the pronunciation would come to one's aid. This was a phenomenon among the Palestinian people as much as any other in the world. Indeed, it was a cause for jesting, at times in good humour, and at others escalating into noisy quarrels and even fist fights. For the quality of language, the choice of idioms, the specific pronunciation and accent, were a source of both pride and prejudice. Who would not be able to identify, even at school, a fellow from Nazareth, Jaffa, Hebron, or Gaza by simply listening to his pronunciation or choice of words? Having said this, I must stress that the Palestinian people constitute one of the most homogeneous in the world. They have never experienced the kind of intrinsic discord that has torn many other societies apart, for one reason or another, largely inherited from the past and amplified by misguided attitudes. Whatever may be said about the Palestinians, and how much they have been unjustly maligned in ancient as well as modern times, they have always been a highly coherent society.

Their souls were, by and large, unafflicted by vice, hate or bigotry towards anyone. This state of mind must have been influenced by their disciplined upbringing and religious background. Sure enough, they have had their share of intra-community quarrels, escalating at times into vendettas. But they are also inordinately shrewd and intelligent, even if they did not have the benefit of education. They were fully engaged in their day-to-day lives, with the usual mixture of elements, pleasant and unpleasant, serious and trivial, along with successes and reverses, modest as both were.

Going to school in the Old City of Jerusalem in the 1930s I took the mystique of Jerusalem for granted, not knowing naturally enough, that it was unique, less still what fate had in store for it and its people. I was made aware that the accident of my birth in Jerusalem linked me not only to my own forefathers, but also those of many families, stretching back through 1,400 years of recorded history.

I was also to learn that my family, though Muslim, had been entrusted with custody of the keys of the Church of the Holy Sepulchre. A member of the family must open the gate of this shrine, one of the holiest in Christianity, at dawn and close it at dusk.

According to popular consensus, as I recall it in those days, this honorary duty was entrusted to my family by the Caliph Umar in the 7th century AD. This was to ensure that there would be no trespassing in later years by zealous Muslims or those misinformed about Islam's unequivocal veneration and tolerance of Christianity and its places of worship. But I am told that in certain church records in Jerusalem they assign the date of the award of the Holy Sepulchre custodianship to the era of Salahuddin who is also known as Saladin, a mere 800 years ago.

I have never researched the various historical records to ascertain which is the accurate date. In several of the travel books that I have read, the origin and cause of this assignment are explained in terms of keeping peace amongst the various Christian denominations. Their passionate and perennial rivalries over jurisdiction – even if it involves merely a matter of centimetres or metres within the sanctuary of the church – are legendary. It is remarkable the extent to which people, in an ancient city laden with history like Jerusalem, are prisoners of their past, their legacy and their profound spiritual inheritance, ready to give everything to protect these historical links. Perhaps policy makers would be well advised to recognise and respect the power of such attachments, and give them the respect they deserve.

The city of Jerusalem has, perhaps, more established dynasties that can trace their lineage far back into recorded history than any other. It may be that they were destined to be there all along to serve as guardians of a great religious movement, and a great faith which ordained Jerusalem as its first *qibla* before Mecca was ordained by the Holy Book, the Quran, to serve this end. Jerusalem still embraces the third holiest Islamic sanctuary, the Aqsa Mosque and its environs, upon which God has bestowed his blessings. Moreover, the sanctuary, more specifically the Dome of the Rock, was the place to which the Prophet of Islam, Muhammad, journeyed from Mecca in a symbolic nocturnal religious mission, and from which he made his ascension to heaven, at God's behest, to witness some of His glorious creations. No wonder then, Arabs and Muslims over countless generations, have spared nothing in the way of sacrifices in the cause of its preservation. And only the ignorant and the uninformed could imagine that they will be less motivated by compulsive religious and historical imperatives to do so again and again.

To the Arab and Muslim worlds, the loss of Jerusalem is equivalent to the loss of an integral component of their religious beliefs, not to mention the closing of the most memorable, sustained, and cherished chapters of their history.

And while on this point, the Dome of the Rock is one of the most magnificent monuments of all time that man has created as a place of worship to God. It combines Arabesque, Islamic, and Byzantine art in harmonious and breathtaking beauty, radiating a sense of exhilaration. One needs to be an accomplished artist, which I am not, to comprehend it. But historians say that 14 centuries ago the Umayyad Caliph Abd al-Malik ibn Marwan allocated the taxable revenues of Egypt for seven years to finance its construction and embellishment. Later generations and empires were no less generous in financing its upkeep and restoration.

I have talked about the genealogy of the people of Jerusalem from firsthand knowledge. But I am also mindful of the fact that old and established families inhabit other towns and villages of Palestine. Many families go to great pains to draw up their family trees and Palestinians generally pay, or used to pay, considerable amounts for the prestige of maintaining and verifying their ancestral lineage. The tragedy of dispersal must have dealt a heavy blow to this predilection, but I am in no position to assess how much. With massive uprooting who can accurately measure what does or does not remain of a people's traditional values and norms? It can only be surmised that this obsession must have waned a good deal.

But the irony is that those throughout Palestine who cannot establish a verified lineage probably outstrip everyone else in terms of the number of years that their families have lived there. For it is known that the indigenous inhabitants have been married to the land for literally 7,000 to 8,000 years of registered history.

The town of Jericho alone, a traditional winter resort for the people of Jerusalem in the Jordan Valley, has already unearthed seven-to-eight layers of towns either devastated by conquest or natural calamities, only to be rebuilt on the ruins of the old. Jericho ranks as one of the oldest known cities in the world. This is archaeology, not myth; it is science, not fiction. The latest (August 1980) Israeli archaeological team, who unearthed what they presumed to have been King David's house 3,000 years ago, found at the same spot abundant Canaanite artistic remains. These pre-date the Israeli find by at least 2,500 years. The Canaanites were the earliest forefathers of present-day Palestinians. But they are also the people whom Israel, alas, claims do not exist, and have never existed. By corollary, they have no entitlement, even partial, to their ancestral homeland. Hearing Israeli leaders like Messrs Menachem Begin, Moshe Dayan, and Mrs Golda Meir, to mention but a few of those who were learned and should have known better, question publicly the existence and national identity of the Palestinians leaves one at a loss about how to react. Should one react with bewildered anger or resigned amusement to such pathetic statements? Such Israeli leaders act as though they are totally oblivious to the universally recognized principle of international law, which stipulates the entitlement of a people to a country derives from long and continued possession. Their facetious pronouncements – for I am sure they know better – are in stark contradiction to the very scriptures upon which they based their claim for a return to the Holy Land.

The presence of the Jewish people in the Holy Land in ancient days, and Israel's short-lived rule in recent times in small segments of Palestine, are well known. Extensively documented too is Judaism's monumental contribution to the development of religious thought, so further elaboration is unnecessary. But one of the ironies of history is that by repudiating and evicting the present-day Palestinians, Israelis, knowingly or not, are also repudiating many of the people whose cause they claim to espouse. When the Israelis were exiled by the Babylonians in the endless obscure political struggles of those ancient times, it was the elite and not the masses who suffered exile. The masses, as was only natural in those tribal societies, intensified their assimilation with the rest of the indigenous population, whether Canaanite, Jebusite (the founders of Jerusalem), Amorite (the founders of Hebron), Aramaic, Phoenician, Nabataean, Philistine, Syriac, or other smaller groups. Some embraced Judaism, others subsequently Christianity, and others still Islam. Before the advent of monotheism, many people were secular, agnostic, or idolatrous. Under Hellenistic influence many turned to philosophy to help them comprehend mundane as well as metaphysical dimensions of existence. But Judaism, Christianity, and Islam supplanted them all because they were consonant with the soul of the land and its people. That is why, as Arnold Toynbee explained, the region of greater Syria, at the eastern end of the Mediterranean Sea, readily embraced Christianity and Islam. That is also the reason why he describes Judaism as an offshoot of Syriac civilisation, which he ranks as one of the greatest distinct civilisations of those ages. And over and above their neighbourly relationships, they were, for the most, part Semitic cousins who had originally heralded from the Arabian Peninsula, Mesopotamia, the Fertile Crescent lands, and Egypt. The Arabs and the Jews, for example, are from the seed of Abraham, the majority of whom came to Palestine from the Arabian Peninsula, with the rest coming from Mesopotamia (Iraq).

It is yet another historical irony that when Abraham made a covenant with God through circumcision, and all the land of Canaan was promised to him and his seed, it was his son Ishmael who was circumcised. His other son, Isaac, had not then been born. Ishmael is the acknowledged forefather of many Arab tribes.

Pursuing this historical exploration a little further, for this is what the Palestinians and the world are being dragged into; the Covenant with God was specific – certainly more specific than United Nations Security Council Resolutions 242 and 338 – in that it delineated the Land of Canaan as the reward.

If one assumes that the current land of Canaan, after a supreme act of land transfer, is confined to what is presently the occupied West Bank of Jordan, which comprises a mere one-fifth of Palestine, what about the remaining four-fifths, as originally granted by heavenly dispensation?

The answer is that it was inhabited and stoutly held by the Philistines, and the Israelis never succeeded in making inroads into their territory. The legendary fight between David and Goliath, in which David overwhelmed his giant opponent, was a comforting compensatory act, but no more. It did not carry with it any heavenly sanctification for the taking over of the lands of the Philistines, even if it were possible, which was not the case. I wonder sometimes, how many people in the world realised that the state of Israel which emerged in 1948 encompassed the entire lands of the Philistines, very largely by conquest, and in excess of what had been allocated to it by the United Nations under the partition plan of 1947. So, four-fifths of Palestine was taken over without even a pretence of historical entitlement or heavenly sanctification.

As for the land of Canaan, I am not going to enter a historical and theological dispute as to who promised what to whom. As the veteran and wise Saudi Ambassador, the late Jamil Baroudi, never tired of reminding UN forums: God is not in the real estate business. But one can say for certain that there was never a monolithic or exclusive Jewish presence in the territory that is today's occupied West Bank. The indigenous Palestinian people lived side-by-side with their Jewish neighbours. The year 1948 is infamous. It stands out in 7,000 to 8,000 years of history as the only one in which the Palestinians lost control over their destiny. But even more disastrously, 1948 was the year in which they became uprooted and dispersed far and wide. The ancient Jews, though tribal and brutal, must have been much more discerning towards the Palestinians than the supposedly civilised Israelis of modern times. The ancients must have had certain considerations and restraints. The 20th century breed, by word and deed, seem to be constrained by nothing. Is this what is proudly proclaimed as modern civilisation and true democracy?

Returning to my central tale, life in Palestine in the 1920s moved at a relatively modest pace. The British administration was intent on accomplishing two things. One was the policing of the land, to ensure the gradual implementation of the Balfour Declaration, under which the British government had in 1917 committed itself to the establishment of a national home for the Jews in Palestine. This was done secretly, behind the backs of

Britain's World War I Arab allies. The second aim of the British Administration was to establish minimal infrastructure, such as roads, water systems and some schooling (they had set up no more than a score of secondary high schools in the whole of Palestine by the end of the mandate on 14 May 1948). This did not mean that there was a dearth of high school education for Palestinians. Private schools of high quality, both national and foreign, were to be found in abundance for those who could afford them. But while this form of education offered standard educational curricula, it did not encourage engagement with the local cultural and historical heritage. Instead, there was alien cultural indoctrination. For example, history lessons paid far greater attention to how many women Henry VIII of England had married and beheaded, than to the history of Palestine itself, ancient, medieval and modern. For the Palestinian Arabs, this resulted in total cultural alienation, mitigated only by the role of the handful of national schools and the deep-rooted traditions. The reader will be surprised to know that not until I had read a book in 1975 by a prominent Israeli author, Amnon Cohen, entitled *Palestine in the 18th Century* did I learn that northern Palestine and, particularly Galilee, was in the 18th century one of the major cotton producing areas in the world. For the purchase of its high quality produce the three foremost European industrialising countries of the era, Britain, France, and Holland, vied to purchase it. The backbone of industrialisation in its incipient stages was textile manufacturing and here we find Palestinian farmers partaking in this process. It had always intrigued me that in almost every Palestinian city or town one can find a special market place named *Suq al Qattanin* (the market of cotton dealers). But I had never given any thought to its ubiquitous prevalence as a direct consequence of its cultivation in abundance, in Palestine itself.

Legendary stories of how the Palestinians in 1799, under the command of al-Jazzar in the north, had defeated mighty Napoleon's naval expedition when he tried to storm the city of Acre, the regional capital of Galilee, had, of course, been passed on from generation to generation. But we were unaware, and we were not told at school, that the victory was not the result either of a divine miracle or even inherent fighting ability, although there was no shortage of the latter. A Palestinian, in hindsight, would have been entitled to expect his own schooling to instruct him in modern and analytical, but simple terms, that the Palestinians in Galilee had scored their victory because they possessed a 15,000 strong, highly trained regular army, spontaneously aided by the indigenous inhabitants of the region in the face of an external assault by a major power.

Regular armies are correlated to advanced, motivated, and prosperous communities. Modern European books attribute the outcome of the battle at Acre to the might of the Ottoman Empire. Palestine, at that time, was a province in the empire. While not detracting in any way from the Ottomans' overall military prowess in the era before decline set in (after all it was a major power), it was so over-stretched in Eastern Europe and elsewhere that the provinces had to make their own security arrangements. On a balance sheet, Palestine was a net contributor to the empire in manpower and material and not *vice versa*. This was the case at the time of Galilee's encounter with Napoleon.

What makes this attitude of deliberate alienation the more objectionable is that Palestine was not even a colonial territory. It was recognized in 1922 by the League of Nations (later becoming the United Nations) as a Class A Mandatory Territory, a trust territory, qualified for and entitled to independence – more than three-quarters of a century ago – but allegedly requiring a transitional period of training to become an independent country *par excellence*. This was, I need hardly state, a thinly-disguised excuse to enable Jewish immigrants, under the protection of the sharp bayonets of the British army, to gradually but systematically dislodge the indigenous Palestinian inhabitants.

This ultimate objective was accomplished in two phases: the cataclysm of 1948, consummated two decades later, in 1967, by Israeli occupation and colonisation of the whole of mandated Palestine.

I may have strayed too long in history, so I want to return once more to Jerusalem to continue my tale.

Up to 1929, as I well remember as a child, Arab-Jewish relationships were as normal as could be in almost every walk of life. An old bearded plumber named Shabatai still sticks out in my memory as a frequent visitor to carry out whatever repairs or maintenance were required in the house. My late father, Zaki Nusseibeh, was one of the elected members of the Municipal Council of Jerusalem and chairman of its Municipal Court. Along with the other four or five Arab Council members, including the Arab Mayor of Jerusalem, Ragheb Nashashibi, their relationships with their Jewish colleagues were business-like and friendly. One of my father's 25-room houses was leased to a famed Jewish physician (I remember his name to be Dan Ziger) in the Herod's Gate quarter, a few hundred metres outside the old walled city. He utilised the premises as a hospital, an ideal location where only big mansions stood with tall cypress trees and gardens. The atmosphere was serene and quiet; the only sound came from the fresh breeze tenderly moving the leaves and branches of the trees. Even shopping for new clothing which my father was fond of doing personally for his children – a day or two before the Bairam feast (at the end of the holy fasting month of Ramadhan) and other festivities – was mostly done, as I recall, at Levy's garment shop in the vicinity of Jaffa Gate. It was interesting to watch the two gentlemen strike a bargain, good-naturedly and, it seemed to me, shrewdly, for both were versatile in the ways of the world. The main shopping district for both the Arabs and the Jews was in the Jaffa Road and the parallel Mamilla Road, just outside the western walls of old Jerusalem. In retrospect, alas, this atmosphere of genuine harmony and friendly coexistence turned out to be a calm which preceded a storm, one of many which both communities were fated to endure.

Before getting into a narrative of this earliest of storms, it seems necessary, if only for the historical record, to describe the Jerusalem of that era and its gradual but impressive development beyond the confines of the historic walled city, largely between 1920 and 1948 when the mandate ended and the British departed.

Prior to the mandate, the Old City was where the overwhelming majority of the inhabitants resided. It was even considered adventurous to stray for long distances in what later became New Jerusalem, particularly West Jerusalem. An Arab historian of Jerusalem and Hebron, writing five centuries ago, describes vividly how those lands in West Jerusalem had been turned by enlightened local governors of the city into prosperous and beautiful orchards where families would have picnics and spend their summer vacations.

The years following the arrival of the British in 1917 witnessed continuing population growth and an acceleration of Jewish immigration, putting pressure on living space within the Old City and the few quarters in its immediate surroundings beyond the wall. This, in turn, prompted a spurt of construction in what came to be known, after 1948, as Israeli West Jerusalem. Although this part of the city was largely occupied by the Israeli forces in the course of the 1947-48 internecine fighting, at least 70 percent of New Jerusalem was built, owned and inhabited by its Palestinian Arab residents. This is on record in Chief Justice Sir William Fitzgerald's report, prepared in 1945 at the request of the British authorities, for the purpose of zoning the Arab and Jewish areas for separate municipal councils within what was to have been an overall international regime for Jerusalem and its environs as an integral part of the 1947 partition scheme. If title deeds or private ownership possess any validity or credence, in a supposedly law-abiding international system, they are meticulously arranged and spelled out in detail in the 1945 report for all to see and read. In 1974, I accompanied the then permanent representative of Jordan to the United Nations, the superb Ambassador Abdul Hamid Sharaf, to one of the UN basements to collect a handsomely tubed and ribboned copy of the microfilmed title deeds of the Palestinians. The Jordanian mission had paid $15,000 for its acquisition. It very closely resembled college degrees awarded at commencement ceremonies, but was enclosed in a tube. I mused and reflected in silent pain as I said to myself: 'Here within the confines of a small and light tube are dwarfed and buried, who knows for how long, the travail, the sweat and the elemental human rights of hundreds of thousands of human beings, of successive generations of hard-working Palestinians.'

What an extraordinary sleight of hand it was to exchange the homeland, the homes, the plantations, the savings, the investment, the labour, the rights, and the hopes of a whole people for a few tiny dots, a small and worthless piece of paper, converted to a more enduring material in a microfilm, but worthless all the same. These homes and the ownership of them, ostensibly in the hands of the custodian of 'absentee property', were awarded at nominal prices to outsiders who migrated to Palestine after the Palestinian exodus of 1948. The newcomers supplanted the legitimate owners, some of whom still live in the squalour of refugee camps. These are the brutally victimised Palestinian refugees. To some of them each year the world community contributes a few kilos of flour, sugar, and edible fat. Once in a while, believe it or not, such luxury additions as a few pounds of rice and kerosene are added, if and when available, and all at the wish or whim of contributing member states which brought this catastrophe upon the Palestinians in the first place. But the Palestinian people are too formidable and versatile to survive on a seven-cent-a-day donation from the United Nations. Their friends will rejoice and their enemies will be dismayed when they learn that, from scratch, they are staging a re-birth, exemplified in achieving one of the highest per capita educational attainment records in the world. Hard toil, sacrifice, and a sense of purpose can move mountains, and this is precisely what the Palestinian Arabs have done, rising from the ashes to which their enemies had reduced them.

After 1967, the Israeli occupation authorities, evidently not sated with the spoils of 70 percent of New Jerusalem – Arab, but mistakenly assumed to be Jewish and Israeli – turned their wrath and greed upon what had been reduced in 1948 to a vastly shrunken Arab Jerusalem. They called it at first East Jerusalem and annexed it to the former illegal acquisition. The Israelis have succeeded, with the help of lavish tax-free donations from abroad and particularly from the United States, which the Israelis callously regard as their milking cow, in colonising and expanding the already shrunken Arab Jerusalem fifteen-fold. This has happened, with rare exceptions, on confiscated Arab lands, including state domain.

Not many of the older generation are still alive to reminisce about the unique serenity of the Old City and its surrounding quarters, or about districts of New Jerusalem that are criss-crossed by tree-lined streets and characterised by the exquisite elegance of villas, each with its own garden. In those years, Sheikh Jarrah, Herod's Gate quarter, Qatamon, upper and lower Baqaa, Talbiya, the so-called Greek and German Colonies (also largely Arab-owned), just to mention a few, probably ranked among the most elegant residential quarters in the world. Architecture and inherited skilful masonry achieved a feat once again, but in new forms and modern styles to keep up with changing times. A visit to Amman today would show modern villas which, in many instances, would surpass those of New Jerusalem which I have described. Time, after all, does not stand still and progress surges ahead inexorably. The Palestinians are proud to have contributed to this process in partnership with their Jordanian brethren.

It saddens one to see that the Arab quarters in West Jerusalem have since suffered considerable dilapidation for lack of adequate upkeep and because the Israelis have over-crowded the houses, with several families in each, to accommodate the heavy influx of oriental Jewish immigrants.

There are sad tales to be told of the massive adversity suffered by the Arab inhabitants of Jerusalem, not solely in material terms, but in the sheer psychological anguish of the aftermath of all that has happened in the city. A close friend of mine, Dr Ali Aaqleh, an accomplished doctor in obstetrics who owns and operates a thriving hospital in Amman, felt a compulsive urge after the Israeli occupation of the West Bank to visit the house where he was born 60 years earlier, in Lifta quarter in West Jerusalem. He told me he wanted to renew his links with his roots and to see, after a quarter of a century of absence, the garden, the playgrounds and the landscape in which he had spent his childhood and his early youth. Having obtained the usual permit from the Israeli military occupation authorities he crossed the bridge on the River Jordan and raced towards his house to fulfil his dream (or was it a hidden nightmare?). Upon arrival at the house he rang the bell, overwhelmed by emotion. The Israeli residents of his house opened the door and asked him who he was. He identified himself and requested permission to visit the house for a few moments. The residents replied tersely that the house did not belong to him but to them, to which he replied: 'I am not coming here to recover the house. I have my house in Amman in which I live.' He assured the residents that he was over 60 years of age and the only purpose of the visit was to enjoy a brief moment of remembrance and spiritual reconstruction of his early years. The residents did not budge and remained adamant in refusing him entry. He departed with tears flowing. When he narrated his experience to me, and I know him to be almost always unemotional and composed, the tears flowed once again before he regained his usual composure. In human terms, one would have expected the residents of his house to display some understanding and allow him the few moments he had requested to revisit the scene of his early life. And besides, it is a deeply-entrenched custom in the Middle East to usher in a visitor or guest for at least a cup of coffee, if not a meal. Similar tragic experiences are so common that I will not devote any further space to narrate them. There have been exceptions to this traumatic cruelty; but it is the pattern of the behaviour of the majority that counts and not that of the rare Good Samaritan.

CHAPTER 3

GATHERING STORMS: A DECADE OF TURBULENCE

The year 1929 could rightly be described as a turning point, shattering generations of friendly Arab-Jewish co-existence and cooperation, and heralding a long, unending chapter of strife. It was not so much the tragic events which accompanied the brief 1929 uprising, cruel as these were, that were significant. The real importance of the uprising lay in the fact that it brought to the fore, and into the minds of the people at large, a sudden realisation of an impending irreconcilable collision. Up to that point only a few people had been aware of this. Zionist leaders of various shades had hardly been making a secret of their ultimate designs to take over Palestine and more. The Palestinian Arab leadership was equally vehemently convinced that this was indeed what those designs were, notwithstanding soothing statements by the British authorities and some moderate Zionist leaders to the contrary. With the country still overwhelmingly populated by Palestinian Arabs and in their physical possession, alarmist forebodings and dire warnings sounded somewhat unrealistic.

Indeed, a division within the ranks of the Palestinian Arab leadership cantered on this point, with differences between what came to be classified as the moderates and the extremists, the latter being the more pessimistic in their assessment of Zionist intentions. The moderates were fortified by the *status quo* at the time which appeared to render the most vociferous and extreme Zionist declarations as hollow cries, largely unrelated to facts on the ground.

In this atmosphere of certainty versus uncertainty the 1929 uprising erupted and came to be known in Palestinian Arab records as *Thawrat al-Buraq* (the uprising over the Buraq Wall) the area of the Wailing Wall.

I was still a child at the time and do not remember anything beyond hostile gatherings in contiguous Arab and Jewish quarters. Stone-throwing, fist and stick fights erupted here, there and everywhere until they had encompassed the country in its entirety. The focal point had been the area of the Wailing Wall, adjacent to the Muslim holy sanctuary and the thickly inhabited Arab quarters surrounding it.

It should never be overlooked that in a religiously-oriented city like Jerusalem, sensitivities are acute and inflammable. They are almost incomprehensible to largely secular cities in other parts of the world that are less imbued by theological traditions and history. It is in recognition of this unique situation in Jerusalem that, over generations, a meticulous and delicate *status quo* evolved, governing the preservation and management of places sacred to the three great monotheistic religions.

In 1929, bands of Jewish youths armed with improvised weapons – in those years the use of firearms was inconceivable – breached the imperceptible but acknowledged city lines, spilling over into historic and religious Muslim shrines. The residents of the Arab quarters fought the marauding Jewish youths, and many scores from both sides suffered injuries. The flames sparked by this incident spread throughout the length and breadth of the country and resulted in tragic attacks and counter-attacks which the British security forces eventually managed to contain. The events in Hebron were singularly tragic because it was the first time in history that the small Jewish community was set upon by surging crowds, resulting in several scores of killed and wounded. I do not believe many people outside the field of social psychology are well-versed in William McDougall's penetrating analysis, published in the 1920s, of mass psychology. This, once ignited, forms a collective mind and volition of its own, at variance with the individual minds of those engulfed in the mainstream, even though they are its individual component.

This is precisely what happened in Hebron, which is particularly religious and has a special reverence for the *Haram al-Ibrahimi* (Sanctuary of Abraham), the historical burial place of Abraham which adherents of the Islamic faith revere as their own prophet and forefather of many Arab tribes through his son Ishmael, according to the teachings of Islam. This explains why there had never been anti-Jewish animosity, not only in Hebron but also throughout the Islamic world. The British formed a Royal Commission which studiously examined the juridical issues and the *status quo*. The Commission, while deploring the bloody rioting, came to the conclusion that the Jews in the Wailing Wall area had, indeed, been the transgressors.

It is incontestably a fact that the Magharibah quarter (adjacent to the wall), and well beyond, have for 14 centuries been Arab, administered for the most part by *awqaf* (Islamic charitable foundations) to cater for Muslim pilgrims and house seminaries of religious instruction and practice. It is a cultural and human tragedy for those owners and residents, that five Arab quarters in the area adjacent to the Wailing Wall were totally destroyed by Israel after its occupation in 1967. The destruction, resulting in the displacement of 6,000 residents, was carried out to expand that area near the wall and the neighbouring Jewish quarters overlooking the Haram al-Sharif holy sanctuary to many times their original size. Of the area in question, 70 percent, ironically, is Arab-owned.

Despite these changes, the medieval wall around the holy sanctuary and the Old City (12 metres high) remains a hallmark of the picturesque landscape of Jerusalem. The wall is the work of successive empires and states. In its present form it bears the work of Suleiman the Magnificent, one of the great Sultans of the Ottoman Empire in the year 1500. Beneath it lie Arab and Roman foundations of earlier walls.

The Jewish belief that the southwestern and northwestern segments of the wall are remains of the second temple enclosure destroyed by Titus in AD 70 is, as mentioned earlier, simply a misconception. The Jewish temples that were destroyed had been built primarily of Lebanese cedar timber which, in terms of durability, can hardly have endured the ravages of millennia in the way that stone can. The walls of the Old City are hardy stone structures and their genealogy can easily be identified as belonging to the Roman, Byzantine, Crusader, Arab-Islamic, and Ottoman-Turkish eras.

Israeli archaeologists, since the 1967 occupation, have been systematically and assiduously digging deep beneath the structures, the walls and even the Aqsa Mosque and the

Dome of the Rock, to the point of posing a serious danger to their foundations. Have those excavations unearthed relics of the temples? None whatsoever. The only remains discovered were of two Arab Ummayad palaces, adjacent to the east of the Aqsa Mosque and numerous relics of other civilisations as expressed in stone-carved remains, coins dating back to the Abbasids, Fatimids, Crusaders, Mamluks, and Ottomans. And beneath them all surfaced Roman columns, some of which had been used in sections of the Old City's gates and walls. The acts of destruction by the Babylonians and the Romans must have been thorough. How else can we explain the fact that after decades of ceaseless digging beneath almost every square centimetre, at depths of almost 13 metres, even beneath the Aqsa Mosque itself, not a trace of Jewish relics has been found? Indeed the diggings proved beyond any doubt that the foundations of the mosque are built on the solid rocks of the ground in that area.

A continuance of this exercise in futility on the part of the Israeli authorities can only result in a cultural and historical calamity, by destroying structures dating back more than a millennium which make Jerusalem the unique and historical city which it is.

Returning to recent history, the 1930s were characterised by turbulence, rumblings, ominous forebodings and mass resistance. The rising tension culminated in 1936 in one of the longest strikes of the 20th century, lasting six months. It brought the whole of Palestine to a virtual standstill. Every segment of Palestinian society joined the strike. Even the normally reticent and highly disciplined Palestinians who held senior posts in the civil service backed the protest. They presented the British high commissioner with a signed memorandum warning of dire consequences if the mandatory power persisted in implementing its policies of unbridled support for the increasingly menacing Zionist objective of eventually supplanting the indigenous and lawful inhabitants of the Holy Land.

The six month all-out strike had been preceded in the early 1930s, particularly in 1933, by massive demonstrations in Jerusalem, Jaffa, and other Palestinian towns. The Higher Executive Committee, headed by the venerable and elderly Kazem Pasha al-Husseini, had called for these massive demonstrations and participated at the forefront of them.

The most violent encounters were between the people and the British security forces in Jaffa, where crowds battled the security forces with sticks, stones, and iron bars wrenched from shop and house shutters. The crowds several times forced the security forces back to their barracks, only to be counter-attacked. During the back-and-forth confrontation, my father, a member of the Higher Executive Committee and in his mid-60s, was trampled upon in the stampede and left unconscious, as were some of the other leaders. My father later recovered, finding himself in a house of strangers. But the occupants had summoned medical assistance and accorded him full hospitality.

It subsequently became apparent to the Palestinian leadership that strikes, demonstrations, petitions and all other forms of peaceful protest would be of no avail and would not dissuade the British government from implementing the Balfour Declaration, the 1917 commitment by Britain to create a home for the Jews in Palestine.

The flow of Jewish immigration from Europe was swelling, peaking in 1936 at 60,000 immigrants in a single year. The immigration was a direct consequence of the rise to power of the Nazis in Germany and their increasing anti-Jewish rhetoric.

The Palestinian people were left with no survival option, if they were to avoid being deluged and overwhelmed, but to launch an armed rebellion. Simultaneously they came to the conclusion that their struggle should not be directed against the Jewish minority but, principally, against the then superpower which had been forcibly implementing and assisting the Zionist designs.

Jerusalem after dusk normally enjoyed quiet, breathtaking, and uniquely exhilaratingly cool nights. One night in 1936, between 8 and 9pm, scattered rifle shots rang out in the clear evening sky. The shots were few. But, as I well recall, their sound was a departure from the normal quiet of the city. More importantly, they sent a signal to the mandatory authority that an armed rebellion had begun. I do not think that those whistling rifle shots were aimed at any particular target, military or civilian.

To me, at the age of 14, as to everyone else, this was a unique, unprecedented, and singularly defiant moment. For in the mid-1930s it was inconceivable that any people would challenge by arms the mightiest power on earth, the British Empire, on whose dominions, it was said, the sun would never set. Even a populous sub-continent like India had been carrying on its struggle for freedom by non-violent civil disobedience. Relatively populous Egypt was also conducting a political struggle for independence by non-military means. And to the world's surprise, the Palestinians, a relatively small people, had embarked upon one of the fiercest, most tenacious and most prolonged armed liberation movements of that era.

I am talking about three-quarters of a century ago. Today it is ironic, though laudable and profoundly satisfying, to see almost all former colonies or trust territories, represented at the United Nations as sovereign independent states. Only the proud and redoubtable Palestinian people still await a seat. Israel has usurped their seat. Belatedly and grudgingly the United Nations accorded the Palestinian representatives (the Palestine Liberation Organisation – PLO) the status of 'observer', which it still holds.

Since this is not intended to be more than a personal synopsis of some of my recollections, I shall not delve at any length into a narration of that great rebellion which, by 1938-39, placed four-fifths of the country, its arteries and even its institutions under the effective authority, if not the formal or acknowledged control, under British military control. After all, the mandatory authority had assembled somewhere around 50,000 troops in addition to a vast security apparatus. Many senior British officers gained their practical training, particularly in anti-guerrilla warfare in the mountains, hills, plains, cities, towns, and villages of Palestine. Field Marshall Montgomery, to mention but one name, was serving as military commander of Haifa.

I had been receiving elementary schooling in Rawdha College since 1929, a prestigious national and nationalistic private school in Jerusalem. It was equalled only by Najah College in Nablus (now a university). My years at Rawdha left a deep imprint upon my historic and national orientation. Unlike high quality but bland government schools, or equally excellent foreign schools such as St George's, Rawdha College was imbued with a mission: to impart knowledge and a sense of pride and belonging to our great Arab heritage, in addition to the standard curriculum. I also attended a semester at Rashidiyya, a government high school, second in prestige only to the Arab College on al-Mukaber hills in southern Jerusalem.

The turbulence and rebellion of 1936, which brought about frequent dislocations and closures, convinced my father that Jerusalem was no longer the place to acquire sustained and uninterrupted education. A celebrated school, Victoria College in Alexandria, modelled on English public schools, was the answer. My younger brother, Mahmoud, and myself were enrolled and sent there.

The years that I spent at Victoria College were memorable indeed. The college offered first class education and educators, character building, sports, debating societies and the richness of life in every field. The self-discipline demanded by the college was, to me, a priceless acquisition. Justifiably, Victoria College has been considered the most elite school in the whole of the Middle East.

In 1938, at Victoria College, we began to sense the gathering storm that was to engulf the entire world a year later. We had been assigned underground shelters to which we had to rush at an instant's notice, and gasmasks, in preparation for dire things to come. The exercises were taken seriously by our teachers, heightening our sense of excitement. These shelters stood us in good stead in 1939-40 when Italian bombers raided targets in Alexandria – largely ineffectually – and were engaged by the roaring anti-aircraft guns along the Egyptian coastline. The British army was in control at Abu Quir and many other bases, and the exigencies of the war were such as to require a military takeover of Victoria College's buildings and premises. The college improvised a temporary campus at St Stephano

Hotel along the corniche, at which I attended a semester and sat my final examinations. The school also opened a branch in Cairo which remained the main centre for the duration of the war.

CHAPTER 4

THE QUIET BEFORE THE STORM

Palestine and its capital, Jerusalem, had been in the throes of rebellion, violence and a dogged fight that was intended to run to the finish when World War II broke out. The British government, anxious to obtain the willing support of the Arab world in its life-and-death fight against Nazi Germany, issued the MacDonald White Paper in 1939. This followed a round of conferences in London, with the Arab and Jewish leaderships in attendance, which envisaged an independent Palestine governed by Palestinians and Jews in proportion to their numbers in the population, banned further Jewish immigration and restricted land transfers. There was one condition about which some of the Palestinian leadership expressed unhappiness, namely, the *proviso* that the independent state of Palestine, in which all citizens, regardless of creed or race, would enjoy equal rights and opportunities under the law, would take effect after an interim period, roughly *co-terminus* with the duration of the war.

The Palestinians, having successfully sustained an all-out and very costly struggle for independence – which, alas, eludes them to this day – pressed for immediate independence. The British argued that the exigencies of a global war had rendered the interim period imperative. They, in effect, said that even if Palestine had been independent, the British Empire, fighting for its existence, would have been compelled to occupy it, as it had subsequently occupied Iraq and Iran. In any event, an independent Palestine, as spelled out in the White Paper, remained the official position of the British government until Jewish terrorism during and in the aftermath of World War II, coupled with awesome American pressure, drove the British, the trustee power, to return the 'sacred trust' to the United Nations, the successor to the League of Nations. Britain, in message to the secretary-general of the United Nations, on 12 April 1947, requested a special session on the question of Palestine.

During the World War II, strange as it may sound today, Jerusalem and the rest of Palestine, a pivotal base for the British war effort, enjoyed unprecedented peace and prosperity. The deadly struggle was being relentlessly waged in almost all other corners of the globe, while Palestine and the Middle East remained a haven of peace for a change. This is not to suggest that Palestine was not at the centre of the war. On the contrary, it was a hive of activity in every field of production and preparedness, and all the people's energies were harnessed in the service of the war effort, particularly in the Middle East theatre. The British skilfully and successfully harnessed the energies of the entire Palestinian people, Arabs and Jews alike, men and women, towns and villages, providing employment for all.

I was accepted by Cambridge University, but just two weeks before I was to depart to the United Kingdom, World

War II broke out. My departure was postponed and I spent 1939 and 1940 studying for my Oxford and Cambridge Higher Certificate (renamed today as the 'A' level). Having successfully finished this assignment and with no end to the war in sight, my elder brother, Anwar, himself a graduate of an English public school (Perse School) and Cambridge University, suggested that I enrol at the American University of Beirut (AUB). His most convincing argument, and he is a superb advocate, was that the AUB had excellent tennis courts and I was a very keen tennis player, holder of championship titles in Jerusalem as well as the winner of the international championship for juniors held annually in Alexandria.

I must attest that the AUB proved, for me, to be a far richer and more profound experience than I had originally thought it would. Here was a university on one of the most beautiful campuses in the world. For close to a century it had educated generations of superb Arab leaders. It was there that the Arab nationalist movement and awakening had flourished, sustained by successive generations of educated Arabs who subsequently shouldered the grave responsibilities of leadership in many countries of the region.

The AUB had the further unique advantage of imparting the best of Western scholarship against a background of a relatively traditional Arab society. Palestinians constituted the highest proportion of the student body, after the Lebanese. But in those years, when Arab nationalism prevailed over regionalism, provincialism and other forms of division, it hardly occurred to the Palestinians or their Arab brethren to make the slightest differentiation.

It is with pride and gratitude that I acknowledge my indebtedness to this outstanding centre of learning.

After graduation, my first job was with the press department of the Palestine mandatory government and the Palestine Broadcasting Service in Jerusalem as senior programme assistant. They were both challenging assignments to the extent that they kept me as fully as possible in the picture as to the traumatic events happening all over the world in a huge global war. The experience also stood me in good stead for the later period when we, the Palestinian Arabs, found ourselves involved in a struggle for our lives and very existence. In November 1947, United Nations General Assembly Resolution 181 was passed to partition Palestine and create a Palestinian Arab state along with a Jewish state, with Jerusalem and its environs as *corpus separatum* for 10 years, pending a new reappraisal. When, subsequently, the Palestinians were left on their own after the departure of the British, my colleagues and I continued our work in a professional manner, without the benefit of a government, for none existed, and without in any way diminishing from the high quality standards of credibility and news objectivity which we had learned from the British. It was an effective and subtle approach of which we are rightfully proud, notwithstanding occasional errors of judgment.

Before violence erupted in November 1947, Jerusalem must have been one of the most exhilarating cities in the world to live in. In addition to its intrinsic and serene beauty and lack of pollution, peace and quiet prevailed on all fronts. It was enjoying an unprecedented economic boom, and offered a very dynamic social, cultural, and sporting lifestyle. Life was blissful; there were few worries to detract from the richness that the city offered. Relations between Arabs, British, and Jews were, once more, as normal and business-like as they had ever been since the 1920s. Indeed, it could have been the ideal psychological launching ground for post-war independence with citizens of all creeds in cogent and willing co-existence.

But it turned out that there were two planes of reality: a visible one of concrete mutual accommodation; and an invisible one, in the form of an underground movement carefully and professionally organised by groups within the Jewish community. The most notorious and ruthless, though smallest in size, was the Stern Gang. It surfaced in 1944, committing a series of terrorist acts which were primarily, if not wholly, directed against the British mandatory power. Its actions raised concerns, but they were not considered serious or pervasive enough to significantly undermine the overall atmosphere of tranquillity in the country. The country simply dwarfed the impact of one small terrorist group.

Work, football matches involving various well-established clubs and social life continued without interruption. One of the most exciting events that I remember vividly was an encounter in 1943 between a visiting team of British footballs, who described themselves as the 'Wanderers', and an all-Palestinian team from clubs around the country. The Wanderers were a first-rate side. One of the players was Tom Finney (later Sir Tom), who went on to become one of the leading footballers in England. His performance was unforgettable. The game was played on the YMCA ground in Jerusalem. And even though the British 'ace' team not unexpectedly won 5-3, the Palestinian side presented formidable opposition. The Wanderers beat a select British army team decisively and all other challengers. Queues for the match in Jerusalem extended all the way from the YMCA to Mamilla Street a kilometre away, and it took almost half an hour to gain entry.

At the YMCA itself, sporting, cultural, and social activities were thriving, and I managed to take part in some tennis and table tennis championships. In football I played for the 1st XI of the 'Arab Club', renamed Ahli Club, founded in 1927 by my cousin, Ibrahim. But I was regarded as not much more than mediocre and was politely dropped from the side.

From 1945 to 1947, the impact of Jewish terrorist activities, still targeting mainly the British, increased in frequency and intensity. The Irgun Zvai Leumi, headed by Menachem Begin, subsequently Israel's prime minister and comprising an estimated 5,000 underground membership, carried out sustained, ruthless and indiscriminate bombings, assassinations, and even the hanging of British soldiers from tree branches.

The worst terrorist act, up to that moment, was the blowing-up in July 1946 of the southern wing of the King David Hotel which had been the headquarters of the British administration. Almost 120 people, mostly senior British, Arab, and Jewish civil servants were killed instantly or were buried under the debris of the building. The body of a Mr G Walsh, director of supply, was thrown out by the explosion and splattered on the walls of the YMCA building opposite. Most of the victims were Palestinian Arabs, being the majority in the civil service.

For a few days after the explosion, army engineers used their equipment to remove the debris, stopping at regular intervals to monitor if any victims were still alive. A few did survive. It was a very ugly experience and because my office was at the Daoud building was very close by I would stop to watch this painful operation. I must have been one of the lucky ones, since just before the bombing I had been on my way to the King David for a drink, as I was in the habit of doing at lunchtime. Shukri Qutteineh, a veteran correspondent of *Al-Difa'* daily newspaper, stopped me in Mamilla Street and we had a chat. That 10-15 minute conversation was, in hindsight, what saved me from being blown up, as the bar and the Sudanese barman were casualties of the explosion which followed minutes later.

The main military Jewish force about which very little was published or known – at least by the Palestinians, including their leadership – was the Haganah. The first public disclosure of its estimated strength of 70,000-80,000 well-organized troops was made by the British journalist John Kimche in March or April 1943, just before the end of the mandate, as I recollect. It is difficult, even today, to ascertain the kind of division of labour which had existed between the Haganah and the other and much smaller terrorist splinter groups. Formally, the Jewish Agency would condemn a terrorist act if it happened to be particularly heinous.

At the Daoud building, owned by a Bethlehem Palestinian, there were also close to 70 foreign journalists covering events from their offices there. At the age of 24 it was more exciting than frightening to watch and even be the target of incessant firing, mortar shelling and explosions.

But our building increasingly became the target of bomb threats by Jewish groups, principally because the Arabic news services were operating from there. After the partition resolution in 1947, Britain's abandonment of its 'trust' and the inexorable disintegration of governmental authority impelled us to act virtually independently, in the service of our own cause. Our ties to the government became little more than nominal. Such were the dangers we faced that the daily routine was to vacate the whole building to allow British army engineers to conduct a thorough search for possible explosives.

The British director of the news services, Colonel Alex Jose, who was a good friend, asked me politely if we minded moving our offices to the German Colony, an Arab quarter in Qatamon, West Jerusalem. These premises had been used by the English section for news and programmes. I replied that we did not mind since it would safeguard the lives of the corps of foreign journalists and other innocent third parties.

We continued our work from the new premises until 15 May 1948 when the last morning news was broadcast punctually from West Jerusalem. The reason was that immediately after the departure of the British high commissioner from Jerusalem at 8am that day the Jewish regular forces launched their all-out advance on the whole of Jerusalem, cutting off the electricity supply which powered our transmitters. We had no alternative but to depart to Ramallah, a town just to the north of Jerusalem, under very heavy fire, taking with us some of the essential equipment which was not available there. The trip involved a huge risk, but we were determined to carry out our duty, as usual, regardless of any danger.

A Jewish settlement, Nevi Yacoub, lay mid-way astride the main, in those days single-lane road between Jerusalem and Ramallah. The Jewish armed groups manned concrete watch tower right on the edge of that curved and narrow road.

It had become the habit of the armed elements in that settlement to fire on every other car passing along that main artery, with the aim of killing, wounding, or maiming the maximum number of civilian passengers. But they stopped short of stopping all traffic by firing at every car. As with Russian roulette, there was a 50-50 chance of survival. Five of my colleagues at the Palestine Broadcasting Service and I made a two-hour stop at Shufat, a suburb of north Jerusalem on the morning of 15 May 1948, in the hope that a British or Jordanian army convoy would pass in their withdrawal from Palestine in deference to the United Nations resolutions and afford us some safety. Unfortunately, none came; withdrawal had apparently been completed, at least at our end. I had no alternative but to tell my colleagues that our arrival in Ramallah was imperative to prepare and broadcast our scheduled 2pm newscast. Even though we were responsible to no authority but ourselves, I felt very strongly that it would be a terrible betrayal of our people if we failed to be on the air on that first day on which we became accountable to our own sense of duty alone.

Since driving up the road to Ramallah was unquestionably a matter of life-and-death, because of the Jewish ambush at Nevi Yacoub, the late Mr Muhammad Adeeb al-Amiri, our older colleague, suggested that each one of us should be given the option of deciding whether or not to complete the journey.

It is a testimony to the sense of dedication, duty and patriotism that the six of us unhesitatingly decided to proceed, in the full knowledge of the mortal danger lying a few kilometres ahead of us. We instructed our driver, George, to continue driving even if he was hit by a hundred bullets, to look unwaveringly ahead, and to avoid drawing attention to us as we passed the Nevi Yacoub death-trap. There could not have been a more disciplined individual, given that George was a government employee and not a soldier or a commando.

There were a few tense moments as we passed the settlement but, to our great surprise, no firing came from that heavy machine-gun emplacement.

We were lucky. The car which preceded us was fired upon and also the car which followed us, with a number of passengers hit. Two days earlier, one of the foremost garment merchants in Jerusalem, Fayez Muhtadi, lost his life while driving through this treacherous trap. His shop was in the Italian Building on Jaffa Road.

I and other colleagues at the broadcasting station in Ramallah used to drive to Jerusalem on many nights during this period of fighting, after finishing our news schedule at 11pm, to feel that we were at the centre of the battle, rather than tucked away in the safety of the Teggart building, re-named al-Muqataa by the Palestinian Authority. We were constantly under fire, but luckily emerged unscathed.

When the Jordanian army reached Ramallah on 18 May 1948 it provided us with British army uniforms with the insignia of war correspondents. In this attire we accompanied the army to many of its combat zones, accepting all the risks involved. In what turned out to be an extremely cold winter, those army uniforms were a great blessing, because there was no heating whatsoever at our offices or lodging.

CHAPTER 5

PALESTINE VIVISECTED

On 29 November 1947, I was at my desk at the Palestine Broadcasting Service, situated in the vicinity of the Italian hospital, Mea Shearim, and the Russian Compound, routinely editing the evening news bulletin, when the wire services of the news agencies bombarded us, and the rest of the world, with news of the UN General Assembly's decision to partition Palestine into two states, Arab and Jewish, with Jerusalem and its environs as a *corpus seperatum*.

To put it mildly, my other Palestinian colleagues and I heard this outcome with consternation, considering that we had all lived in the belief and hope that Palestine, whole and undivided, would at long last gain its independence, as a trust territory, in accordance with the British White Paper of 1939, which had been the official policy of the British mandatory government. It was our profound conviction that Arabs and Jews could live in amity and peace under one united or federal government, with equal rights for all and discrimination against none. This was stipulated in the minority report of the United Nations Special Commission on Palestine (UNSCOP) in August 1947. Indeed, the United States government had itself, through its representative at the United Nations, Senator Warren Austin, proposed a cantonisation plan, whereby the country would remain geographically intact, but with a feasible system of decentralisation, to accommodate demographic realities on the ground. Dr Judah Magnes, Chancellor of the Hebrew University in Jerusalem, had suggested a binational state, but regrettably his advocacy fell on deaf ears, in both camps.

In hindsight, I am convinced that neither Arabs nor Jews during that tempestuous period had the cool-headedness, vision, or wisdom to strike the necessary compromise. The Palestinians were against the vivisection of Palestine, which is a small, compact country. Partition would devour its body and soul. It is endowed with plains, coastlines and mountains, lakes and rivers. One passes from 300 metre peaks in upper Galilee, to the lowest spot on earth at the Dead Sea, all in perfect harmony and complementarity. Jerusalem, this jewel of cities, is interrelated in all aspects of life as a single, undivided city, geographically and demographically: water, electricity, sewerage, health services, telecommunications, trade, shopping centres, agriculture, tourism, and all else that one expects in city life made it one and indivisible. When partition was adopted and internecine fighting began, the tenants living in the lower floor of our house were Dr and Mrs Segre. Dr Segre, an engineer, and his wife were of the Jewish faith. We did our utmost to ensure their safety with the combatants on our side until the situation deteriorated into fixed war lines and prudence dictated that they depart to a safer haven on the other side of the city, which they did with the help of their security forces.

Jerusalem was a leader among Arab cities in the installation of modern amenities. It was the first city in the Middle East, for example, to have a complete sewerage system installed in 1929. The garden of our house where I was brought up, opposite the American Colony Hotel, had a beautiful flower garden which I loved as a child. This was taken over by the municipality, with my father's willing consent, because the new sewerage system was to pass through it. Then, the telephone was installed, if I remember correctly, in 1927, early enough by world standards; electricity was there even earlier because I do not remember any other system of lighting preceding it in my house. But the streets and alleys of the Old City were lit every evening by oil lanterns on lampposts. My father had been awarded the contract to light them, and I remember his employees holding ladders, the oil, and the matches with which they lit every one of them every evening and put them out at dawn. It was a lucrative though small business, an antecedent to what the government awarded to the Palestine Electric Company. The company implemented the Rutenberg scheme, the brainchild in the 1920s of Pinchas Rutenberg to generate power through a hydroelectric project using the waters of the River Jordan. The concession covered almost the whole of Palestine, with the notable exception of Nablus city which established its own company.

It was not easy, either physically or psychologically, to break up something that had been in existence from time immemorial, and was running smoothly. The Zionist Jews, on the other hand, had their own agenda too, even though their leadership had publicly declared their acceptance of the partition plan. The memoirs, documents, secret papers, and books have subsequently disclosed that the pioneer leadership of Israel, David Ben-Gurion, Golda Meir, Menachem Begin, Shimon Peres, Moshe Dayan and others secretly welcomed the Arab leadership's rejection of partition, and exploited the Arabs' miscalculations and misjudgement to forge a war in which the Palestinians, totally unarmed and ill-prepared, would be the certain losers. When, in the wake of the partition decision, sporadic rioting erupted in Shamaa quarter close to St Julian's Road leading to the YMCA and King David Hotel, Jewish forces started shelling Arab quarters, neighbourhoods met to assess the gravity of the situation, with each one declaring what arms were available for self-defence. There were hardly any, because the British mandatory power, under defence ordinances, had imposed the death penalty on anyone caught in possession of even a bullet. Scores of Palestinians received the death penalty by hanging for possessing firearms during the great 1936-39 rebellion. My mother informed me that during the 1930s my father had possessed a small revolver, I forget its make. When the British issued their defence ordinances – more accurately martial law – my parents found it prudent to hide this lethal weapon. The revolver was wrapped in white linen and buried in a big earth-filled flowerpot and placed with other flower pots on the eastern balcony opposite the American Colony Hotel. We later emptied the pot and recovered a dilapidated, rusty contraption, fit for permanent burial. Besides, I had no previous training with firearms. This was the most that we could provide for self-defence, even though our house was a war front and suffered almost total destruction twice, once in 1948 and again in 1967.

The generation of officers and men, who had fought in the ranks of the Ottoman army during World War I had, by 1948, either passed away or were so advanced in age as to be useless as part of a fighting force. The younger generations of Palestinians under the mandate were never given military training. The exceptions were those who had joined the police force, but their training was strictly civilian law enforcement. During World War II, the Jewish Agency had obtained the British government's approval for creating the Jewish Brigade – a division's strength – as part of the Allied armies. This eventually became the backbone of the Haganah which played the decisive role against the Palestinian Arabs and the poorly equipped Arab armies when the moment of decision arrived. The political leadership of the Palestinian people was largely in exile or in detention, and the Palestinian people were thus deprived of the opportunity to request the creation of an Arab brigade, parallel to the Jewish one, to gain military experience which would have afforded them a semblance of protection when their survival was at stake.

The Palestinians' lands were squandered largely without resistance and by inexcusable default. I saw city after city, town after town, village after village, suburb after suburb, and building after building fall to Jewish forces because there was no-one to defend them. On a Monday in April 1948, the British commander in charge of the Daoud building in Jerusalem where I worked requested me to inform my elder brother, Anwar, chairman of the National Committee of Jerusalem, that the British army contingent was withdrawing from the building, as part of the overall withdrawal from the country. He would naturally have informed Anwar's Jewish counterpart of the impending move, as the building was at a crucial crossroads between King George Street and the street leading to Talbiya and Baqaa quarters. I asked my brother if he could send a small contingent to guard the building since after all, it was an integral part of the Arab quarters in West Jerusalem. He replied: 'But from where am I to get such a force? The only contingent we have is that in charge of defending Herod's Gate quarter and it is a mere 25-man strong force, commanded by the Veteran Commando, Bahjat Abu Gharbieh. Thus, the Daoud building was taken over by Jewish forces unchallenged. Qatamon, at the farthest end of West Jerusalem, had a defence force of 80 men under the leadership of Ibrahim Abu Dayyeh, a well-known commander. During 8-10 May 1948, a few days before the end of the mandate, Jewish forces, at something like battalion strength, attacked this contingent. The battle raged for three days and ended only when all but one of the defenders had been killed and their meagre stock of ammunition had been exhausted. The only survivor was Ibrahim, the commander, who suffered serious wounds. My brother, Anwar, and I went to visit him where he lay, on a mattress with serious back wounds, in total exhaustion. He had not slept for three days and nights while the engagement was on. I mention this particular episode, not to narrate history, but only to show how haphazard, isolated and static Palestinian defences were, if they existed at all. By contrast, the Jewish forces had a central mobile force which could be dispatched to reinforce and relieve those requiring support, within a coherent plan. Palestinians fought with utmost bravery and self-sacrifice but, to no avail.

They had, under the command of Abdul Qader al-Husseini, this legendary commander, the nearest thing to a strike force, *al-Jihad al-Muqqaddas* (sacred Jihad), headquartered in the town of Bir Zeit. But it was less than 1,000 strong, poorly equipped, and somewhat detached from the day-to-day combat which was under way in almost every Palestinian city, town and village. It was no match for Israel's regular forces, although in guerrilla warfare it had been pretty effective.

With this Qatamon force decapitated, and with the British and Jordanian armies, which were guarding consulates and vital installations, withdrawing with the approach of 15 May 1948, buildings and whole villages were being destroyed (the Deir Yassin massacre in April 1948 being the most notorious event). The Arab civilian population of West Jerusalem found itself naked and vulnerable: women and children started their trek towards East Jerusalem and the relative safety of the walled Old City, each carrying a few bundles of their most precious possessions. Anwar, as chairman of the National Committee, requested Bahjat Abu Gharbieh to stop their influx, especially through the Musrara Arab quarter near the American consulate. When he tried to do so, they replied, politely but firmly. 'What do you have that will enable you to safeguard our lives and defend our homes and our children,' they asked. 'If you provide us with that protection, then we will go home promptly, but don't expect us to go there without a soul to defend us.' Bahjat had no alternative but to let them pass and desert their homes – as it turned out – for ever.

Narrating these facts will, perhaps, answer those who have alleged that the Arab governments ordered the civilian population of Palestine to abandon their homes, and return only after liberation. I doubt whether those governments cared a hoot about the safety of the civilian population, less still knew much about their ordeal. The truth of the matter is that every single Palestinian family had to decide on its own whether or not to accept the risk of war and act accordingly. As far as my own family was concerned, my mother, younger brothers and sisters and other close relatives, I insisted that we stay put in our homes until the end of April, a couple of weeks before the end of the mandate. But the situation was becoming darker by the day, and the British security presence was fast disintegrating. I said to myself: obstinacy may be a virtue, but only up to a point; and wisdom is the better part of valour. Repeated attempts had been made to blow us up. Other homes in the vicinity were targeted, including a 300-year-old historic palace which belonged to my eldest brother, Hassan, opposite Sheikh Jarrah mosque. And what will happen, I wondered, when 15 May arrives and the Israelis begin their all-out invasion? I decided, with the approval of Anwar, to let the women and children – almost 20 in all – leave temporarily for Lebanon, while we would stay on to weather whatever was in store. Two mini-buses were hired to transport them to Lebanon and, as their vehicles passed through Amman, then a modest city of 50,000 (today 1.5 million), the crowds, roused by the Palestinian struggle, cheered them enthusiastically. Little, I surmise, did they realise that those they were cheering as heroes were forerunners of the massive catastrophe which befell the Palestinian people a month or two later, in the form of the mass exodus of refugees, heading off in all directions. Their misfortune has haunted the entire landscape of the Middle East, if not the world, up to this day.

In any event, the family rented a house in Itat, near Aley on Mount Lebanon (a very beautiful spot) and the Red Cross were prompt in providing them with generous assistance. They acted in this way, to their credit, in every corner, in Palestine and beyond, wherever Palestinian refugees dropped anchor. A year later, Resolution 194, adopted by the UN General Assembly on 11 December 1948, provided for the repatriation of the refugees to their homes and compensation for losses incurred. It also set up an agency for those wishing to return, the United Nation Relief and Works Agency (UNRWA). This was to cater to the needs of the Palestinian refugees, replacing the Red Cross. I have had a great deal to do with this agency, as undersecretary and then minister of reconstruction and development, responsible for the Palestinian refugees in Jordan. The duties of this United Nations agency was to have ended immediately after repatriation, but, alas, because of the failure of the international community to resolve the Palestine issue, in all its aspects including that of refugees, the agency is still functioning some 60 years after its establishment. And the end is not yet in sight, with the refugee population expanding from 750,000 in 1948 to around 4.25 million registered refugees in 2008 primarily in Jordan, Syria and Lebanon.

There is another episode that will help to illustrate the feel of the situation at that time. A couple of weeks before the end of the mandate, my colleague at Palestine Broadcasting, a very gentlemanly man, Spiro al-Issa, asked me to accompany him to his new house in the Qatamon quarter of West Jerusalem. He was a few years older than me and had recently married. He bought a house which he furnished tastefully with modern saloons, dining room, bedrooms, Persian carpets etc.

I went with him to inspect the house, in which he had not yet lived, and he was joyous that everything looked neat and beautiful. He then said: 'I am locking the house temporarily because I do not know what will happen over the next few weeks. It is safer to lock it well since most probably our work at the broadcasting will be conducted temporarily from Ramallah, instead of our studios in Qatamon.'

He locked the house with a relaxed smile and said: 'Things will return to normal in a few weeks' time.' Little did he know that the smile which covered his face as he locked the main door of the house was a farewell smile and a point of no return.

It was reported that in the aftermath of the 1948 cataclysm and the plunder of the Palestinian Arab quarters of West Jerusalem, the Persian carpet market in New York was fully occupied for two years, selling these plundered carpets; and Israel does recognize that this had happened.

The good Spiro al-Issa died many years ago, without ever seeing his house again or being compensated for the losses incurred. His brother, Saeed al-Issa, also a colleague, was a highly gifted poet and after 1948 joined the BBC Arabic Service, to which he was a great asset.

The Palestinian refugees belonged to different categories, reflecting the diffusion and stratification of Palestinian society. The rich and the reasonably well-to-do did not even register as refugees and launched their new lives in various pursuits and directions. The former civil servants during the mandate lived off their pensions and savings, because they were too old to start from scratch again.

The professional class restarted their careers, but only slowly. But the vast majority were rural refugees who had lost their villages and their agricultural lands, in addition to gainful employment in various installations and structures like ports, airports, refineries, government offices, and so on. They were literally destitute and had become totally dependent on UNRWA for their survival, health, and education. They were lodged in tent camps and for many years refused cement structures because to them, such a change symbolised resettlement outside their homeland. They even resisted the planting of trees, although most of them were seasoned farmers and loved farming. This feeling of alienation, siege and abandonment persisted for decades, but has mellowed somewhat with the passage of years, the passing away of the older generation and the overall awareness that repatriation, though internationally recognised as a right, is not easily attainable and must await a new turn in the wheels of fortune. In the meantime, normal lives must go on.

A ceasefire, which had not always been observed, ended abruptly after only three days when Israeli forces attacked on the central front: Lydda, Ramleh and their large cultivable plains. Talat Ghussein, who later in life became Kuwait's Ambassador to Washington and was renowned for his embassy's lavish hospitality, visited me at my office at the Teggart building in Ramallah where our temporary studios were located. He is a close relative and a dear friend from school days in Jerusalem. His father was leader of Palestine's youth party and a member of the Arab Higher Committee. The British exiled him to the Seychelles Islands, together with other Palestinian leaders.

Talat told me that he had just arrived from Ramleh, on urgent business in Ramallah. He added that he had left behind a huge pile of harvested wheat which belonged to the Bustami *waqf* foundation administered by his family. It was worth several thousand Palestine pounds (sterling). He wondered aloud whether the existing truce would last sufficiently to enable him to sell the crop or that it might end abruptly and cut him off completely from Ramleh. His worst forebodings came to pass and he at once found himself a refugee. Those of us at the broadcasting station arranged for him to apply for a job in the English news section. He was given the job over scores of other equally qualified candidates who had been rendered unemployed as a result of the dissolution of the mandatory government, and with no Palestinian government to take its place. Twenty days later, Talat came to me and said: 'Hazem, I want to thank you for helping me get this job. But, as you know, I have my mother and six young sisters to support, and I cannot do this with the kind of salary I receive at the broadcasting station.' His salary was a meagre 40 Palestine pounds a month, but this was the standard rate more than half a century ago. He added that with his town of Ramleh lost, he had no alternative but to seek a more lucrative job in order to support his large family. He asked me not to mention this to anyone, adding he wished to depart quietly without any goodbyes. I respected and understood his wish. He travelled first to Damascus where his family had taken refuge. From there, he landed a job with the government of Yemen, during the indescribably medieval and closed rule of Imam Yahya. He tolerated that stifling life for no more than one year, before heading to Kuwait to hold the job of secretary-general of the Development Board and eventually other important posts. Not that life was easy in Kuwait either: during the 1950s one had to cope with intense heat of 50° centigrade or more in summer, without air-conditioning, running water, proper housing, and other amenities of life that became available after the petroleum revolution of the 1970s. In the meantime, he had to put up with a life of hardship, as the Kuwaiti people themselves did. But, to the credit of Kuwait and its wise rulers, particularly Emir Abdullah al-Salem, the first ruler after independence in 1962, the Palestinian community, which expanded to half a million over the years, were accorded every hospitality and friendship which enabled them to flourish and help their kinsmen in the Palestinian territories of the West Bank and Gaza Strip, and other countries where Palestinian refugees settled after

1948. The story of Talat Ghussein epitomises the uprooting, the hardships, the uncertainties, and the challenges which confronted hundreds of thousands of Palestinian households in the aftermath of their dispersal.

Meanwhile, a substantial portion of the Palestinian people remained in their homeland, in the West Bank and Gaza Strip, which had been spared occupation thanks to the Jordanian army in the former, and the Egyptian army in the latter. My home and most of my father's real estate were in what is now East Jerusalem. The sense of being a refugee, therefore, did not strike me as sharply as it did the inhabitants of West Jerusalem and the refugees whose homes were in what became Israel, over 78 percent of the mandated territory of Palestine. For a year or so, we lived in East Jerusalem and the rest of the West Bank under a Jordanian military administration, but many of the governors were Palestinians, because of the familial relationships which existed between Jordan and Palestine – one people in two countries.

At the broadcasting station, we were put on the official payroll of Jordan's civil service, along with other structures and functions of government. It was universally recognised that the West Bank, cut off from the sea and the rest of Palestine, could not survive alone, with no means of sustaining itself and without sea or land outlets to the outside world, except via Jordan. Delegation after delegation went to Amman to meet King Abdullah I to seek unity with Jordan, and political conferences were held in several West Bank cities as well as towns requesting it. Their pleadings were answered and a free and fair election, to the integrity of which I can truly attest, was held in 1950. The result was the establishment of a house of deputies with equal representation for both territories. The parliament on 24 April 1950 adopted an Act of Unity under a Hashemite constitutional monarchy to be named the Hashemite Kingdom of Jordan, but with the *proviso* that the said unity should not prejudice the final outcome of the Palestine question, compatible with Arab aspirations, international legitimacy and norms of justice.

I, for one, and the vast majority of Palestinians in the West Bank supported this unity, with its *provisos*, as the best deal possible in the aftermath of a monumental catastrophe. But there still remained some psychological ramifications, a dichotomy, principally over the question of identity. The central government in Amman instructed us at the broadcasting station to drop our distinctive identifying call sign of: 'This is Jerusalem, the Palestine Broadcasting House'. This name over decades had become a trademark, and it seemed to us, the three senior directors at the broadcasting – Azmi Nashashibi, Muhammad Adeeb al- miri and myself – that foregoing the name of Palestine, and changing the call sign to 'the broadcasting service of the Hashemite Kingdom of Jordan', was tantamount to the abandonment of Palestine, at least symbolically. We could not accept the change and refused to implement it. The government, fully understanding our predicament, did not react impulsively, but instead, created a new department, the Department of Press and Publications, which became part of the Ministry of Foreign Affairs.

The three of us were transferred to the new department, in both Jerusalem and Amman, and a new director of broadcasting, later Governor and Ambassador, Ihsan Hashem, took over the post. On the day that he took up his post the name was changed. The move, we later learnt, caused tears to be shed in every Palestinian habitation, whether in Palestine or outside of it. For the change of name – a mere symbol – had inflicted a deep wound in their consciousness and also sharpened the realisation that Palestine had faded away and was there no more.

On 24 February 1949 on the island of Rhodes, Egypt the leading Arab country, signed a permanent Armistice Agreement with Israel, under the auspices of Dr Ralph Bunch, assistant secretary-general of the United Nations for political affairs. Lebanon followed suit, on 24 March 1949, Jordan on 3 April 1949 and lastly Syria on 20 July 1949.

The Armistice Agreements, although without prejudice to the ultimate solution of the Palestine question, in fact ended the war for good, and the United States, Britain, and France, obligated themselves in the tri-partite declaration of 25 May 1950 to oppose any resort to war in the region for a solution of the problem.

They pledged to guarantee the territorial integrity of all the states in the region as they existed at the time of the declaration, without prejudice to the final territorial settlement, or the demands of any of the contending parties. The mechanism for a solution was assigned to a United Nations Palestine Conciliation Commission, comprising the United States, France and Turkey. The Commission, after extended negotiation between the Arab states concerned, including Palestinian representatives, and Israel, succeeded in inducing all the participant parties to initial on 12 May 1949 what came to be known as the Lausanne protocol. Ahmad al-Shuqairi, first chairman of the Palestine Liberation Organisation, Waleed Salah, attorney general and subsequently Jordanian Minister of Foreign Affairs, Farid Assad, banker and businessman, and lawyer Aziz Shihadeh were the Palestinian representatives attached to the Arab delegations at the conference, and were staunchly in support of the protocol; indeed, they persuaded the Arab states to accept it.

The protocol stipulated that all parties should accept the 29 November 1947 General Assembly decision to partition Palestine, as the basis for a solution of the Palestine question. But Israel, under the leadership of David Ben-Gurion, reneged on the signature of its delegation and refused to implement the agreement, which mandated withdrawal from Palestinian territories occupied in excess of what had been allotted to it under partition. He also refused to repatriate the Palestinian refugees to their homes under UN resolution 194 adopted by the General Assembly on 11 December 1948. Israel also rejected the idea of an international regime for greater Jerusalem stipulated therein, which comprised mostly Arab quarters, and suggested the internationalisation of East Jerusalem, which had been saved for the Palestinian Arabs by the skills and heroism of the Jordanian army. Thus, a long stalemate began, freezing the problem in all its ramifications but building up enormous tensions which found expression in guerrilla activity, military coups d'état, the 1956 Suez war, incursions and counter-incursions, social and political rumblings and upheavals, and the final eruption of the disastrous war of 5 June 1967, in consequence of which Israel completed the occupation of the whole of Palestine, and other Arab territories.

In the meantime, with a permanent armistice in place, a deadly and almost deafening silence fell upon Jerusalem and other territories of the West Bank. The roar of guns and the rattle of firearms, part of life for so long, could be heard no more. At this point the human dimension of the tragedy came into focus. The Old City, already congested with its own inhabitants, saw its population multiplied many times by the inhabitants of West Jerusalem who had taken refuge there with relatives. Others had sought shelter in some of the huge monasteries, which are a hallmark of the city, and under any roof that could give them safe temporary shelter. By contrast, the Arab quarters, outside the walls to the north, east, and south were virtually deserted. Most of their inhabitants had evidently sought the security which the high wall of the Old City seemingly provided, or had gone abroad. I settled in one of the two big houses which my family owned in the Herod's Gate quarter, with 50-year-old pine trees, aging but strong and imposing. The streets were literally deserted, with only groups of marauding stray dogs disturbing the quiet of the empty streets. Whenever I walked in the evenings to visit the handful of friends who had remained in their homes I carried a stick to help me ward off those aggressive barking dogs, and I must confess that during these walks I was uneasy, to put it mildly. Living alone in a 25-room house is somewhat daunting, even frightening. Every noise, tick or move resounded and re-echoed like a whisper in the dark, and there was not a soul to talk to or communicate with. These quarters, without people, became a shadow city and this state of affairs lasted for several months until Jerusalemites started steadily yet hesitatingly their trek back. Electricity generators for united Jerusalem had been in the Musrara Arab quarter which Israel had occupied. East Jerusalem now had to improvise its own electricity generation, and provide new sources of water from Ein Fara in the Ramallah subdistrict, to replace the Ras el-Ein reservoir in the central plains, which was cut off from East Jerusalem.

The inhabitants of Jerusalem, a highly sophisticated, versatile and experienced community, suddenly found themselves jolted into dispersal: uprooted physically from their homes, civil service jobs (Jerusalem was the capital city), commercial pursuits, real estate, the professions and services, etc. The Old City and a much shrunken Palestine could not possibly absorb them, or afford them the kind of future to which their endowments entitled them. They migrated to all corners of the globe, according to each families' or person's assessment and prospects. Many immigrated to the United States and integrated well into its melting pot. Many others went to Saudi Arabia and to the various gulf emirates, which the oil revolution had placed on a course of undreamed of development and prosperity. Their contributions to their new host countries were significant and substantial. When I visited Kuwait in June 1962, as Foreign Minister of Jordan to partake in the first independence celebrations, I visited the Emir Abdullah al-Salem at his austere office. In the course of the conversation I felt I should thank him for the hospitality and brotherhood which Kuwait had shown to our people, Palestinian and Jordanian. He did not let me finish and said: 'It is me who should thank you, for it is your people who have contributed so much to the building of Kuwait.' What a great pity that such deep bonds should have been so rudely shaken and undone by what seemed to be an ambivalent or even hostile attitude when Iraq invaded Kuwait in 1990. I am certain that the vast majority of Palestinians in Kuwait did not, in any way, share the regrettable utterings made by some of the Palestinian leadership during the crises, even though their community of close to half a million were expelled, and made to pay the price for the error of the few. In any event, the Palestinian migrations have not been in vain: they joined the ranks of billionaires, millionaires, well-to-do entrepreneurs, and professional classes in all walks of life, including academia. Jerusalem would have thrived and been enriched with their presence, but unfortunately the city has been denied their contribution.

Those years in the middle of the 20th century were turbulent and traumatic. Years of tension and turbulence – putting one's life on the line in the service of duty, the whistle of bullets over one's head, the explosions, the uprooting, the uncertainty – culminated in the *nakba* (catastrophe) which befell the Palestinian people. And while I weathered the war and turbulence because I was totally immersed in them, and had no time even to get sick, the silence and the pent-up feelings were evidently too much to bear. I suffered what amounted to a nervous breakdown. Although I did not consult a doctor for treatment, when I mentioned my ailment to Dr Asaad Bishara, a friend in Jerusalem, he gave me a packet of vitamin B tablets. Whenever I took one, my face flushed red and left a rash. I threw the vitamins away and depended on my own stamina for recuperation. Evidently the vitamins in the government's store had passed their sell-by date. There was no government to check on such an essential service.

So, one phase had ended and a new one was set to begin.

CHAPTER 6

A New Start

With the accumulated return of many Jerusalemites, a semblance of a community began to emerge. Three newspapers, *al-Dif'*, *Falastin* and *al-Jihad*, resumed publication which had been suspended in May 1948 after their departure from Jaffa, their original headquarters. Raja al-Issa, owner and publisher of *Falastin* newspaper – the oldest of the three publications– told me that all the publishers, owners and writers had had to abandon everything when the Jewish forces closed in on the city and occupied it. They had had to start anew, with hardly any assistance from anyone. The papers were modest in size because their constituency was relatively small. As mentioned earlier, I became director of the press department in Jerusalem, affiliated to the Ministry of Foreign Affairs. My assignment included press censorship, and I was required to affix my stamp to every article of political or military importance. But, to my credit, and I am very proud to put this on record, I never prohibited a single article or imposed censorship on any item. I did this out of a deep conviction in the freedom of expression, including the right of dissent. I was thoroughly imbued with the ideas of John Stuart Mill in his celebrated work *On Liberty* and, of course, other classical libertarians. My experience in the press department of the mandate government, the Palestine Information Office, also fortified me in this conviction. It was at this post that I edited *Muntada* (forum) during World War II, in which I solicited the writings of the most accomplished Palestinian writers, including such luminaries as Isaaf Nashashibi, Khalil Sakakini, Dr Ishaq Musa al-Husseini, Iskandar Khouri al-Bajjali, Ali Dajani, and Abdul Rahman Bushnaq. Dr Martin, a British university professor, seconded to work at this department, was my senior but also my counterpart. He never questioned me for a moment about the content of the contributions because any subject was acceptable, short of seditious ones which there never were.

Returning to 1950, on some occasions the editors of the newspapers would draw my attention to some material which they felt might embarrass them in front of King Abdullah I of Jordan. They hoped that I would censor such material, without embarrassing themselves in front of the writers whose articles they did not wish to publish. Thus, they could put the blame on censorship. But I never afforded them this luxury. My advice generally was: 'If you feel that the material is worth publishing, but are afraid of the king's reaction, go ahead and publish because he is understanding, wise and good-hearted, although short-tempered. The ultimate penalty – and this was generally the case – is that you will be recalled to Amman to meet the king. He will give you a piece of his mind, with a scolding which will make you blush. He will then invite you to lunch and go out of his way to assure you that his displeasure is over, that there is no rancour in his heart and that the whole matter is closed.'

This may sound banal and not worthy of mention. But this is far from the case when we recall what came to be the fate of Arab journalists in later decades under the authoritarian regimes in certain parts of the Arab world. The penalty for dissent, for an indiscretion, and for criticism can range from long imprisonment and incarceration, to even bodily mutilation and liquidation. The secret apparatuses and tools of oppression which were perfected in East Germany and other countries with totalitarian regimes were transferred to our region. There is no way of telling to what extent such evil practices have inhibited freedom of expression at the source through self-censorship. In the absence of a minimum standard of respect for human rights, one should not expect an ordinary journalist to be a hero, a Mahatma Gandhi or a Nelson Mandela. They are brave, but not reckless or suicidal.

But there is another source of inhibition which has weighed heavily on free expression, namely the corruption of money. With the huge surpluses accumulated with the explosion of oil prices, many publishing houses, newspapers and magazines, as well as writers, broadcasting stations and television networks, have been seduced by the glitter of gold and the promise of riches. If those instruments are subdued or seduced, who is going to watch over the conduct or the misconduct of public affairs and the welfare of the citizens?

With the return of normalcy, or what came to be taken as normal, and adjustment to the new state of affairs in a shrunken Jerusalem in the framework of peace and quiet, I felt that it was high time for me to get married. I was 28 years of age, already late by Jerusalem and Middle Eastern standards, and I started in earnest searching for a partner in life.

In the ultra-conservative and closed society that existed in that era, a man could not find his fiancée at a random social gathering, a dancing party or at work, because the two sexes were still mainly segregated, except in a few colleges. Arranged marriages were still the norm, and one should not dismiss some of the positive aspects of such a system, including a thorough investigation of the prospective husband or wife. For if one asked for the hand of a girl in marriage, both families would begin extensive inquiries as to his or her character, family background, temperament, health, education, career, and, last but not least, her looks. It is a more thorough and on-the-spot investigation than is available at present on the internet.

One day, an aunt of mine, Ruqiya, one of whose nieces, Ammuna, had been married in Nablus, came to the house of my elder brother, Anwar, when I was there. She said, trying to hide the thrill in her voice while choosing her words carefully, she had heard that I was looking for a prospective wife. She added that she did not wish to intrude (intermediaries are generally careful lest a marriage goes foul and they are blamed for the recommendation) but because she cared for my happiness she felt a duty to suggest the name of a very beautiful 20-year-old in Nablus, Qadar Taher Masri, from the renowned Masri family. She gave me a picture of her (she was a brunette with green eyes), adding that she was highly intelligent, and a graduate of the Friends College in Ramallah, a Quaker School.

Anwar, who is a prompt decision-maker and a pragmatist, immediately said: 'Let's make the one-hour drive to Nablus now and see what comes of it.' I was afforded the opportunity to see Qadar discreetly, and I must say I fell for her at first sight. On returning to Jerusalem we deliberated on the next step, which was to ask her family for her hand in marriage.

Her father, a well-known prominent businessman was dead, and we had to make the proposal to her eldest brother. After waiting some time for a reply – which greatly unsettled me, because I was bent on this marriage – I was given a positive reply. My engagement lasted for six months.

It is worth mentioning here that the value system of Palestinian and Jordanian society, and I presume other Arab societies, requires reticence before acceding to a proposed marriage. This is to stress the great value that a family put on their daughter and their great love of her; so it is only with reluctance that they give her away in marriage. Later in life a wife could thus boast that she was not given away lightly.

Anyway, we celebrated our marriage in Nablus, in the presence of almost 200 guests from both families and friends, all attired in their best, most fashionable and lavish dresses. The orchestra of Palestine Broadcasting, where I had worked for years, was there to help us celebrate the wedding. We spent our honeymoon in Austria, a beautiful country which, in April 1951, was still marked by the scars of war. Vienna was a mass of damaged buildings, including the cathedral. Many of the inhabitants bore war injuries. Yet Vienna and the Viennese wore a brave face, with spotless cleanliness, and excellent coffee shops, with the most delicious pastries for which Vienna is famed. The opera house was also in shape and functioning. We attended the opera and, in addition to the Viennese, the audience included American, Russian, British, and French officers. I was impressed by the fact that the Russian officers were all wearing the formal evening dress, since many of us were under the impression that the communist regime would not attach much value to such formalistic attire. Vienna was divided into four zones, indicated by signs which read: You are entering the British zone, or the Russian zone, etc. This all ended in 1955 when the World War II Allies agreed to withdraw their occupation forces and Austria declared its neutrality.

The Austrian people are steeped in history. When we met a number of Austrian professors, to whom we were introduced by a mutual friend Dr Hussam Eddin Dajani, who had graduated in Vienna, we were surprised by their intense nostalgia for the Austro-Hungarian Empire. This collapsed after its defeat in World War I. What remained of it were memories of a great past, the magnificent palaces of the Hapsburgs, and the big head of its capital shorn of the vast body of its former empire.

Upon my return to Jerusalem, and while scanning the newspapers, I read an advertisement which stated that under a US-Jordan Exchange programme (Smith-Mundt) a scholarship for a qualified Jordanian was available at the Woodrow Wilson School of Public and International Affairs, at Princeton University. I had completed my undergraduate studies at the AUB and obtained a law degree at Jerusalem's law school, sponsored by the government. But Dr Constantine Zuraiq, my professor of history and historiography at the AUB, never tired of impressing on his students the importance of obtaining a PhD if we wanted to fully round off our education. He himself had studied for his PhD at the Oriental Department of Princeton University. With this background, the advertisement about the scholarship appeared to me as God-sent and the fulfilment of a cherished dream. Emerging from the catastrophe, I could not possibly make it financially on my own. I immediately showed the advertisement to my wife and her response was even more enthusiastic. Remaining in Jerusalem would have meant living for a while in the family house until we could arrange an independent home for ourselves. Besides, as a bride, she naturally and quite understandably did not wish to live with the extended family.

I went to Amman and came up before the selection panel, which was chaired by Dr Fawzi al-Mulqi, the then foreign minister and later prime minister. With my qualifications, including an extensive career in government, the panel found no difficulty in selecting me for that scholarship. Such selection might not be so easy today, with thousands of qualified people to choose from; but this was not the case in the early 1950s.

The scholarship, possibly costing the donors $4,000, was for one year. But my experience at the Woodrow Wilson School was so enriching that my wife and I decided to go all the way so that I could study for a PhD. I had obtained my Master in Public Affairs (MPA) at the Woodrow Wilson School in the first year, I then shifted to the Department of Politics where I obtained an MA and completed the requirements for the doctorate in another year. My PhD dissertation was published by Cornell University Press in 1956, and entitled *The Ideas of Arab Nationalism*. For a couple of decades it was the major reference book on the subject. The publishers, after many reprints, sought my permission to publish it in paperback, to give it greater circulation amongst university students. But, foolishly, I refused, thinking that this might detract from its standing. I did not know at the time that the best classics and memoirs were being republished in paperback.

My choice of the thesis topic was prompted by two considerations. First, for two years my wife and I were on our own, with meagre assistance from home. To earn some money

I translated two Arabic books into English, for the American Academy of Learned Societies. One was *The Independence Movements in Arab North Africa* by 'Alal al-Fasi, leader of the independence party in Morocco, and the second *The Philosophy of Jurisprudence in Islam* by Subhi Mahmasani, president of the Supreme Court in Beirut. These, close to 700 pages, I completed during two consecutive summer holidays, in the simmering heat and stifling humidity of the Princeton Firestone Library where, in those days, there was no air-conditioning. My wife, Qadar, saved us precious money by typing the books, although she had no previous training in typing. But she was well-versed in playing the piano, and this was a great asset for typing. Moreover, she took a job at the Educational Testing Service for a year, and another at the Firestone Library. She thoroughly enjoyed the work and this supplementary income enabled us to stay longer in the United States. I said jokingly to her that, in appreciation of her assistance, I was dedicating my book to her, which pleased her. But when she read the dedication which said 'To my wife, without whose disturbance this book would have been finished long ago', she requested that the dedication be withdrawn.

We lived three happy years in Princeton, a town with a population of no more than 15,000. We lived in three locations, the first at Wiggins Street, the second at University Place and the third at Prospect Avenue. The rent for those apartments was, if I remember correctly, less than $100 a month, and other living expenses, including the supermarket, would be roughly the same. My wife cooked food at home, and most of the produce from the A & P and Acme supermarkets was already clean and ready for cooking. We lived comfortably but austerely, avoiding luxuries, unnecessary expenditures and waste. Our recreation outlets were the two cinemas in town, the Play House and the Garden Theatre, on Nassau Street, which we attended three times a week. The other pleasure was walking or bicycle riding. We had a radio in the apartment, but no television set for fear of being distracted from study. Bayard Dodge, the celebrated president emeritus of the AUB when I was a student there, also refrained from acquiring a television set because of the same apprehension. President Dodge, as we used to call him, was in retirement at Princeton, but was fully engaged in translating into English an Arabic Classic (*Fihrist ibn al-Nadim*), a chronology of the most important works in Arabic. We used to meet almost daily during the summer at the small library of Princeton's Oriental Department, which was chaired by the celebrated Dr Phillip Hitti, author of *History of the Arabs,* the best book on the subject in English, along with many works on various phases of the history of Syria and Lebanon, from where he came in the early part of the 20th century. Dr Dodge belonged to a rich family which owned tin mines, and his salary at the AUB was reputed to be a $1 honorarium per annum.

Coming from Jerusalem, with its temperate climate, particularly at night, it was not easy for me at first to adjust to the weather in Princeton or, for that matter, the entire East Coast of the United States. I could not afford air-conditioning which was just beginning to enter the market. Princeton in 1951-54 had only a few air-conditioned premises, among them being the two cinemas and a department store.

In 1953, my wife gave birth to our first child, Laila, at the Princeton Hospital, under the care of a distinguished lady, Dr Monroe. She was so loving and caring that she always made a point of asking about Laila's health, and giving whatever advice was needed throughout our stay. Soon after, a number of my wife's girl friends and colleagues came to me and asked me to take my wife to the movies and not to return to the apartment before 7.30pm. I obliged but not knowing what for. When we returned and opened the door, we were surprised and excited to see that the apartment had been beautifully decorated, as at Christmas, ten of Qadar's colleagues were putting beautifully wrapped presents into a circle in the middle of the room. They contained babywear of kinds. The friends had also brought a delicious cake which we ate together in celebration. I remember this gesture in fondness and deep appreciation, because it radiated warmth and sincere friendship, and the feeling of sharing, which is important on occasions of joy, sorrow, or sickness. It also showed another side of American society which can appear to be characterised by uncaring and impersonal relationships, leading frequently to a sense of loneliness, seeming indifference and alienation. At the same time an impersonal lifestyle has its advantages, preventing unnecessary and unwelcome intrusiveness, and affording the kind of privacy which is absent in the closely-knit traditional societies of the East. There, everybody interferes in everybody else's business, and social duties and obligations are unbearably demanding.

Another observation I noted about America in the early 1950s was the fact that racial segregation was still paramount. I remember some exclusive clubs with signs which read: No blacks allowed.

On buses, a few seats at the back were reserved for blacks, and none of them even attempted to violate this accepted norm. There was one black student at the Woodrow Wilson School, Harris, a very genial character. Another black person, also very friendly, was in charge of maintenance at the library. Many more, of course, lived in the town itself. It was in my opinion quite offensive and humiliating to segregate people on the basis of the colour of their skin, particularly on public transportation, where the offensiveness was so glaring, inhuman and ill-considerate. This would be unthinkable in our part of the world, where all people of whatever race or colour are equal, in the sight of God and humans. The best amongst them are the best in character and conduct alone. When I visited the United States and lived there in later years, what I described above had disappeared for good, another milestone in the journey towards equal rights for all that Abraham Lincoln began with the abolishment of slavery.

Learning at the Woodrow Wilson School and other departments of Princeton was a joy and privilege. The three-hour seminars for graduates, three times a week, would bring together around 20 students, with three highly accomplished professors, each taking charge for one hour, but all participating in the overall discussion.

The programmes of public and international affairs, social sciences, economics and international relations were integrated into one combined approach in dealing with public or international issues. We learned that analysis should be rigorous, but not inflexible, and scores of factors must be taken into consideration in the process of decision-making. Dean Wallace, Professors Harold Sprout and Gardner Patterson, and Professors Levy and Tubin, acted in concert, throwing light on the issues, from the viewpoints of their particular fields of specialisation. We would all be required to participate actively in the discussions, and occasionally each student would make an oral presentation. There were three subjects every term and the readings for each one of them, every week, required a minimum of 40 hours, with a staggering 30 more if all the additional and optional material was to be covered. I do not think anyone had the time to read all the material, but it was the goal all the same. I used to read and write regularly from 7.30am until 5pm, with no respite, apart from an hour for a light lunch. A nap or a doze (our Mediterranean habit) was unthinkable, and if one did nod off inadvertently, one would wake with a guilty conscience.

There could not have been a better preparation for the higher echelons of public service, and I am certain that graduates from the course excelled in their various careers because they developed into a powerhouse of mental agility. The emphasis of the curriculum, and it is important to mention this here, was on the elements of national power in their combined totality as the paradigm for judging nations and the guide for dealing with them. National interest, balance of power, and a legalistic and moralistic approach were, of course, all germane. But, in the final analysis, the strength or weakness of nations is what matters. So the essence is nation-building, as part of a perpetual race for equivalence, if not ascendancy.

While the criteria mentioned above reflect the real world as it is (*real politik*), I often wonder whether this was always the case in the way international relations was approached in academia. At the AUB in the mid-1940s, the course was based on an historical narration by an eminent British professor, Roger Soltau, with minimal analysis. I surmise that the emphasis in academia was on national interest, but within a system of law and morality. This appears to have been the case if one looks at the establishment of the League of Nations in the 1920s, with all the lofty principles of President Woodrow Wilson's 14 points, including the right of all peoples to self-determination, which made him a hero in the eyes of the people of the Arab world. It was assumed that World War I had been the war to end all wars. That was the utopian vision of the post-war years. International law was regarded as the arbiter of most issues, and expertise in it was the accepted preparation for a career in diplomacy.

In the aftermath of World War II there was an even greater emphasis on the solution of all issues by peaceful means, with machinery in place to punish transgressions, under a system of sanctions, to be applied in full or in part, on the aggressor. The only recognition of the element of power was the right of veto, bestowed on the major five powers (major powers at the time the UN Charter was promulgated in 1945), because war amongst them was inconceivable.

Therefore one might have expected a greater emphasis on law and morality in the academia of post-World War II. But this was not the case, and the explanation stems from the fact that what followed the war was not peace but an awesome, attritional and sustained Cold War, with war threatening annihilation in the atomic age. While I was in Princeton, in the early 1950s, the skies were being watched not only by sophisticated radar systems but also by the naked eye from the highest tower in town. Such was the state of alertness which, in retrospect, appears overreaching and exaggerated.

Upon completing my PhD requirements, it did not take me long to choose 'The Ideas of Arab Nationalism' to which I made a reference earlier, as the subject of my thesis. I had been born at a crucial period in the evolution of the Arab nation, after the break-up of the Ottoman Empire in the aftermath of its defeat in World War I. At Rawdha College in Jerusalem, even the 50 or 100-lines punishment imposed on a pupil involved glorifying the Arab nation. When I was at Victoria College, an English school, in 1938, the Egyptian Minister of Education, Muhammad Haikal, an author and writer on the Arab and Islamic legacy (not to be confused with the celebrated journalist and writer Muhammad Hassanain Haikal), visited us. The headmaster, Mr Ralph Reed wished to impress on him that Victoria College's students hailed from all over the Middle East and beyond. Mr Reed asked every student in the classroom to stand up and recite his name and nationality. Every pupil obligingly mentioned name and nationality, Iraqi, Egyptian, Saudi, Sudanese, English, German, etc, until my turn came. I said my name and added that my nationality was Arab. Mr Reed was somewhat taken aback. He was a very firm headmaster and asked me again to state my nationality. I repeated: 'I am an Arab, sir.' In the face of my insistence (shall I say audacity?) he had no alternative but to ask: 'Which country do you come from?' I answered coolly: 'Jerusalem, Palestine.' Such was the intensity of Arab consciousness, triggered by developments since the first inchoate stirrings of the Arab national movement, in the closing decades of the 19th century. Successes and reverses, achievements and thwarted aspirations were the legacy of the Arab Revolt, led by Sherif Hussein of Mecca, in 1916, which had crystallized the deep-rooted yearnings of the Arabic-speaking world, from Morocco on the Atlantic to the Arab Gulf states on the Arabian Sea and the Indian Ocean (with a population at present close to 300 million). The yearnings were for national and Arab identity that had hitherto been submerged in the Ottoman identity. There was also a desire for a cultural renaissance and the restoration of Arab lands to the world map after centuries of stunted growth, de-Arabisation and marginal Arab existence. Arab nationalism had become a popular cause, a living force in the consciousness of the masses. As students at the AUB in the early 1940s, there were three ideologies or movements, competing for the loyalty of the student body: Arab nationalism, Syrian nationalism which advocated unity of *Bilad al-Sham* (greater Syria), and the Communist party. The majority of students were too bourgeois to embrace communism; the Greater Syria party, though the best organized, was too confining in its ultimate goal; and that left the Arab national movement in the ascendancy. Dr Constantine Zuraiq was the ideological mentor and I, along with the majority of students, joined the Arab national movement and became its leader in my last year at the AUB. We held a large gathering in West Hall towards the end of the year at which I spoke, along with three others representing Palestine, Lebanon and Iraq. It fell just short of being a party. The other speakers were Yahya Hamoudeh (later PLO chairman), Abdul Qader Najjar from Iraq and another fellow student from Lebanon.

The fundamental break with the ages-old universalism of the Islamic states was not easy to absorb, as the Arabs regarded themselves as the 'substance of Islam', as proved by the part they played in the rise of Islam, and its sequential monumental civilisation. The Holy Quran was conveyed to the Prophet Muhammad in Arabic, and Arabic was the language of Islamic civilisation. The great amalgam of many races within 'the house of Islam' rendered irrelevant any early racial overtones, in addition to which Islam, as a doctrine, has always vehemently opposed distinctions on the basis of race and colour. The criterion is virtue and the message is universal. 'But it [the Quran] is naught else but a reminder unto all mankind' (Sura 81:27).

The Arab League, created in 1944, was a poor substitute for substantive Arab integration and consensus, in that it simply ratified the vivisection of the Arab world carried out by its former western Allies. Even Syria was cut up into four separate entities, Syria, Lebanon, Palestine, and Transjordan under the secret Anglo-French Sykes-Picot agreement during World War I, in a reckless division of the spoils between the two colonial powers. During the 1940s, extensive political movements emerged throughout the Arab world, and the activities of our movement at the AUB were an authentic microcosm of thoughts and deeds elsewhere. There were three major objectives:

First, our determination was to win independence from foreign tutelage, whether in the form of mandates, protectorates or outright colonisation. Most Arab countries were under one form of foreign dominance or another. So, it was only natural that independence was the priority goal.

Secondly, we were determined to work for Arab unity, which had been thwarted by the European powers, in the aftermath of World War I. Before the war, even though we were subjects of the Ottoman Empire, *de facto* unity existed, and there were no national borders.

Thirdly, having been exposed to Western culture and ideas, and conscious of the glaring backwardness of our own societies, we nourished grandiose plans for reform, covering all aspects of life.

Supporters of the Arab national movement conceived of reform and progress in general terms; they did not lay down precise frameworks, and their ideology was devoid of 'isms' and detailed socio-economic prototypes. These were to come later on, when President Gamal Abdel Nasser came to power in Egypt after the 1952 revolution, which aspired to achieve far-reaching social and economic transformation. But all Arab movements were united in their quest for modernisation. They believed in a building on what was best in the newly rediscovered Arab heritage, while catching up with the breathtaking contemporary civilisation and culture of the world.

By and large, they accepted Western liberal democracy as the best system of government, one fully compatible with the golden age of the Arabs' past as they perceived it. Not surprisingly, therefore, as one Arab country after another achieved independence, they established political and economic systems on the pattern of Western liberal democracy. But, traumatised by the Palestinian catastrophe, Arab nationalists turned against the existing regimes, accusing them of criminal incompetence, if not outright treason. The mutual suspicion developed into hostility, with the result that the flowering of democratic institutions which, ironically, had been a platform common to both, was further curtailed. Earlier in the century, when the older generation rebelled against despotic Ottoman rule, one of their foremost objectives was the reinstatement of liberal constitutional government. Later generations fought with equal determination against oppressive, undemocratic colonial rule. And yet, when both external adversaries had been successfully removed the Arab nationalists of different generations found themselves deadlocked in a struggle for power which undermined their erstwhile shared goal.

Lethargic Arab societies had to be rebuilt from their foundations to make possible far-reaching change at an accelerated pace. This urgency explains the dizzying phenomenon of military coups, underground movements and outright hostility to existing regimes throughout the length and breadth of the Arab homeland; but in the process, the early shoots of freedom and democracy, to which all aspired, were destroyed.

One of the foremost Islamic reformers of the latter part of the 19th century, Sheikh Muhammad Abduh, epitomises in one expressive sentence what he and other reformers had in mind in their yearning for modernisation and reform. He had visited France and was impressed by what he saw. Upon returning to Egypt, he was asked to give his impressions and he replied: 'In France I found Islam but no Muslims; in Egypt I find Muslims but no Islam.'

In general, ignorance and backwardness afflicted the Arab and Islamic worlds. There is no incompatibility between Islam and modernity, as some present-day commentators seem inclined to suggest. Their common enemy is backwardness and the entrenched weaknesses and flaws which accumulated so massively over centuries of immobility.

In my book on Arab nationalism, written in 1954, I allocated three chapters to the all-important question of social and economic reforms. Indeed, they constitute the ultimate synthesis of the book and its message. Likewise, all the other chapters are seized with the imperatives of democratic reforms, human rights and freedoms, not as envisioned by a solitary writer or a musing poet, but as a true reflection of a long line of Arab thinkers and reformers going back to the 19th century.

It is, therefore, somewhat disconcerting to find the Arab world today, and particularly in the wake of the terrible bomb attacks perpetrated by a few deranged individuals in New York and Washington on 9/11 2001, being overwhelmed by sermons pointing out the need for reform. The implicit message seems to be that reform represents uncharted territory, and that 300 million people living in the cradle of civilisation need to be taught how to lead better lives. How can anyone lecture the Palestinian people on the worth of liberty and freedom when they have been fighting and spilling their blood profusely in their relentless struggle to attain them? Outside prodding for reforms should not be dismissed as unduly intrusive, because we are all living in one global world, where intrusion sometimes, if for a good cause, may be commendable. But this should be done with humility, dialogue and goodwill, and not at gunpoint, as in Iraq and Afghanistan.

CHAPTER 7

THE CALL OF JERUSALEM

Upon obtaining my doctorate degree at Princeton, in the summer of 1954, I was offered the post of associate professor at a prestigious university by Professor Victor S. Thomas. My wife and I were gradually, but irresistibly, being sucked into the way of life in United States, particularly college life, notwithstanding all its hard work, austerity and challenges, or perhaps because of them. I had extended my stay in the USA for two years in order to complete my graduate programme. As a result I had declined an offer from my government to accept the post of director-general of broadcasting, after completing my programme at the Woodrow Wilson School of Public and International Affairs during my first year in America. The council of ministers in Jordan subsequently informed me that I had been dismissed from my post in the Ministry of Foreign Affairs for failing to return. So no post was awaiting me in Jordan, and with a relatively attractive offer of teaching, with many times the remuneration which a job in Amman or Jerusalem would offer, I was hard put to decide.

And yet, once more, the call of Jerusalem was so overpowering that it guided my decision to decline the offer and prepare to return home. I knew that my wife had become enthralled with life in America, its freedom, its privacy, its good neighbourly relationships, and the warmth and genuineness of its ordinary citizens. I knew, too, that if I had given her the opportunity to decide with me on the offer to stay, she would have persuaded me to accept it. I, therefore, declined the offer summarily, and informed my wife of it as a *fait accompli*. I do not usually act unilaterally but in this instance the call of the city of my birth was overwhelming, and I decided to live with the consequences, good or bad. As I said earlier, East Jerusalem, in which my home is located, remained in Arab hands after 1948, and therefore I would be returning to familiar territory, to home.

It was not without emotion that we bade goodbye to Princeton, after three consecutive happy years, in the course of which we hardly left the town, except for shopping trips to Philadelphia, or visits to relatives and friends in nearby cities. During the peak of a heat wave we spent a day in Asbury Park in the company of two close friends in Princeton, Professor and Mrs Farhat Ziyadeh, American citizens of Palestinian background. In the park we enjoyed the refreshing breeze of the Atlantic, but also watched the selection of America's beauty queen, a very laborious process, in suffocating and unbearable heat, for hours on end. How much more pleasant and exciting it is to watch the highlights of such contests on television, in the comfort of the home, rather than being forced to endure the whole tedious performance.

For our return home, Dr Hitti suggested, on the basis of his own experience, that we travel on one of the Dutch cargo ships operating regularly between New York and Beirut across the south Atlantic, with a stop at Casablanca before entering the Mediterranean Sea via Gibraltar. The ship had a dozen or so first class cabins for passengers and crew. There were two Indonesian attendants to serve our cabin, which we sorely needed because our daughter, Laila, was only one year old. The food, by the way, was rich but too spicy for our tastes. Passing by one of the lighthouses in the Azores, I wondered how long an occupant or occupants would have to endure the loneliness of being stuck out in the mid-Atlantic, with only whistling and withering winds and roaring waves for company.

We landed in Casablanca, and did some shopping in its ancient *suq*, where craftsmen excel in picturesque leather manufacturing of every type. The call on Casablanca coincided with the exiling of King Muhammad of Morocco by the French. He was an extremely popular king because of his modesty and caring nature, as well as the leadership of his people for complete independence. Believe it or not, some superstitious Moroccans told my wife and me that they could see the face of the king drawn on the moon. Such is the power of believing. The trip, enjoyable but tiring, took 18 days, and when we docked in Beirut, two of Qadar's brothers, Nashat and Zafer, were there to welcome us. We were thrilled by the reunion, and had dinner with them in one of the exquisite restaurants of Mount Lebanon. We then continued our journey home to Jerusalem the following day by plane. I hope the mayor of Beirut will not be upset if we say that our first impression of the downtown neighbourhood, by comparison with the part of America from which we had just come, was unfavourable. Bear in mind that I am talking about an impression half a century ago, which still sticks in my memory. In fact, we love Beirut, have dear close relatives there, and wish it all the best. Also, the area around the docks in any port city is never particularly clean.

Our plane for the journey to Jerusalem was a two-engine propeller-driven Dakota, the pride of the fleet in spite of the intense vibration during flight. We landed at Qalandia, a modest airport a few miles north of the city. From the window we saw waving crowds in the terminal building, and I said to myself that tourism must be thriving. But it turned out that the crowds were there either to bid farewell to or welcome loved ones. Air travel was still a novelty, prompting hearty welcomes or emotional farewells.

My first post upon return was chairman of the Jordan delegation to the Mixed Jordanian-Israeli Armistice Commission, which was established by virtue of the Armistice Agreement of 3 April 1949. This stipulated that the accord would not affect the final borders or the territorial settlement, or the demands of any of the contracting parties. But it did rule out all acts of belligerence, infiltration or transgression, at least in words, pending the conclusion of the final settlement.

My new post was of ministerial rank, which indicates the importance attached to it by the government of Jordan, and my accountability was to the Ministry of Defence. My staff consisted mainly of military officers: Colonel, later, General Muhammad Ishaq; Captain Muhammad Daoud, later (September 1970) prime minister of a military government which clamped down on the unruly Palestinian militias; and other rotated officers of different ranks. I was the only civilian. The Israeli delegation was constituted in a similar way, but with one civilian legal counsel, Yosef Tekoa, who later became Israel's ambassador to the United Nations.

The headquarters of the MAC (Mixed Armistice Commission) was a shabby house owned by an Armenian and rented to the UN in the no man's land just behind St George's school, a few hundred metres from my house, opposite the American Colony Hotel. It was a similar distance from the famed Mandelbaum gate, which was the crossing-point between Jordan and Israel during the armistice regime. General Edseem Burns, a Canadian, was chief of staff of the United Nations Truce Supervision Organization (UNTSO) and was responsible for the four MACs between Israel on the one side, and Egypt, Syria, Lebanon, and Jordan on the other. Commander E. H. Hutchison was the chairman of the Jordan/Israel MAC. He was a navy officer with great courage and was always ready to put his life on the line whenever fighting erupted in Jerusalem or elsewhere. Colonel Charles Brewster, also an American, succeeded him in this post during my tenure.

The choice of the building was intended to make it equally accessible to both sides. My delegation would enter the building from the eastern entrance, while the Israelis one would enter from the western one. Each delegation had one or two rooms to serve as offices, or rest rooms when meetings went on late into the night or the early morning, as they often did. In the mid-1950s, while the armistice was in effect, it was frequently violated by one side or the other. The Palestinians were prone to infiltrating their former home towns, Ramleh, Lydda or even Jerusalem, while the Israelis retaliated with massive force, as in the West Bank villages of Qibya in 1953 and Hussan a year later, resulting in the destruction of scores of homes, and heavy losses of life.

In such serious cases, the aggrieved party would bring the matter to the UN Security Council, to await its action or inaction.

The atmosphere of tension and violence, and the absence of any political initiatives to resolve the conflict naturally impacted on the atmosphere prevailing at the MAC meetings. It was grim and acrimonious, and although we were seated opposite each other at a narrow table, neither delegation spoke to the other, but spoke at each other, with the chairman acting as the pacifier and casting the decisive vote. We took our state of war seriously and considered any human relations beyond the rigid and the formal as unpatriotic, if not treasonable. I am writing this in 2008 when Palestinians and Israelis meet naturally and as a matter of course to discuss all kinds of issues. But this was not the case in the tense atmosphere of 1955. Being gregarious and friendly by nature and temperament, I did not find this job to my liking, but I had to serve as best as I could.

In 1975, eight years after Israel had occupied East Jerusalem and the rest of the West Bank, my mother fell sick in Jerusalem, and I felt duty-bound to visit her. I had been reluctant to visit Jerusalem under occupation, and yet life had to go on. My family obtained the necessary permit from the military government and, on the agreed date, I went to the Allenby Bridge (renamed the King Hussein Bridge by Jordan). Large numbers of my family were there to welcome me after years of absence. There was Anwar, Hisham and Muhammad, in addition to sisters Ziba, Sama, and Hala. Mahmoud and Dr Ahmad were outside the country.

After the routine checks at the bridge by security and customs officers, and these are usually very stringent indeed, one of the Israeli officers asked me to accompany him to the premises at the bridge where intelligence officers conduct their investigations. I entered the room to be welcomed heartily by a general, tall and well-built, and surrounded by a group of senior Israeli officers. The general asked me directly and with enthusiasm whether I remembered him. After a good look, my answer was no. The man before me, I later learned, had become the military governor of the occupied West Bank. He said: 'I remember your face, your voice, even your very words when I was your opposite number at the Mixed Armistice Commission, and when I signed your entry papers I decided to come down specially to greet you.'

He was General Aryeh Shalev, and I had not recognised him because his reddish hair had turned white. Anyway, he instructed his assistant, Dr Amnon Cohen, a renowned Arabist and author, to take care of me and see what he could do to meet my requests. He offered me a green card for immediate return to the West Bank if I wished to. But I declined the offer and insisted on the right to return to my property in my home city, Jerusalem. Dr Amnon replied that, while he understood and appreciated my request, it was beyond his jurisdiction, inasmuch as such permission could be granted only by a cabinet committee at the highest level. And that is how the matter remains up to today. Several attempts were made subsequently to follow up on my request to return but, they were all turned down. When my elder brother, Anwar, died in 1986, I was in Jerusalem to receive condolences. One of the visitors was Minister Ezer Weizman (later president) of Israel. He asked why I had not returned to Jerusalem, and I replied that it was because his government had refused my requests. He promised to do what he could but, apparently, to no avail.

Another point which must be mentioned here is that a Jerusalemite like myself, a displaced person, is denied the right of return, despite categorical United Nations resolutions to the contrary. He also fails to receive the protection afforded under the Fourth Geneva Convention of 1949, and his properties in Jerusalem are seized and sequestrated. Thus, a Jerusalemite faces double jeopardy: refusal of his right of return and confiscation of his private property, ostensibly on grounds of his absence, which is not of his own choosing. There can hardly be a more incongruous, arbitrary and blatantly unlawful phenomenon. It is, in fact, as one moderate Israeli leader, Yossi Beilin, described it, highway robbery.

I am talking about East Jerusalem, a district described by the Security Council in a 1980 resolution as occupied territory, along with the rest of the West Bank. In 1994, Jordan and Israel concluded a full peace treaty, signed ceremoniously at Wadi Araba, which ended all states of belligerency. Under international law, when states of belligerency are ended, private properties belonging to nationals of the erstwhile warring states are restored to their owners.

The British government, following the two world wars, restored to the Germans and the Italians the properties which had been held in abeyance in Palestine, pending the conclusion of the war. Any other behaviour would have been a flagrant violation of individual human rights and the inherent right to private property enshrined in all laws, human and divine.

What is more inexplicable is that these measures affecting absentee owners involve discrimination towards members of the same family. Thus, confiscation is waived in the case of my brother, Hisham, who happens to be an

American citizen, but applied against myself and my other brother, Dr Ahmad, because we are Jordanians. I would not have given this seemingly private matter so much space had its predicament and ramifications not been applicable to innumerable other Jerusalem compatriots. It is an issue that demands utmost public concern.

After almost two years of service with the Mixed Armistice Commission, I was transferred in 1956 to Amman, to assume the post of undersecretary of the Ministry of Reconstruction and Development.

The name is, perhaps, a misnomer, inasmuch as it connotes the ministry in charge of the affairs of Palestinian refugees in Jordan. But King Abdullah I, an ardent pan-Arabist, tempered only by statesmanship, did not accept categorising an Arab, from whichever country, as a refugee in another Arab country. To emphasise this point, he named the largest refugee camp in the Jordan Valley, the *Karameh* camp, meaning the 'camp of dignity' and deleting the term refugee.

I would have preferred a post in Jerusalem itself, but the only possibility was that of governor, which was not vacant. All the higher echelons of government were located in Amman – cabinet, ministries, parliament, army, intelligence and vital economic institutions. There was no escaping the conclusion that Jerusalem was no longer the capital of Palestine. It had ceased to be so with the withdrawal of British administration in 1948, and the failure of the Palestinians to establish a state of their own. This had caused it to shrink geographically, demographically and functionally.

To compensate the Palestinian people for Jerusalem's change of fortune, and in recognition of the city's unique religious status it was named the spiritual capital of Jordan.

It would not have been practical for me to commute daily to work between Jerusalem and Amman, a distance of some 83 kilometres. So I rented a house in Amman – there were precious few available for leasing – and settled there with my small family, my wife, Qadar, my daughter, Laila, and my son, Haitham, who was born at the Augusta Victoria Hospital on the Mount of Olives in Jerusalem in August 1955.

The Ministry of Reconstruction and Development was a hive of activity, involving the livelihood, health, and education of hundreds of thousands of Palestinian refugees, in both the East and the West Banks. The identification and eligibility of a refugee for assistance, meagre as it was, was still in a state of flux and confusion, and the refugees were generally angry and edgy. Their mood impacted on society as a whole and its social equanimity. The refugee population, together with the settled Palestinian population of the West Bank, constituted a majority of the total population of the kingdom, and had been franchised as citizens, under the Act of Unity of 1950. No government, therefore, could afford to alienate them. Added to the destitute refugees were the inhabitants of the towns and villages of the armistice lines who, overnight, had lost their fertile lands and livelihood and had become destitute. The state of Jordan, lacking in resources, found itself encumbered with the colossal legacy of the Palestinian problem, and, if not for modest outside assistance, could have crumbled under its weight.

The United States was the largest donor to UNRWA, so the post of commissioner general was invariably held by an American citizen. I had the pleasure of cooperating with two of them, Mr Henry R. Labouisse, who at some point became a secretary in the American administration, and Dr John H.

Davis, an eminent academic and administrator. Mr Labouisse was a man of great gentleness and understanding, and one could not have hoped for a better choice. His contributions at that early unsettled juncture in the lifes of the refugees were invaluable. Aside from using official channels, I could always contact him by telephone at his headquarters in Beirut whenever a problem arose regarding the refugees, and he would find a solution.

There was a stream of congressional delegations visiting Jordan and inspecting the refugee camps. I remember a visit by Senator Albert Gore Sr, among others. Welcome as these visits were, sometimes I felt they made too much of an issue of checking the validity of refugee cards, considering that the value of each was a mere 7 cents a day in rations. UNRWA, with our assistance, made every effort to delete invalid and duplicate cards, but without, we felt, being too intrusive and inquisitorial in doing so. There was a limit to how often one could count the members of a family of five or six individuals crammed into a shabby tent or asbestos-walled room. One had to take into account the human rights dimension of privacy as well.

UNRWA, in cooperation with the United Nations Educational, Scientific and Cultural Organisation (UNESCO), carried out a successful general education programme for hundreds of thousands of refugee children. Under the programme they received elementary and preparatory education, in hundreds of UNRWA schools. The education also included vocational and teacher training programmes.

As part of the education programme, students received subsidised secondary education at government schools. A university scholarship programme afforded college education to 326 young refugee men and women in Arab universities and I am proud to state that during my tenure as permanent representative of Jordan to the United Nations I obtained a resolution from the General Assembly to grant an additional 600 scholarships per annum to young Palestinian refugees.

While appreciation and gratitude are due to UNRWA and UNESCO for the signal success of their educational programmes for refugees, it would be unfair not to acknowledge the great role played by Jordan, Egypt, Syria, and Lebanon, as host countries, in enhancing the level of education in their respective territories. Suffice it here to say that the Palestinian refugees in the West Bank, the East Bank, Gaza, Syria, and Lebanon are second to none in their rates of literacy (around 90 percent), one of the highest rates in the Arab World, and much of the rest of the world.

UNRWA made education its top priority, and laudably so, while the providing health services, in close cooperation with host governments, was its second priority. Third was the provision of relief and welfare services for the neediest families.

UNRWA's mandate from the General Assembly included not only relief but also rehabilitation. This issue was raised at one of the meetings of the advisory council in Beirut, constituted of the four host countries and five ambassadors representing the donors—the United States, Britain, France, Belgium, and Turkey. The representative of Turkey, a retired general, remarked that the host countries were perpetuating the agony of the refugees for political gain. He added that the sum of $200 million was earmarked by the United Nations for rehabilitation and yet Arab governments were declining to utilise the funds. I replied that if such a sum, substantial by the standards of the time, was indeed available, my government had no inhibitions about it being used for the improvement of the lives of the refugees, without prejudice to their other inalienable rights, including return and compensation. Some refugees were, indeed, fearful that rehabilitation would impinge on their right of return but we tried to convince them that living in dire conditions was not the road to salvation.

I negotiated with senior UNRWA officials on ways and means of implementing the programme. I asked how much funding was available, and the answer was: as much as could be spent. We established a technical department to study the feasibility of possible projects, and appointed Abdullah Kardous, a former district commissioner in Palestine during the mandate as director. Two Jerusalemites, Zaki and Zafer Budeiri, both engineers of high quality, were in charge of the technical aspects. Under the terms of the programme, the recipient of funding for a project, in his own field and of his own choice, would in exchange, hand back his ration card.

We proceeded with implementation in earnest and with zeal. It was an advanced step compared to a programme of relief whose ultimate end was to keep body and soul together, imperative as this goal was. Under this programme, housing projects were built, including one in the Sheikh Jarrah quarter in Jerusalem. Many grants were awarded to fund the development of crafts and services of every sort, including taxi operations. To help bedouin refugees, mainly from Beer Sheba in the Negev desert, but displaced to Jordan, we gave grants to a score of clans to buy livestock for breeding.

After less than a year and after we had managed to allocate around $4 to 5 million, the deputy director-general came to inform me that the funds had been exhausted, and we would have to close down the programme. I was surprised and asked what had happened to the $70 million which the agency had indicated was available. He said that the total represented the pledged amount, but various states had not paid up. We were disappointed because, amongst other projects, I had an ambitious plan to plant 5 million olive trees to cover the hills of the West Bank and contribute to the earnings of its inhabitants. The West Bank, like Galilee, is well suited for the cultivation of olives and other fruits.

At one point, UNRWA informed me that because of budget shortcomings it would have to discontinue relief assistance to newborn babies. I protested that this category was the most vulnerable, and no-one could contemplate depriving a baby of the basic necessities of life. But, naturally, he who pays the piper calls the tune, and so the agency went ahead with its decision, and stopped relief assistance to newborn babies. But I did win one important concession, that all Palestinian children should have their names registered as refugees with the agency, regardless of whether or not they were to receive assistance. Thus we safeguarded in the official registers the true number of Palestinian refugees, with the total to date more than 4 million.

It was during this year that my second daughter, Lina, was born. This date coincided with the imposition of a curfew in the Zarqa region of Jordan, to the north of Amman. I was returning from a meeting of the advisory council of UNRWA in Beirut when I saw barricades blocking the main highway to Amman because of disturbances in an army camp. But the officers in charge were extremely kind and understanding and permitted me to continue to Amman. These were the troubles described by the late King Hussein in his first autobiography, *Uneasy Lies the Head*.

The important post of undersecretary of the Ministry of National Economy became vacant, with the resignation of its eminent incumbent, Hamad Farhan. I had completed a mere one year when the government decided to transfer me to this important post, with equally strong challenges, but ones that were less emotionally draining than those dealing with the plight of Palestinian refugees.

CHAPTER 8

SETTLING DOWN

Taking up the new post entailed not only a change of venue but an affirmation that Amman, and not Jerusalem, was destined to be my permanent home and the focus of my career. My wife and I decided to build a villa, instead of moving from one apartment to another. My brother, Hisham, a highly talented architect and a graduate of the University of California (Berkeley), had just arrived with an American engineering consulting company to carry out a study for the government on the most efficacious methods of extracting potash and other minerals from the Dead Sea. It was a pioneering mission in largely uncharted territory, because nearly all other potash extraction in the world was being carried out from land mines. The exception was the Israeli project, in operation since the era of the British mandate, also in the Dead Sea.

We seized on the opportunity of Hisham's presence in Amman to seek his assistance in building the villa. Hisham was a man of great friendliness and selflessness, and he instantly obliged. He drew up the architectural design, with the help of two other Jerusalem engineers, Zaki and Zafer Budeiri.

A contractor built the villa in 1956-57, in less than a year. It was considered at the time of its completion one of the more elegant and stylish villas at the third circle in Jabal Amman. That area comprised the best and the most beautiful villas, with rose gardens, fruit trees and flowers of every variety. Members of the USAID mission were impressed with its residences and dubbed it the 'marble mile'. Our house today is the premises of the Austrian Embassy in Amman which purchased it from my wife, its owner. We built another house, on the fourth circle. The new mansions and villas of Amman's new quarters today, several decades later, are even more sumptuous, and I wonder what superlatives might have to be used to give them their due. But I have been informed that when four American presidents, Ford, Bush, Carter, and Clinton, attended King Hussein's funeral in 1999, they visited the US embassy in the Abdoun district (one of the new quarters). They reportedly expressed surprised admiration at seeing such luxurious and elegant housing. Jordan, in the minds of many, is associated with deserts and camels. The truth of the matter is that the people of Jordan and Palestine place considerable value on house ownership, the more embellished the property is the better. The stone façades convey an impression of cleanliness, symmetry, and durability and, as I mentioned earlier, Palestinians are experts in stone cutting.

The Ministry of National Economy was tasked with planning and overall supervision of the economy, focussing mainly on private enterprise, but fortified by the injection of public funding and investment incentives, because capital formation was still in its incipient stages. The staff of the ministry was highly qualified economists, financiers, and legal experts; it was small but efficient, with the minimum of bureaucracy, and maximum latitude for individual decision-making. It is to the credit of this ministry that over many years it launched and initiated almost all the country's major projects: expansion of phosphate mining, which put Jordan as the second largest exporter of phosphates in the world, after Morocco; the launching of the potash project; oil refining; oil exploration, in cooperation with foreign companies but with very meagre results so far; medium and small industries; trade and commerce; and, finally, formulating the laws and regulations governing business activity in the country, with particular attention to consumer protection where monopoly situations exist.

In the mid-1950s, turbulence and tension enveloped the entire region, culminating in the invasion of Egypt after the collusion of Britain, France, and Israel (the Suez Canal war of 1956). The United Nations ordered the withdrawal of the aggressors, thanks to a rare confluence of interest between the two superpowers of the day, the United States and the Soviet Union, leaving a temporary, uncertain and dangerous vacuum in the region. When Egypt and Syria united under the United Arab Republic on 1 February 1958, Iraq and Jordan, the two Hashemite monarchies, responded 13 days later by establishing the Arab Union, a confederation of the two kingdoms. At the initiative of Iraq, and particularly at the behest of my schoolmate and close friend, Adnan Pachachi, former Iraqi minister of foreign affairs, the federal cabinet took a decision to appoint me undersecretary of the Ministry of Foreign Affairs of the federal union. As I was later informed by a cabinet member, Khalousi al-Khairi, the decision was to have been announced officially on the radio at 7am on the morning of 14 July 1958.

During the morning of this very day, a bloody military coup d'état took place which not only overthrew the monarchy but was also accompanied by a savage massacre of the entire Hashemite monarchy in Iraq, men, women, and children. The unspeakable brutality encompassed also Jordanian cabinet ministers and senior officials who had already taken up their posts in Baghdad: 75-year-old Ibrahim Hashem, prime minister; 74-year-old Suleiman Tuqan, minister of the Royal Court and better known as the mayor of Nablus, the largest city in the West Bank; Adnan al-Husseini, an administrative commissioner; and others.

I have often thought how lucky I was that my appointment had not been two weeks earlier, in which case I might have faced the same fate. This was my second lucky moment of escape from imminent destiny, the first being the Nevi Yacoub ambush in 1948, which I have already described. There is yet another instance of a miraculous and hair-raising escape which I shall narrate in the course of this chapter.

Although the greater part of development was taking place in the East Bank, being then the less developed territory in the kingdom, Jerusalem and the rest of the West Bank had their share of development or renovation. This included the construction of a new road linking Jerusalem and Bethlehem. This was a zigzag road that traversed difficult mountainous terrain behind Government House, at Jabal al-Mukaber. On the former road one could drive from Jerusalem to Bethlehem in a mere five minutes along a direct route via the Baqaa Arab quarter in West Jerusalem. Israel seized this district in 1948. Furthermore, the government restored electricity and water to Jerusalem and many adjacent towns and villages in the area that, along with Jerusalem, had been cut off from their former sources of supply. In the East Bank, one of the most urgent projects was the building of a highway from Amman to Aqaba, the only outlet to the sea, the Red Sea. The West and the East Banks had lost access to the Mediterranean, their former trade route, and had to reroute their trade via Aqaba, Beirut, or Latakia on Syria's Mediterranean coast. This involved crossing international borders, red tape, delays, and considerable expense. As president of the Development Board, I pushed all concerned hard, with the full backing of the prime minister, the *ex officio* chairman of the board, to expedite its execution. We were in desperate need of this road, for access to other countries of the Middle and to the Far East. The modest port of Aqaba port also took pride of place in our scale of priorities and was transformed into a modern, functioning facility, serving not only Jordan but land-locked Iraq as well.

The Suez Canal War had created a new strategic situation. The British and French, hitherto the dominant powers, had lost their former influence and had been succeeded by the Americans. Conspiracy theories held that the United States was, from the start, and even prior to Suez, planning and conspiring to replace the two former powers. But quite apart from conspiracies and rumours, Britain did not have the resources to sustain its presence, and a mere decade later had to withdraw even from the jewel of its possessions, the fabulously rich Gulf States.

The Eisenhower Doctrine, proclaimed in 1957, sanctified the new strategic reality by offering aid in various forms to countries that opposed communism. Even though the United Arab Republic and most Arab states had rejected the United States' projection of power and dominance, as a continuum of old colonialism, Jordan, weakened by the dissolution of the union with Iraq, and Lebanon, facing an insurrection against the Western-backed government, were more than happy to accept American assistance.

In the wake of the coup in Iraq there were widespread reports that one was imminent in Jordan, as a result of collusion between certain Jordanian military factions who were in league with Iraqi forces stationed in the country. One could feel the tension, and King Hussein had no alternative but to seek assistance from Britain, Jordan's former ally, while Lebanon invited American assistance. The British sent squadrons of Hawker Hunter jet fighters to Jordan, while the United States sent marines to Lebanon. These moves created a stir in the region and evoked considerable hostility. President Nasser was at the peak of his popularity, and every utterance he made was listened to by the masses of the Arab world from the Atlantic to the Gulf. Even moderate Saudi Arabia joined the chorus of opposition. This created a unique situation, a virtual encirclement of Jordan and a physical blockade of its trade routes. Syria had shut it borders, and Saudi Arabia closed its air space. The most critical consequence was a shortage of fuel upon which modern living, industry, agriculture and services depend.

The government appointed me chairman of a committee which comprised a representative of Britain, Wing Commander Jock Dalgleish, former trainer and advisor of the Jordanian air force and a close friend of King Hussein, and the United States was represented by an admiral. Jordan also received a donation of $5 million as an emergency contribution to help ease the effects of the blockade. We would meet every evening between 5 and 8pm at my office at the Ministry of Economy, located at the first circle on Jabal Amman. Our agenda consisted of deciding on how and when to import petroleum products, and how much we should acquire. Then we had to decide how to distribute the small quantities that arrived to meet the most urgent needs of the country as a whole. In the initial stages the shipments were made by air, because shipping by sea to Aqaba would have been too slow. Saudi Arabia declined to permit air shipments to fly over its territory, and the Americans flew the aircraft through Israeli airspace.

The petroleum crisis lingers on in my memory. Government agencies, municipalities, public utilities, and even farmers in the Jordan Valley pleaded for a few barrels of diesel oil to operate their engines. Ali Dajani, director of the Amman electricity company, informed me in desperation that unless he obtained two or three barrels that evening, Amman, the capital, might spend the night in darkness; hospitals would be without their essential refrigeration; broadcasting would go off the air, and indeed all other essentials and amenities of life would be considerably affected. How much, I mused, are we in the debt of Edison, the original discoverer of electricity, and without which life is mere elemental existence.

Abdul Majid al-Udwan, an owner of a banana plantation and an orange grove, fearful that his crops would wither in the heat of the Jordan Valley literally begged for some diesel oil for irrigation. As one who owns a farm in the Jordan Valley and appreciates what its survival means to an owner, I went out of my way to help him, in spite of the competing priorities and claims.

We continued with this *ad hoc*, day-to-day, hand-to-mouth improvisation for several weeks until oil could be ferried by tankers to Aqaba. I believe we did a good, efficient and a fair job, and the crisis was overcome with the minimum of damage.

It was decided later by all the parties concerned that it would be better if responsibility for oil supplies reverted to the private sector, where it belongs. In winding up the programme, we found out that there remained in the fund a sum of $500,000. I suggested that instead of returning this balance to the donor it would be a good idea to spend it on the construction of storage facilities in Aqaba, just in case another crisis was to arise, and the two other members of the committee agreed. Thus Aqaba was provided with a storage facility which it sorely needed.

During quiet moments at our daily committee meetings I often inquired from Wing Commander Dalgleish, to satisfy a personal curiosity, about the relative merits of different military aircraft. There was lots of talk in the region about Soviet Migs, British Hawker Hunters and American F-4 Phantoms. Wing Commander Dalgleish, a superb pilot, asked me whether I was interested in watching a display over Amman of the British Hawker Hunters. I replied that I would very much like this. I am sure he had obtained clearance from the relevant authorities for a display of this kind. Anyway, he said that, aside from my wife, I could bring along to the military airport at Marka anyone I wanted to, which I did. It was a remarkable display, with jets breaking the sound barrier and performing aerobatics, diving to just above the ground and then zooming up again into the unfathomable skies, like a whistling whirlwind.

The citizens of Amman, uninformed about this display, were taken aback fearing that the rapid and collective sounds of 12 aircraft may have been the result of explosions caused by hostile elements, for the state of tension had not subsided altogether. But these apprehensions were allayed when the facts about the display were announced.

The United States government endorsed its intrusive policy in the region by allocating $40 million per annum in assistance to Jordan. The sum seems trivial by current standards, but it was equivalent to the government's budget five decades ago, and the total today would be worth 10 times this amount. A large aid mission came to Amman to act as partners in the implementation and supervision of the projects selected under this programme. To regularise this expanded operation, two steps, were taken.

An administrative agreement was negotiated with the head of the US mission, and we both benefited from the legal advice of Amin el-Hassan, a competent and versatile lawyer. It was a lengthy, cumbersome document, with too many ifs and buts, which I tried to whittle down and simplify.

It was agreed that in order to execute this programme, with its operational as well as planning dimensions, one control department or authority, namely a rejuvenated development board should be established, in which final authority and authorisation would be vested independently from the routine-laden Ministry of Finance. To mention some of the structures and functions of the Development Board will give an idea about the extensive scope of its jurisdiction and activity. They included the East Ghor Canal authority in the Jordan Valley (later renamed the Jordan Valley Authority), the water authority, public works operations and equipment, the national resources authority, the establishment of the agricultural loaning authority to replace a defunct loan agency known in the early 1950s as the development board, and the establishment of an Industrial Bank.

The arm of the new Development Board was so stretched that the Finance Minister at the time, Hashem Jayyusi, complained to the prime minister that I, as president of the Development Board, could employ at will hundreds if not thousands of employees of various skills and specialisations, while he could hardly appoint a janitor, because of the constraints of the government budget. What he did not realise, or did not wish to do so, was that while he was managing a routine civil service machine, we at the board were establishing, creating, rejuvenating and implementing a large and ambitious development programme, with adequate funds to see it through.

Having established the Development Board, I shifted from the Ministry of Economy to head the new authority as vice president, the president being, *ex officio*, the prime minister who chaired the meetings. The 12-man Development Board consisted of the prime minister and four ministers, including the minister of finance, representing the government, plus five members representing the private sector in industry, agriculture and finance. Najmuddine Dajani, a very capable economist (later minister), was appointed secretary-general.

We also established a planning division, to which we enlisted the most capable economists to prepare a five-year programme for economic development (1962-67). To attract the best talents, we paid them much higher remuneration than our own economists, their superiors. Hanna Audeh, who later became finance minister, was appointed head of the planning division. His credentials included a degree from a well-known Dutch institute specialising in the field of planning.

In presenting the plan to the prime minister in 1962, I acknowledged with deep appreciation, the generous assistance that the Ford Foundation, represented by Hugh Walker, had extended to the Development Board, and to the ministries which had cooperated in the preparation of this programme. The foundation had selected and made available to the board some of the most talented, the most experienced and the most knowledgeable experts in the United States. They included professors Ben Lewis, L J Zimmerman (the Dutch Institute), Clark Ploom, who worked tirelessly editing and re-editing the plan, Joel Dirlam, Andrew Watson, P Sargant Florence, William Snavely, Dascom Forbush, Terence Young, and John Hilliard. In continuous succession, over a period of two-and-a-half years, they placed their extensive experience, expertise and dedication at the disposal of the board, in close cooperation with our staff and ministry representatives.

The Development Board also decided to reform Jordan's fiscal system, and a Royal Fiscal Commission was formed under the chairmanship of Suleiman Sukkar, a veteran minister of finance and banker. As well as Jordanian members, the commission included Dr Phillip Taylor, Dr Walter Heller (former chairman of economic advisers to the White House) and Dr Ward Macy as advisers from the Ford Foundation. The commission's intensive and able survey of Jordan's fiscal system, in the summer of 1960, was an invaluable aid in the country's development effort, and in reforming Jordan's fiscal policies. I also acknowledged gratitude to R. S. Porter of the British Middle East Office for his advice and assistance to the department of statistics, which provided us with one of the principal ingredients for our own planning and, principally, the national income survey.

The top priority of the five-year programme was the expansion of gross domestic output. The goals of reducing both unemployment and dependence on foreign aid were second and third. The plan was submitted to the House of Representatives and obtained its endorsement.

But prior to that, I deemed it necessary, for a multiplicity of reasons – not least of which was to do with public relations – to convene a gathering attended by a select group of leading international figures to assess the programme and provide any input they could. They included Paul Hoffman, the famed director of the Marshal Plan, who was invited to address parliament, the chiefs of planning in India and Iran, the president of the University of Rome, and the director-general of the United Nations Development Programme. For three days we met in the cabinet room of the prime minister's office, discussing, debating, assessing the issue, and listening to suggestions from the various participants.

On the final evening of our three-day conference, and as the guest participants were paying tribute to our work and thanking us for the hospitality afforded them in Jordan, the telephone rang and the speaker was none other than the much loved and admired King Hussein. He asked me to come immediately up to the Royal Palace, as a new government was being formed with Wasfi Tal as prime minister. I had been chosen to hold the portfolio of Foreign Affairs. I do not remember how I managed to extract myself from the gathering, but I did so as tactfully as I could, offering a few words of gratitude to our guests, apologising for the interruption and handing over the closing of the session to the Secretary-General Najmuddine Dajani.

This was, to all intents and purposes, the end of my close association with the task of economic and social development, not only for the East Bank but also for Jerusalem and the West Bank, united as they were under one flag.

The years spent at the Ministry of Reconstruction and Development, at the Ministry of National Economy, and finally, and perhaps most productively, my three years at the Development Board, are the most cherished in my memory. They were years of positive action, of construction and reconstruction, of giving hope, growth and gainful employment to so many people hitherto in dire need. The country of undeveloped resources and manpower, of innumerable refugees, and of abundant frontline villages, was beginning to stir into life and gradually move away from despair. Houses were being built, farms and industries were being established, schools were being opened and expanded, and a fully-fledged Jordan University was being inaugurated in 1962 by King Hussein, a precursor of some 25 universities across the length and breadth of Jordan.

People, having caught their breath and begun to feel confident were sending their sons and daughters abroad for study or work. They were successfully building up communities in both the West and the East, particularly in the Gulf region. The government of Jordan was streamlining its operations and seeking assistance from wherever it could obtain it. In 1960, a delegation was sent to the Federal Republic of Germany with the minister of economy as chairman, me as vice chairman, and a sizeable delegation representing important fields of activity. The minister and I had a productive meeting with German

Chancellor Ludwig Erhard. We were impressed by his grasp and vision, and surprised to notice that there was not a file or a paper on his desk. We were told that the day-to-day business and the hustle and bustle of business transactions were conducted in an adjacent building. In the atmosphere of calm, a leader or a minister can think, plan and act clearly. In our part of the world, a minister still insists on signing every paper, deciding on every appointment, and taking every decision. I participated in several cabinets, under three different prime ministers, and I regret to state that a council of ministers may still busy itself with the most trifling of problems, which would be better left to much lower echelons in the hierarchy of decision-making. Centralisation stifles initiatives, squanders precious time, and detracts from focusing on the major issues at hand. Is it the penchant for power, lack of discernment, or sheer bureaucracy which afflicts so many systems in the world?

As Jordan began to stabilize, after years of turmoil and uncertainty, on 6 August 1960 the offices of Jordan's prime minister were blown up in a massive explosion. This criminal act destroyed the wing housing the offices of Prime Minister Hazza al-Majali and the press department just beneath it. The prime minister was killed instantly, as were 12 other employees of the office, including some who had accompanied the delegation to Germany, Assem el-Taji, Maaita and others. I was lucky.

This was my third miraculous, hair-raising encounter with destiny, which I promised to narrate. I had just spent a two-week holiday with my family in Beirut. Upon my return, and on what turned out to be the day of the bombing, I wanted to pay a courtesy visit to the prime minister and to ask him to sign some papers, in his capacity as chairman of the board.

When this had been done, I asked the prime minister to excuse me, as I had other urgent business, and my brother, Muhammad, chief engineer of the Jordanian army in the West Bank was waiting for me, because he had an appointment at the Ministry of Defence. However, Hazza Pasha insisted that I should accept his hospitality for a cup of coffee, according the tradition of Arab hospitality. I insisted, equally vehemently, on taking my leave, and stressed that the waiting room adjacent to the office was full of visitors who wanted to see him, as his military aide would confirm. So, with the two insistences cancelling each other out, he let me go, with the promise that this would not happen next time.

I left the building and joined my brother who was waiting for me outside. No sooner had the car started moving than we heard the deafening sound of the nearby explosion which wrecked the prime minister's wing, destroyed other parts of the complex as well, and caused heavy smoke to billow from the wrecked building. I was there a mere five minutes before and would have remained there if I had succumbed to the prime minister's genuine kindness and hospitality. But it must have been God's wish that I should survive, in my third brush with death.

Hazza al-Majali was one of the most decent men that I have known. He was friendly, unassuming, a genuine patriot, and a firm believer in democracy and dialogue. Like other Jordanian compatriots, he was a strong supporter of Arab unity and the inevitability of its realisation. He had supported unity with Palestine and with Iraq in the early 1950s, and mid-decade, as prime minister, backed the British-sponsored Baghdad Pact, which would have united the Arab and Islamic states, in a close strategic and military alliance to confront any

Soviet expansion in the milieu of the Cold War. The pact would have brought together Iraq, Jordan, Turkey, Iran and Pakistan, in addition to Britain. Other Arab states might have wished to join at a later date, particularly Egypt and Syria. The United States would have been a non-official but strong supporter. I am certain that if this alliance had seen the light of day it would have stabilised the entire region, and might have brought about a fair solution to the question of Palestine, acceptable to all parties half a century ago. Unfortunately, both the Arabs and the Jews opposed it, for their own self-seeking motives. Egypt and Saudi Arabia opposed the pact because it would have strengthened the Hashemite regime in Iraq, and this was anathema to Saudi Arabia, while Nasser's Egypt resented the fact that the initiative for the alliance was to be given to Iraq, rather than to Egypt, as leader of the Arab world.

Israel presumably opposed the proposal because it would have brought to its borders a mighty alliance of states, capable of thwarting any ambitions of expansion, particularly into the West Bank, which it coveted, as later developments showed. Hazza al-Majali was forced to resign by mass demonstrations, but made a political comeback a few years later, only to be felled by his adversaries.

The squandering of precious human life has been a common occurrence in the contemporary history of the Middle East. In most instances the killing has been carried out for no reason beyond, perhaps, differences of opinion, an inexplicable hate or envy, or even an unpalatable statement. Prominent victims of conscience and of political opinion come to mind as notorious examples of such despicable behaviour: King Abdullah I of Jordan; Hazza al-Majali and Wasfi Tal, both prime ministers of Jordan; President Anwar Sadat, Prime

Minister Mahmoud Naqrashi, and Cabinet Minister Amin Uthman (an Old Victorian) of Egypt; King Faisal of Saudi Arabia; Druze leader Kamal Jumblatt and Prime Minister Rashid Karami of Lebanon; Dr Abdul Rahman Shahbandar, a Syrian nationalist politician; lawyer Hassan Sidki Dajani of Jerusalem; Sami Taha, president of the Palestine labour union of Haifa in 1946; and Zafer al-Masri, my brother-in-law, a potential leader of promise, who was mayor of Nablus. The list could go on and on.

Some of the above were murdered because they had had what were considered by many at the time to be treacherous contacts with Israelis. One cannot help but wonder how the course of history might have changed if some of those early contacts had been allowed to develop. Musa al-Alami, one of the foremost leaders of Palestine, told me how Ben-Gurion came to him in Jericho, in the wake of the 1967 war and told him that Israel was willing to withdraw from Jerusalem and the West Bank, in exchange for full peace and normalisation. But Musa al-Alami said the general atmosphere was so inflamed that he could not and did not communicate this message to those in power, smouldering under the defeat of 1967.

Awni Abdul Hadi, Palestinian leader and member of the Arab Higher Committee, the highest Palestinian decision-maker in the late 1940s, told me how all the members of this senior body were willing to accept the UN Partition Plan, Resolution 181 of 29 November 1947 but because of their dispersal or exile outside of the country they never had the chance to meet and take a collective decision. At the same time, they were afraid to declare individually their opinions, thus allowing the country to drift into chaos and catastrophe. How different the turn of events would have been if everyone had stayed put and allowed the two-state solution to be implemented on the ground, with no refugees, and with economic union. We could have avoided all the dire consequences of war and terrorism, dispersal and suffering, all of which have afflicted the entire region and impacted so much on the rest of the world.

This, of course, would have been conditional for its success on an extension of the presence of the mandatory power for a transitional period of two-to-three years (with UN approval), pending the creation of the institutions of state and its security apparatus. But, for Britain to have withdrawn hastily and ignominiously in six months, leaving behind death, destruction and disintegration of state and society, was perfidious, and unbecoming of a major power, with a trust accorded to it by the world community to safeguard and promote the welfare of mandated Palestine and its people.

But, in the final analysis, the blame must be placed on the absence, on the Palestinian side, of democratic institutions to study, debate and decide on the most feasible course of action, with full freedom of expression, and without fear of physical or moral harassment. This was woefully absent.

CHAPTER 9

From Economics to Politics

The decade of the 1960s was the one in which I became immersed in the intricacies of international politics. This is not to say that I had not been involved before that, but this time I was in a position to take decisions and act upon them. I had met several world leaders in the years leading up to 1948, in the salons of Katy Antonius, widow of George Antonius, the celebrated author of the classic book, *The Arab Awakening*, and formerly a senior Palestine government official. Her beautiful residence in Sheikh Jarrah, commanding a panoramic view of Jerusalem, was a regular meeting place, in a most relaxed and enjoyable atmosphere, for Palestinian leaders and intellectuals, and international visitors. Katy, a charming, beautiful and distinguished lady of middle age, was the daughter of a Lebanese intellectual who owned one of the most important and successful publishing houses in Egypt, *al-Muqattam*, which also produced a daily newspaper and a monthly journal. Katy gave sumptuous parties – lunches, dinners and receptions – the year round. We used to convey our views to the visitors at these social occasions, and they conveyed theirs, to the mutual benefit of both.

Musa al-Alami was one of the prominent figures I met at this time. He had represented Palestine at the newly created Arab League in 1944, and had established Arab offices in major Western cities to explain and expound the Palestinian cause. He offered me a post in one of these offices in London, Washington, or New York, but I declined because of my studies at the government-sponsored law school in Jerusalem.

When I took up my new post, as Minister of Foreign Affairs of the Hashemite Kingdom of Jordan, I told Wasfi Tal, a prime minister of courage and integrity that public office, with all its appurtenances, prestige and public lustre, did not particularly enthral me, and that I had accepted the post in order to be able to serve the Palestinian cause. I then asked for a week of private time to work out, articulate and formulate a work plan for serving this cause. He readily agreed, and I spent the week all alone preparing what came to be known as a White Paper, eventually published as the official policy document of the Jordan government. The book, consisting of 37 pages, and published with the blessing of King Hussein, encompassed three fields: a. Jordan's basic positions towards the Palestinian question; b. inter-Arab relations; c. the ideological encounters going on in the Arab world, pertaining to social and economic change, progress and reforms.

The original study that I had prepared provided for the establishment of a United Kingdom of Palestine and Jordan, as the political framework to be substituted for the existing name of the Hashemite Kingdom of Jordan. The reason was to acknowledge Palestinian self-identification, while preserving the unity between the two banks of the river Jordan. Wasfi and I argued the merits and demerits of the proposed change in a long meeting with the king. I said that if the proposed framework was not adopted, then the Palestinian people would be seeking the restoration of their self-identity, outside of the existing unity between Jordan and Palestine, and this is precisely what eventually happened. Prime Minister Wasfi Tal argued strongly against my proposal, on the grounds that it could be divisive in relations between Palestinians and Jordanians, thus encouraging dual loyalty and separatism.

The king listened intently to both arguments, and I had the feeling that he was sympathetic to my proposal, which would have preserved unity under the Hashemite monarchy. But Wasfi had the advantage of the *status quo* and the built-in inertia to any change, particularly when it was so far-reaching.

Thus the need for Palestinians to have representation of their own and the right to self-determination was reinforced. The creation of the PLO in 1964 came as the natural answer to this need, and Jordan participated actively in its creation.

I should mention here that the vast majority of Palestinians, citizens and refugees, were living in the Hashemite Kingdom of Jordan, with its East and West Banks, including East Jerusalem. The principal objective of the plan was to give top priority to the question of Palestine, which had remained dormant, deadlocked and unresolved in the decade-and-a-half since 1948, during which Israel had consolidated its hold on all the Palestinian territories, including areas specifically earmarked for the Palestinians. There was also the tragic plight of the Palestinian refugees, living in the abject squalour of refugee camps, in several locations.

The Jordanian House of Representatives endorsed the plan, which I had presented to it, as amended by the prime minister and excluding my proposal that the name and constitutional status of the kingdom be changed.

When news of the plan was announced, all Palestinian communities, in the Arab world and the diaspora, received it with considerable enthusiasm and support. Delegation after delegation came to Amman to convey support, including a delegation representing the Arab Higher Committee, which, before the formation of the PLO, was the recognised representative of the Palestinian people. The delegation consisted of Munif al-Husseini, close advisor to Haj Amin al-Husseini, Mufti of Jerusalem and president of the committee. It also included, Emile al-Ghori, its secretary-general, who later became a minister in the Jordanian cabinet.

They met King Hussein and expressed to him their full support for the plan. Ahmad al-Shuqairi, Izzat Tannous and Issa Nakhleh, former representatives of the committee to the United Nations and, currently representing the independents, also visited Amman to convey their support.

Nimr Masri of Ramleh and Abdul Rahman Murad of Haifa gave their support in the name of the Palestinian refugees in Damascus. Other delegations representing the refugees in Lebanon, and Palestinian communities in the United States likewise extended support.

If this overwhelming support represented anything, it represented the penchant of the Palestinian people for the restoration of its identity and the name of Palestine within the proposed United Kingdom of Palestine and Jordan. It also reflected support for renewal and resuscitation of the Palestine problem after a long period of torpor and outright neglect.

This may be the point at which I should mention an initiative taken by the administration of John F. Kennedy in 1961 for a solution of the problem of Palestinian refugees. I do not know whether this initiative, formulated by Dr Joseph Johnson, president of the Carnegie Endowment for International Peace, came in response to the activation of this issue, as described above, or in response to secret talks which, it had been disclosed, were going on between the Kennedy Administration and Nasser's Egypt. I have no way of knowing, one way or the other. All I know is that when I became foreign minister in 1962, Dr Johnson visited me at the ministry, and presented me with a plan on behalf of his government for the gradual repatriation of the refugees to their homeland, in accordance with UN General Assembly Resolution 194 of December 1948.

Because of the perennial relevance and importance of this plan to the question of the refugees, and even though I turned it down, as did other Arab foreign ministers, I feel it is useful to give an outline of the proposal, and the reasons which prompted us to reject it. The plan stipulated:

> 1. Every head of a refugee family should be given the opportunity to choose freely and without any pressure from any quarter between return to Palestine or compensation.
> 2. Every refugee must be fully informed about the following matters:
> The nature of the opportunity available to him for integration into Israeli society if he chooses repatriation.
> The amount or value of the compensation that he would receive as an alternative if he chooses to remain where he is.

3. The calculation of compensation would be on the basis of the value of the properties as existed in the years 1947-48, plus interest accruing on them.

4. The United States and other member states of the United Nations, including Israel, would subscribe towards providing the sums necessary for compensation.

5. Israel would have the right to conduct a security check on any refugee who chose to return to his land.

6. Refugees who did not own properties in Palestine would benefit from a lump sum to assist them to integrate into the societies in which they chose to settle.

7. Every government was entitled to withdraw from this plan if it considered that it constituted a danger to its vital interests.

8. The plan would be implemented gradually, and if it were to be scrapped mid-way, the refugees would not be left in a situation that was worse than the one they were in before the beginning of implementation.

When I asked Dr Johnson how many refugees per annum would be able to return under his plan he said the total would be 5,000. This, I retorted, would mean over 100 years for the return of all the existing refugees, let alone their offspring.

Moreover, the sporadic, individual, and gradual return of a refugee over many decades would entail family separations and other difficult choices, including the indomitable task of trying to integrate into an alien and hostile society in which the newcomer would be treated as a second class citizen, as was the case with Palestinians who remained in Palestine in 1948 and had become Israeli citizens.

Returning to the plan for Palestine and regional reaction, relations between Egypt and Jordan at this time were at a very low ebb for various reasons, including the break-up of the United Arab Republic which had united Egypt and Syria. Egypt and Jordan were also at loggerheads over the Yemen war in which Jordan and Saudi Arabia supported the monarchists against the new republican revolutionary regime. It was, therefore, not surprising that President Nasser should have received the plan for Palestine with unbridled scepticism, if not outright hostility. President Nasser, in his first public reaction, and in light of the Palestinian people's support for it, found it necessary to declare: 'Anyone who claims to have a plan for the liberation of Palestine is untruthful and insincere.'

The plan was certainly not a magic one to liberate Palestine, and nobody ever claimed that it was so. But President Nasser, who was drained by the dissolution of the United Arab Republic and under pressure in the Yemen war, felt that he was being challenged and embarrassed in the Arab arena to work for the Palestine question at a time when his hands were so full. Aside from troubles abroad, at home the drastic nationalisation plan had all but obliterated the upper and middle classes of Egypt. At the same time, we in Jordan and Palestine, who were so involved and committed to the Palestinian cause, felt deeply that the Yemeni war was a deliberate diversion of Egypt's resources at the expense of the more vital Palestinian issue.

I wish to state, in all sincerity, that it was never our intention to embarrass President Nasser, who was considered by the peoples of the Arab world as a great and sincere leader;

but, we opposed his country's descent into the quagmire of an open-ended war in Yemen, which was against Egypt's best interests and our own. There is no doubt, however, that Egypt's intervention benefited Yemen greatly, as it had helped to extricate it from the atrophy into which it had fallen, under a medieval monarchy which threw around it a *cordon sanitaire*, isolating it completely from the outside world. In our private conversations, Wasfi Tal never tired of repeating that one of the great ironies was that a forward-looking and progressive government like our own should find itself supporting one of the most backward and reactionary regimes on earth. And yet such were the inter-Arab political convolutions, intrigues, and hostilities that such behaviour seemed justified in a bitter struggle for survival.

The Jordanian government and I were closely involved in the establishment of the PLO. During a conference of Arab foreign ministers in Riyadh in 1963, Ahmad al-Shuqairi, minister of State in Saudi Arabia and a prominent Palestinian leader, asked me if I could invite him to Jordan, with the approval of Prince Faisal ibn Abdul Aziz (later King Faisal of Saudi Arabia). I informed King Hussein of this request and he agreed. Ahmad al-Shuqairi came to Jordan and held talks with the king, Wasfi Tal, and myself. In addition to the meetings at the royal palace, we convened daily in my house in the room overlooking the garden in Jabal Amman.

At these meetings we explored all available avenues for articulating Palestinian identity and action but with a *proviso*, and an important one, that this should not impinge on or undermine the unity and cohesion of the people of Jordan. It was, indeed, a dilemma which needed to be treated with utmost circumspection and care. The people of Jordan consisted of Palestinians and Jordanians, living side-by-side in amity and harmony in all walks of life. The proposal was for power sharing on a 50-50 basis in the cabinet, in both houses of parliament, political parties, the civil service, the armed forces, and the security apparatus. A great deal of integration had taken place since the Act of Unity of 1950, in addition to social, familial, economic, demographic, and geographic realities on the ground.

These were achievements which could not be lightly discarded, and Ahmad al-Shuqairi was fully cognizant and supportive of them. He had a draft framework on which we worked, article by article, and point by point, with mutual and sincere understanding. Thus were the rudiments and the building blocks of the PLO established in 1964.

The first Palestine National Council convened at the Intercontinental Hotel (now the Seven Arches Hotel) on the Mount of Olives in Jerusalem. The owner of the Hilton group, who in the 1960s was contemplating the construction of a hotel on that spot, remarked to the then Jordanian minister of economy that, in his view, it was the most beautiful spot in the world.

King Hussein officially inaugurated the first National Council meeting, and then left the delegates, who included all the Palestinian-Jordanian members of the House of Deputies, to draw up a charter, select an executive committee and elect Ahmad al-Shuqairi, a brilliant orator and an accomplished politician, as the first president of the new organisation. He remained in that post until 1969 when Yasser Arafat, head of the largest Palestinian group, Fatah, was elected president.

In the meantime, I accompanied the king – and I was then serving as Minister of the Royal Court (advisor to the king) – on a three-day tour of the West Bank, together with Sherif Hussein bin Nasser, uncle of the king, and chief of the royal cabinet. I had the privilege on the second day to invite King Hussein, his entourage and members of the cabinet to a luncheon at my family house in Jerusalem. It was almost burned down after being hit by napalm bombs in the 1967 war, but has since been repaired.

Israel claimed that it launched its pre-emptive air strike on Egyptian air force bases in the 1967 June war in retaliation against commando raids by Palestinians, starting in Syria and then Gaza, and Jordan. I have no record or information about what happened on the Syrian armistice line or in Gaza. But I can talk knowledgeably about Jordan, including the West Bank and Jerusalem. I am convinced that Israeli assessments of what they described as Palestinian aggression were exaggerated.

One Friday in 1965 I was in Jerusalem, as I was every weekend, at my family house when I heard a small explosive charge detonated at a distance of 300 metres between our home and Sanhadriya Street opposite, just beyond what was no man's land on the western side (Israel has since built three large hotel there, including the Olive Tree and Royal Plaza Jerusalem just opposite my family house). I inquired about what had happened, and was told that a youth had crossed into no man's land, placed the charge, but against no particular target resulting in no damage worth mentioning. At that time, practically no-one had heard of Fatah, the dominant group in the PLO, and hardly any attention had been paid to what had happened that particular Friday. Arab Jerusalem was booming with tourists from every land, and enjoying unprecedented prosperity. At that time I used to walk in the Old City with its narrow meandering streets, in a human traffic jam, compounded by beasts of burden laden with merchandise of every description, the only means of transport in the *suqs* (markets) there. I spent almost my entire childhood going to school in the Old City, and playing in a children's playground (Saadiya playground) equipped with swings, sand pits and slides, a welcomed donation from the late Mrs Valentine Vester, one of the owners of the American Colony Hotel. And still, every time I went there, in later life, the Old City enraptured me with new facets of its seduction. I noticed large Roman stones straddling the walls on both sides of a street and sniffed the variety of scents that permeate the air. Then I would savour the aroma of the famed food there: *kaak* (bread hoops sprinkled with sesame seeds), *falafel, hummus, mutabaq* (sweet loaves made by Zalatimo Brothers); and *kenafeh* (soft cheese cooked between two layers of orange-shredded pastry).

Walking through the Old City with my brother, Muhammad, in 1965 I remember saying to him that I almost felt like a tourist, coming for the first time and discovering with the curiosity of a stranger what I had not seen before. About 150 metres from the Holy Sepulchre was the ancient Roman Cardo Square, which is submerged in the many layers of the Old City.

On that same spot, and likewise submerged, is a *suq* consisting of 70 shops which belong to the Nusseibeh family from time immemorial, or *al-dahr* in Arabic, as the *waqf* describes it. It probably dates back 600-800 years, and was given as a *waqf* endowment for the benefit of the Dome of the Rock nearby. In the early 1970s, Meron Benvenisti, an open-minded man of high character, was deputy mayor of West Jerusalem. He asked my brothers, Anwar, Hisham and Muhammad, why they did not unearth this ancient *suq*, for all they needed to do was to remove the earth and debris that could be carried away on mules. Unfortunately, this was never carried through. A request went to the Law Courts but was turned down on technical grounds. Perhaps lovers of Jerusalem can channel their energies into securing approval to unearth and refurbish this ancient shopping centre.

Returning to that small explosion on no man's land in Jerusalem in 1965, that incident and a similarly small one in the southern area of the West Bank, in which a pump was blown up, did not justify the massive Israeli retaliation launched against Jenin and Qalqilia in May 1965, and the Latroun area and the village of as-Samu in the south of the West Bank in 1966. Prime Minister Wasfi Tal and I were attending the Arab Defence Council meeting in Cairo when news of the raid on as-Samu came in. Wasfi turned to me and said: 'The battle for the West Bank has begun, and this raid presages it.' In ordinary situations during the 1950s and early 60s, hostile actions were referred to the Mixed Armistice Commission for perusal, but this did not happen in the latter years leading up to 1967. Subsequent developments, culminating in the June war of 1967, have demonstrated beyond doubt Israeli designs on Jerusalem and the rest of the West Bank. And, as always, we Arabs, whether Palestinian, Jordanian, Syrian, or Egyptian, have facilitated Israeli designs through our inept behaviour and uncalculated actions. How else can we explain the rush to join a war at 10am on Monday 5 June 1967 when the fate of the war had already been sealed at 8am by the total destruction of the Egyptian air force?

Naturally enough, we were all deeply saddened and distressed that our homeland had been wantonly lost in such a careless way. I remember a meeting with King Hussein in which I asked how it was that our military attaché in Cairo did not inform us about what happened. To which, in a moment of sullen brooding, the king replied: 'Did you expect our military attaché to inform us when the big man himself (meaning General Abdul Munim Riyadh of Egypt, who was in command of the Jordanian Forces) did not know?' When I served as ambassador to Egypt in 1969, Hussein Shafii, vice president of Egypt, told me how he was the first to inform President Nasser bluntly about the total destruction of the Egyptian air force at around 2pm.

Many authoritative books have been written on this crucial historical issue, so no additions are needed. And besides, it is not within the purview of my remembrances of Jerusalem, even though my city was its ultimate victim. A few days after the fall of Jerusalem an Israeli newspaper admitted nonchalantly: 'We laid a trap for King Hussein and he fell right into it.' This being said, we should not minimise or underestimate the colossal public pressure that was building up in support of the expected war throughout the Arab world through radio broadcasts, the mass media and mass gatherings. This mass hysteria smothered any voice of reason or rationality. Indeed, this public pressure made it difficult, it not impossible, for President Nasser to withdraw from the brink, regardless of his better judgment.

Some of the Arab states were, alas, willing to gamble with the fate of the Holy Land by permitting individual, sporadic raids, while Jordan was being maligned at official Arab meetings and in the press for trying to prevent them, and accused of standing in the way of the liberation of Palestine. In fairness to the United Arab Command, set up at the Arab summit of 1964, under the leadership of Ali Ali Amer, it had repeatedly warned against a drift into war precipitated by such sundry actions while Arab defence preparations were far from adequate or complete. Militarily, he had described the West Bank as 'naked'.

Ahmad al-Shuqairi's elaborate memoirs, rich in information on various stages of the struggle of the Palestinian people for liberation and independence, failed nonetheless to give due credit to Jordan's role in initiating and activating the Palestinian cause in 1962-63, a process that eventually led to the establishment of the PLO in 1964, as the representative of the Palestinian people. As mentioned earlier, we were both walking a tight rope, in the process of reconciling Palestinian needs and aspirations on the one hand, with the indispensable requirement to preserve the unity of the Jordanian state and people on the other. It was a dichotomy which had repeatedly created tensions and crises between the governments of Jordan and the PLO. Many politicians and governments paid the political price for such tensions, before and after 1967. I resigned from the government of Wasfi Tal towards the end of 1966, for reasons relating to this sensitive issue, and because of the government's over-reaction to the activities of the leadership and staff of the PLO, which had set up its headquarters in the vicinity of Jerusalem.

Let me focus for a moment on 1964, for it saw both the creation of the PLO and the birth of the Arab summit.

Following the dissolution of unity between Egypt and Syria, the collapse of the union between Iraq and Jordan, and the war in Yemen, a political vacuum was created which impelled a drastic reappraisal of common Arab action. A serious attempt was made in 1963 to revive some form of federal union between Egypt, Syria, and Iraq, the latter two states being governed by the same Baath party. Lengthy talks were held in Cairo to reach a *modus vivendi* for unity, but these attempts came to nothing.

I was Minister of Foreign Affairs in the newly-formed government of Samir Pasha al-Rifai, a veteran and versatile statesman of long standing. The king wanted a kind of national unity government, capable of dealing with an increasingly tense situation in the Middle East. Inter-Arab relations were at a very low ebb, and Israel was bracing itself for a possible confrontation with the Arabs. Incursions, skirmishes and raids were taking place intermittently along the 650 kilometre armistice line between Jordan and Israel.

As foreign minister, I was following the unity talks going on in Cairo with utmost attention. There is nothing worse than being left out and isolated, as Jordan had been in the siege of 1958. I was urging the prime minister on the importance of making some move, some initiative or an overture to the tri-partite conference in Cairo, a declaration of intent to join if the right conditions were present.

But Samir al-Rifai, who was following the talks intently, and had greater experience with Arab politics than myself, was advising caution and patience. He said we should wait and see if anything came out of the talks. There was a great deal of bickering, and possibly bitterness at the talks, coming as they did in the aftermath of the break-up of the United Arab Republic in 1961. The Egyptian press reported on the differences and difficulties in the discussions. My concern was that if some form of federation were to take place between Egypt, Syria and Iraq – powerful surrounding countries – Jordan's position would become untenable. But before long the talks collapsed without agreement. The prime minister's advice was vindicated and the attention of the government reverted to internal affairs which were equally pressing. A coalition of forces in parliament had mobilised to threaten the government with a vote of confidence and force it to resign. This it did, and parliament was consequently dissolved. This was the first time that a government in Jordan had been forced to resign as a result of a no-confidence vote in parliament, thereby registering a milestone in the democratic evolution of Jordan.

While all these developments were taking place, Israel in 1963 brought matters to the fore when it embarked unilaterally on the diversion of the River Jordan, disregarding altogether the natural and inherent rights of the riparian states, as well as the Johnston Plan of the mid-1950s, drawn up by US Special Ambassador Eric Johnston at the behest of the government of the United States, for a fair distribution and utilisation of the extensive Jordan River basin. Its fountainheads, the Hasbani and Banyas rivers, emanate from Lebanon and Syria, with only Tal-Qadi Spring from Palestine-Israel itself. Israel's project was to divert all these waters outside of their natural basin in the Jordan Valley for irrigation projects in the Beer Sheba area and the rest of the Negev. In terms of international law and internationally accepted practices, the Israeli action was little short of a declaration of war against the riparian Arab states, and the latter were placed in an untenable situation, requiring an appropriate response. Syria threatened to divert the waters running through its territory, and the danger of war loomed large. To avert this possibility and allow for cool-headed deliberations, President Nasser of Egypt, in a broadcast speech to coincide with a national celebration in the Suez Canal area, called for the convening of an Arab summit conference to deal with the situation. King Hussein of Jordan was the first to accept, and gradually all the Arab states, without exception, agreed to take part.

Thus was born the institution of the Arab summit conference, meeting annually in different Arab capitals to discuss common Arab policies and actions pertaining to internal as well as external affairs. In real terms, it is a meeting of member states of the Arab League at the highest level. The first summit was held at the Hilton Hotel in Cairo in January 1964, and I accompanied the king as a member of Jordan's delegation, in my new capacity as Minister of the Royal Court.

The background to the River Jordan crisis, to be discussed in Cairo, had its roots in the previous decade. It was US President Dwight D Eisenhower who in October 1953 had appointed Eric Johnston as a special representative to draw up a unified plan for the utilisation of the waters of the River Jordan and its tributaries, and to distribute such waters between the Arab states concerned and Israel. Johnston visited the area several times, the last being in the fall of 1955. The team of experts under his supervision worked out an elaborate plan, which included soil analysis, recorded in several volumes which I placed in my office at the Development Board as a basic reference on all matters relating to the implementation of the East Ghor Canal and other irrigation projects. Even on the personal level the data was useful: when I bought a piece of land, on which I established a citrus grove in Kafrein in the Jordan Valley in 1959, I benefited from the report's analysis of soil and water there. It graded the area class A, and I was grateful for that advice.

The plan, which was to have been implemented in five stages, each at an interval of two-to-three years, provided for electricity generation from dams to be incorporated into the project. Arab irrigation experts had carried out intensive studies of various aspects of the plan and introduced considerable technical alterations, without undermining its overall objectives. The political committee of the League of Arab States on 30 January 1961 approved the amended plan in principle, at its meeting in Baghdad, but stopped short of giving it outright approval.

In 1974, I was an Ambassador in Rome when Mahmoud Riyadh, foreign minister of Egypt and later secretary-general of the Arab League, visited the city. He was a good friend and a sincere patriot, and I invited him to lunch at the embassy. In the course of the conversation, he told me that the Arab foreign ministers had balked from approval of the plan, even though they were convinced of its soundness and feasibility, for political reasons, fearing negative popular reaction against this unified project. It should be recalled that in 1955, when it was first introduced, there was a public outcry against the plan, spearheaded by the Palestinians themselves who had most to gain. At a conference held in Jerusalem on 20 July 1955, the Palestinian refugees rejected the Johnston Plan, as an attempt to rehabilitate them, instead of repatriating them to their homeland. This rejection of the plan demonstrates the intensity of opposition to rehabilitation, and repudiates suggestion that Arab states exploited the plight of the refugees for political ends.

In any event, the first Arab summit of kings and heads of state convened on 13 January 1964 to consider the Israeli diversion of the river Jordan, from all its political, economic and technical aspects. The summit adopted several resolutions, including one for the implementation of an Arab plan for the diversion of the tributaries.

At a second Arab summit held in early September 1964 at the Palestine Hotel (now the Helnan Hotel) in Alexandria within the fabulously beautiful Muntazah gardens and palaces of the late King Farouk, the conferees approved the detailed arrangements for implementing and financing the Arab plan. The summit also decided to embark on military preparedness, for fear of an Israeli military intervention when the diversion was implemented.

Thus the tense atmosphere and developments on the ground, combined with a host of regional and international policies, declared and undeclared, were converging to prepare the region for an inevitable confrontation between the Arab states and Israel. The question posed, therefore, was not whether a fateful confrontation would occur, but when.

At the same time, relations between the United States and Egypt were fast deteriorating under the administration of President Lyndon Johnson because of his sweeping and unquestioning support for Israel. King Hussein made a semi-official visit to Washington in 1965. He and his delegation had been flown to the US capital on the presidential plane and were hosted at Blair House, the official residence of guests of the White House. President Johnson and King Hussein met privately for some 25 minutes, after which both came to the Oval Office for formal discussions. I was one of the two senior Jordanian representatives accompanying the king, as Minister of the Royal Court, and the other was Anton Attallah, Foreign Minister and a very venerable man, with an extensive judicial background.

President Johnson opened the discussion with an abrupt sentence, which took us by surprise. He exclaimed, without even a word of welcome: 'Why do you Arabs hate us?' I replied very coolly and confidently: 'But, Mr President, who told you that we hate America? To the contrary, we admire a great many things about America and the American people. But we do take exception to American policies in the Middle East, and particularly the Arab-Israeli conflict.' Foreign Minister Attallah added some weighty arguments to the discussion. But a moment later President Johnson was wanted on the telephone to deal with a railway strike which was of concern to him because of the disruption it was causing to basic services. The talks continued with senior government officials.

The Arab summits had slowly become institutionalised, as a form of confederacy in its early stages, particularly on matters of foreign policy and defence, and the Arab states were beginning to deal with external powers with a single voice. An example was the decision of the Arab foreign ministers, at a meeting in Cairo in 1965, to sever relations with the Federal Republic of Germany, following the disclosure that it had supplied Israel with 200 top-of-the-line tanks, in addition to other military hardware. The Arab states considered this deal to have upset the military balance between them and Israel. Efforts were made to dissuade West Germany from proceeding, but to no avail.

It is pertinent to mention here that the Federal Republic of Germany was the largest importer of Arab oil, particularly from Libya. And in 1960, it had concluded with Jordan, as I have explained elsewhere, a generous economic cooperation agreement, which included the establishment of vocational centres and the carrying out of a systematic geological survey.

The accord also covered tourism, agricultural marketing and other items, in a long list prepared by the Development Board, including the development of the port of Aqaba. It was clear to us in our negotiations that West Germany was going out of its way to be helpful. Perhaps, we reckoned, this was because it had given enormous assistance to Israel in compensation for Nazi atrocities against the Jews in World War II, and Jordan was now bearing the brunt of the tragedy of the Palestinian refugees, who had been displaced by Israel. The relations remained severed until 5 February 1967, i.e. four months before the 1967 war. King Hussein was strongly against the severance of relations with Germany, and lost his temper when Wasfi and I tried to convince him that Jordan had no option but to act in unison with the rest of the Arab world. We all regretted having to take this extreme measure against a friendly country, unburdened by any backlog of colonialism and colonial misrule. But we could not be lone deviants in a 20-state Arab foreign ministers' gathering. I made some amends at the meeting when I opposed strongly a proposal by Ahmad al-Shuqairi that we establish diplomatic relations with East Germany. I won the argument promptly and decisively when I asked: 'How can we possibly contribute to Germany's division when we all claim to be proponents of Arab unity?'

CHAPTER 10

Moving Around

Having laid the groundwork at home pertaining to the Palestine plan it was felt that the Arab states should join in the diplomatic efforts to promote the Palestinian cause worldwide. At a meeting of Arab foreign ministers, Jordan suggested that each Arab country should choose a particular region with which it had close ties and interests for its diplomatic effort. I had received an invitation to attend a conference in Bahia Salvador, in northern Brazil, under the title 'The Alliance for Progress'. The conference was attended by leading figures from Latin America, as well as from the United States and Europe, including the president of Germany, David Rockefeller of Chase Manhattan Bank and other leading bankers and economists.

As part of the initiative to promote the Palestinian cause overseas, I used my visit to Brazil to visit other South American states: Argentina, Venezuela, Peru, Chile, Panama, and Mexico. In each of the countries I visited, I met the president, the foreign minister, other senior officials, and last but not least, representatives of the thriving and buoyant communities of Arab extraction, mainly from the lands of Greater Syria, Lebanon, Palestine, and Jordan. These communities migrated to the new world in the latter part of the 19th and in the early 20th century. I was glad to see that almost invariably while they had fully integrated into the societies of their new homelands they still retained a very strong emotional attachment to their countries of origin. Almost every community had established an Arab Club, a Lebanese Club, a Palestinian Club or a Jordanian Club, separately or collectively, depending upon the size and relative wealth of each of the communities. They were all nostalgic about their former homelands, and expressed this nostalgia by retaining various symbols and practices such as national dishes like *kubbeh*, *tabbouleh* and *hummus*. The older generations also retained traditional values and ways of behaviour, but I very much doubt that such observance will outlive them once they are gone.

There are no definitive figures as to the numbers of those communities which hailed from Arab homelands, but they are estimated to be in the range of 20 million, mainly Lebanese. I was also happy to see that they had climbed the ladder of achievement pretty fast, and were considered in the main, as having been signally successful in all walks of life, and particularly in business.

In Argentina, where there is a strong Syrian community, the Syrian ambassador invited a large gathering of leading personages, to whom I presented the Jordan plan for Palestine. They impressed me as being distinguished and serious-minded. One of those present at the gathering was Amin al-Hafez, Syrian military attaché, who a mere three years later became president of Syria.

There was one unexpected and regrettable incident in Argentina which could have marred this visit. After the official reception at the airport, I walked towards my car with the foreign minister of Argentina and Dr Najib Ijha, a Jordanian ambassador who was stationed at the time in Amman and had been sent as my companion on the tour. As we approached the car, I observed from a distance around a couple of hundred youths carrying placards. They were lining the exit from the airport, leading to the motorcade which was to take me to the hotel. At first, I thought that they were a welcoming gathering but, as I drew near, I discovered that it was a hostile demonstration against Jordan and, presumably, against the visit. It was orderly and I saluted them and smiled in order to maintain an atmosphere of serenity at the reception, and to take the demonstration in my stride. But as I was getting into the Cadillac, one or two of the demonstrators threw tomatoes in my direction, but missing their intended target. The next day, the Arab ambassadors in Buenos Aires, as well as the Director of the Arab League mission, visited me in my hotel and expressed deep regret at what had happened at the airport. I learnt later on that an Egyptian military attaché to Argentina, by the name of General Issam, had arranged the protest, capitalising, perhaps, on the tension which existed between Egypt and Jordan in the early 1960s, before the birth of the Arab summits. What the general evidently did not know was that my tour was a part of an all-Arab effort to promote a just solution to the question of Palestine, in accordance with international legitimacy and the relevant United Nations resolutions.

In Caracas, Venezuela, I was likewise accorded warm hospitality by both the government and the Arab community, and a banquet was held in my honour, at the community's exquisite club where speeches were given. Looking back several decades, I recall being impressed by the modernity and cleanliness of the capital itself. But on the outskirts of Caracas, by contrast, one could see slums containing ugly tin huts, in a country blessed with oil. I am sure the successive governments could not have allowed the continued existence of such pockets of poverty amidst plenty.

Peru was equally hospitable, and leaders of the Arab community insisted on presenting me with a silver tray with appropriate inscriptions to commemorate the visit. At the hotel where I was staying in Lima I observed special security measures near my suite and was later informed that the government had been alerted to threats against my life, which necessitated such measures. I was not particularly ruffled by the warnings and, being an optimist by nature, could not imagine who might want to commit such an act against my person. It must have been a false alarm, or an attempt by an Israeli agent to unnerve me, on that lone mission on behalf of a worthy cause.

But the highlight of the tour was in Chile where a substantial and influential Palestinian-Jordanian community lived. As soon as the aircraft stopped its engines near the terminal building, Dr Ijha, my colleague, who is himself from Bethlehem, told me to look out of the window. I could not believe my eyes. There were hundreds of well-wishers crowding every inch of available space, with dignitaries, clergy, the media, TV and radio microphones and, heading them all, two ministers: the minister of foreign affairs and the minister of the interior, in addition to the president of the senate. It was a popular, genuine and spontaneous expression of a profound sentiment of goodwill towards a foreign minister who came from their own terra sancta, Jerusalem and its twin satellite towns, Bethlehem and Beit Jala, from which almost the entire Arab community had originally migrated. My visit clearly aroused feelings of nostalgia.

The reception was far grander than a mere formal, official occasion, and I took this lavish generosity to be a reflection of the success, standing and influence of this community. I was shown a number of industries, projects and banks which belong to descendants of some renowned families: Jarour and Sons; Suleiman Zummar; Hanna Saeed Yacoub; Anton and Khosse; Nazir Hirmas; Raphael Tarout; Khalil Qattan; and many others. I did my best to sell Jordan to them. Jordan in the early 1960s included their own towns, Bethlehem, Beit Jala and Beit Sahour. I explained to them all the incentives that Jordanian laws offer for the encouragement of investment. They were reasonably enthusiastic, but envisaged any potential investment in Jordan as being in addition to, and not in place of, their existing investments in Chile, which were substantial. There was one promise that I made to them and to all other Palestinian-Jordanian communities which I met: that those so wishing could obtain Jordanian nationality without forfeiting their existing ones. When I returned home, I conveyed this proposal to the government and it was approved. The necessary amendments to the law of nationality were enacted to give effect to the dual nationality. I do not know whether this amended law is still in force, but in the context of the requirements of the period the step was a positive incentive to attract investment from our expatriates.

The morning after my arrival, the telephone rang at the hotel and the speaker was Issa Bandak, a former mayor of Bethlehem and formerly Jordan's ambassador to Chile. He apologised for not being at the airport to welcome me. He assured me that he was a close friend of my late father in Jerusalem and that he had very much wanted to welcome me but his dispute with the government of Jordan had prevented him from doing so. The dispute was over the embassy residence which the government believed he had bought on its behalf, while he claimed that it belonged to him, with yearly payments from the government into the embassy account being rent. I thanked him for his consideration and his friendly expressions, and withheld comment on the dispute.

Chile was the only Latin American country where Jordan had an embassy because it was the one with the greatest number of expatriates. Financial constraints at that time precluded the establishment of additional embassies in other parts of the sub-continent.

Today, there are more ambassadorial exchanges and a confluence of interests has spurred the opening of new embassies. On the last day of my visit to Chile, Jordan's Ambassador Kamal al-Humud, a very amiable, experienced and capable man, gave a dinner in my honour to which prominent government figures and leaders of the Jordanian-Palestinian community were invited. In the course of a conversation with the foreign minister of Chile, the latter asked which country I was planning to visit next on my tour. I replied, without giving much thought, that it was Bolivia. The foreign minister was nonplussed and I noticed that there was something on his mind. I said: 'Mr Minister, did something I said cause you concern?' He replied: 'Bolivia has killed three of our ambassadors.' What he meant was that the three had apparently given in to the difficulties of living at the kind of high altitudes that are a feature of Bolivia. I had not been aware of the problem of altitude in the capital, La Paz, which, I was told, was in the range of 4,200 metres above sea level. At this altitude, the air is thin and oxygen is woefully inadequate. People in the know are usually provided with oxygen mask until they have adjusted, if they do at all. I told the minister that I had already committed myself to the visit, and that they were waiting for me. To which he replied: 'Do not worry, for they are used to last-minute cancellations.' So I asked our ambassador to send a cable to the Bolivian ministry of foreign affairs, expressing, with utmost regret, my inability to fulfil the visit because of unforetold urgent business, and promising to make the visit at an unspecified later date. True enough, I was campaigning for the Palestinian cause, but not to the extent of martyring myself where it could be avoided.

The next station on my tour was Panama. Because of a delay, I arrived at 3am. To my embarrassment, the foreign minister of Panama had been waiting for me for hours on end, either at the airport or elsewhere. I apologised for the inconvenience which I had caused him and assured him that the reason for the delay was not of my own making. The minister was understanding.

Colombia had a large community of Palestinian extraction. The country was on my schedule of visits, and we were in constant touch about the programme for it, which was quite elaborate. Unfortunately, I was informed by my government to cut short my tour because of urgent business at home. In truth, being on the move from one country to another and interacting with one community after another, within the space of a day or two was somewhat disorienting, with erratic air travel by night and day, contingent on the schedules of various airlines. In a sense, therefore, I was relieved to be returning home earlier than I had planned, but not before completing the last lap on my way home, the visit to Mexico.

I arrived in Mexico City on a Friday afternoon, which meant the start of a long weekend. I would not have minded that, but for the fact that Mexico City, the capital, is located at an altitude of around 2,700 metres above sea level, not as bad as La Paz, but bad enough for my physical constitution. Jerusalem and Amman are on hills, but both lie at altitudes of less than 1,000 metres above sea level, heights that are tolerable, indeed, stimulating.

In Mexico City, I felt extreme discomfort, breathing with difficulty and walking at a snail's pace like a mechanical robot. But I was not alone in this discomfort, as I observed almost all other guests at the hotel labouring under the same handicap. We were advised to refrain from drinking, as it would only aggravate our predicament. At dinner, I felt a loss of appetite and hardly completed a cup of tomato soup. I went up to bed early, only to wake up at midnight, not knowing what to do until the break of the day.

I tried to make arrangements to spend the weekend in Acapulco, a wonderful beach resort, and found a seat on a plane going there. But there was no guarantee of an early return on Monday morning, and a meeting with the president of Mexico had been scheduled for noon. So I sweated it out in Mexico City, and as I adjusted to the altitude life became gradually easier and more tolerable. The ambassadors of Syria and Lebanon visited me at the hotel and took me on a tour of the sprawling city by car. The traffic jams were massive, if not prohibitive, and I wonder how manageable it is today, decades later, with a doubling of population and automobiles, which must traverse the same old roads of this built-up city. The pollution must be suffocating in a city surrounded by mountains. The meeting with the president was very warm and fruitful, and what added to its amiability was the national drink, tequila, which was served along with coffee.

Looking back, I often wonder whether that tour was worth the effort and, my answer is a categorical yes, particularly if one's objectives are not set too high. Latin America is a beautiful sub-continent and its people are very friendly and warm. Indeed, there is much in common between our way of life and theirs, and I guess a great many of the Spanish and Portuguese inhabitants carry traces of Arab lineage and heritage, dating back to the time when their ancestors crossed the seas, following the demise of Arab rule in mainland Spain in the late 15th century. Over the 800-year period of Arab settlement in the Iberian Peninsula, there must surely have been a considerable amount of intermarriage between the Spanish and the Arabs.

I had originally intended to meet with American Secretary of State Dean Rusk at the end of the tour but it was agreed that such a meeting would be more conveniently arranged in the latter part of September when each year the secretary of state would come to New York to participate in United Nations functions on the occasion of a new session of the General Assembly. An American secretary of state meets with as many foreign ministers as time allows. But, traditionally, Jordan, as a friendly country and one with a close, if not organic, relationship with the question of Palestine, is invariably on his list of meetings.

In the latter part of September 1962, I led the Jordan delegation to the General Assembly session of the United Nations.

It was my first attendance as a foreign minister and the occasion was eventful, particularly for a newcomer. It coincided with Algeria's independence and its accession to membership of the United Nations. I was one of around 40 foreign ministers who went to the airport to welcome Ahmad Ben Bella, the first president of newly independent Algeria. The aircraft, on landing, hoisted on its nose the American and Algerian flags. The delegation included Foreign Minister Abdul Aziz Bouteflika, who later became president of Algeria.

The following day, a solemn ceremony was held on the occasion of Algeria's accession to the United Nations. The General Assembly was packed with leading world figures, including Adlai Stephenson, head of the US delegation who in 1952, had run as the Democratic party's presidential candidate and obtained over 27 million votes, against President Eisenhower's 32 million.

The elected president of the General Assembly, Sir Zafrullah Khan, was a celebrated Pakistani scholar, a great orator and a very modest and unassuming man. He had written the best book in English on the life of Muhammad, and had many authoritative publications to his credit. Seven states had been elected as vice presidents of the assembly, including Jordan. Just before the start of Algeria's accession ceremony he came up to me and asked me to preside over the session. Surprised, I said: 'But no-one deserves to preside over this historic session more than you.' Sir Zafrullah had truly and persistently been the champion of dependent countries in their quest for independence, and he had worked particularly hard on decolonisation affecting Arab and Islamic countries. But Sir Zafrullah answered: 'Algeria is an Arab country, and I want an Arab foreign minister to preside over this ceremony.' And so it came to pass.

While in New York I was surprised to meet up with an old friend from my university days. Professor Farhat Ziyadeh was teaching at the Oriental Department at Princeton University when I was there in 1951-54. He is from Ramallah, as is his wife Suad. My wife and I were friends of the Ziyadeh family during our three-year stay. When he read in the papers that I was coming to New York as foreign minister he came especially to New York to congratulate me and entered the hall of the General Assembly hall to find me on the podium, seated in the chair of the presidency. He almost cried out in surprise. He later told me that my becoming a foreign minister so relatively soon after graduation was in itself a big jump. But seeing me at the summit of the world assembly went beyond all his expectations. Evidently promotions in academia are slower than in politics, all things being equal.

I addressed the General Assembly, as do all foreign ministers, although on occasions the address may be given by a prime minister, or even a head of state. Traditionally, the president of the United States gives the address on behalf of his country which hosts the UN. The addresses in the 1960s were long and tedious, starting with lavish congratulations to the president on his election, generous praise of the outgoing president on his performance, warm welcome to the new member-states of the United Nations. These were many in that decade of decolonisation, raising membership from 45 states in 1947 to 192 today. I must have attended almost a quarter of the UN's sessions, whether as foreign minister, permanent delegate, or roaming ambassador at the request of my government to help the permanent mission on certain specific issues, particularly the question of Palestine, or the plight of the Palestinian refugees. The latter is a perennial item on the agenda of the General Assembly, in accordance with its Resolution 194 of December 1949, calling for their repatriation and, or, compensation.

These issues formed the centrepiece of my address, as well as the addresses of all Arab delegations. There was one additional item, namely, the treatment of the Palestinian Arabs who had remained in their country and become citizens of Israel. Up to the outbreak of the war of 1967 the Palestinian Israelis had been subjected to many forms of discrimination and ill treatment, and lived under military rule. Their daily lives were affected by travel and work restrictions, in addition to the confiscation of their lands and properties. They had the added misfortune of being treated in the Arab world with the same suspicion as Israelis were, and were subject to the same boycott as that towards Jewish citizens of Israel. They were not permitted to visit any Arab country, as though they were responsible for being under Israeli rule, rather than the adjacent Arab states, which had ignominiously failed to save them in 1948. As a Palestinian, I knew better, and as Jordan's Foreign Minister I gave their every grievance my full attention and focus. This was done through the Special Political Committee, which addresses particular items other than those addressed at the regular First Political Committee.

I had the privilege of meeting Secretary of State Dean Rusk for the first time in 1962. Present at the meeting was Dr Muhammad al-Farra, Jordan's Ambassador to the UN. Rusk was a man of great understanding, open heart and mind; and he was a decision-maker. The discussions included bilateral issues between the United States and Jordan, covering economic and military assistance. In my speech at the General Assembly, I had criticised the United States for providing Israel with Hawk missiles. The secretary of state looked me directly in the eyes and asked: 'When you criticised the United States for giving Hawk missiles to Israel, were you simply stating a position or did you feel that your country was genuinely threatened by it?' I said: 'Mr Secretary, I happen to come from Jerusalem, it is my home city, and I have seen houses being blown up over the heads of their residents with simple explosives How, then, do you think I feel when I read in *The New York Times* that America is giving these lethal missiles to Israel?' Mr Rusk replied instantly: 'I understand how you feel, and to begin with these are defensive and not offensive missiles.' I said: 'I understand that, but if my adversary can hit me with impunity while I cannot hit him, then he has the advantage.' To which the secretary replied: 'What can we do, then, to allay your fears?' I said: 'Provide Jordan with the same.' The secretary said: 'Granted.'

When I returned to Amman I reported the conversation to King Hussein who apparently had been briefed about it by the Americans. But then the king said: 'Where are we to get the money from to pay for them?' And the matter rested there. But eventually, in the 1970s, Jordan acquired Hawk missiles which are now part of Jordan's air defences.

I also raised with the secretary the question of Palestine and the urgent need to do something to resolve the crisis. Since the failure of the Palestine Conciliation Commission to solve the Palestinian question on the basis of the Lausanne protocol of 1949, the whole issue had been festering, poisoning the atmosphere in the region and beyond. I told the secretary that we were taking the initiative in Jordan to reactivate the issue and I made reference to the Palestine plan. The secretary, alert and dynamic as he was at every meeting, spoke, and his voice still rings in my ears. 'No-one,' he told me, 'has ever touched this problem without getting his fingers burnt.' As he spoke he pointed to his fingers.

I still cannot explain the context in which the secretary made this cogent remark. Was he referring to John F Kennedy's recent reported efforts towards solving this problem before his untimely death? Or was he referring to an earlier period when great statesmen like Secretary of State George Marshall, Defence Secretary James Forestall and many other State Department officials who were sympathetic to the Palestinian cause found themselves out in the cold, or worse.

I cannot vouch for this but, my information is that Dean Rusk, as undersecretary of state in 1949, was the author of Resolution 194 pertaining to the Palestinian refugees and was, therefore, thoroughly acquainted with the problem.

In 1965, I attended the annual session of the General Assembly, and this gave me the opportunity to meet Secretary Rusk a second time, when we discussed various issues of bilateral as well as regional interest. This time, however, I sprang a surprise on him when I informed him that my government had information from credible sources about Israel's progress towards making atomic bombs. I told him this development would destabilise the Middle East and render more difficult the achievement of a just settlement of the Palestine problem.

The information that I gave to the secretary was based on French sources with direct access to the project. The French had been the main suppliers to the Dimona atomic installations in the Negev desert. From as early as 1950, Israel had made no secret of its pursuit of an atomic programme, and a special committee had been formed to this end, directly responsible to the prime minister. In 1950 I had written a lead article in the Jerusalem daily, *al-Difa'*, warning of this impending danger and expressing the view that by 1965 Israel would have acquired this terrible weapon, thus immobilising any efforts towards a political solution.

Secretary Rusk replied that he had no information regarding this matter. But I insisted and requested that an investigation be launched. The secretary agreed and asked William Macomber, US Ambassador to Jordan, who was present at the meeting, to inform me of the outcome of such an investigation. Two months later Ambassador Macomber called on me at the Foreign Ministry and informed me that the information which I had passed to Secretary Rusk was essentially correct, adding, that the investigation had found Egypt to be running neck-and-neck in this field.

In 1968, the Secretary of State Rusk declared: 'The spread of nuclear weapons would aggravate our difficulties in maintaining friendly relations with parties to a continuing dispute. If one party 'went nuclear', we might have to decide whether to help the other party, directly or through security assurances, whether to sever economic aid to the country acquiring atomic weapons, or whether to stand aside, even though the result might be a war which would be hard to contain.'

How true and realistic the secretary's analysis was, and I have no way of telling whether or not my discussion with him two years earlier had contributed to his categorical statement. But I feel comforted in the belief that I did at least try to bring the problem to the fore at the highest levels.

Moving around, of course, was not confined to my United Nations activities, but also included a wide variety of bilateral, regional and international commitments. In the summer of 1965, King Hussein said he wanted me to represent him at the summit meeting of the Non-Aligned states to be held in Indonesia in celebration of the 10th anniversary of the Bandung conference of 1955, during which the movement was launched. Waleed Salah, Hazza al-Majali and Azmi Nashashibi had represented Jordan at that conference, the principal architects of which were President Jawaharlal Nehru of India, President Gamal Abdel Nasser of Egypt and Marshal Josip Tito of former Yugoslavia. Ambassador Abdul Hamid Sharaf, a very fine gentleman and statesman who became prime minister in December 1979, accompanied me to the 1965 meeting.

The summit was attended by around 35 heads of state and government, including President Ahmed Sukarno, leader of the host county, Chou En-lai, renowned leader of mainland China, Zulfiqar Ali Bhutto, foreign minister of Pakistan, Zakaria Muhyiddin, vice president of Egypt, along with the sister of the Shah of Iran, a very dynamic personality, and many other Third World leaders from Asia, Africa and Latin America.

President Sukarno had arranged a fabulous programme of ceremonies, luncheons and dinners, and classical entertainment performed by some of the finest troupes from China, Cambodia, Indonesia and other south Asian countries. President Sukarno was a highly cultured man who could talk knowledgably about the multifarious philosophies and cultures of the world with the ease and perfection of a famed painter, and would present a masterly synthesis of them. And all this he would do impromptu.

At his summer residence in Bandung, a beautiful retreat with rich green lawns, artificial waterways and a cottage where he produced his important written works, President Sukarno gave a banquet for his celebrated guests. Sitting in the main hall, just before we were invited to move to the dining room, I found myself next to Chou En-lai and President Sukarno. I wanted to take this opportunity to convey to Chou En-lai our profound gratitude for China's support of the Palestinian cause. Ahmad al-Shuqairi had visited China the year before, and had been given assurances of such support, which he narrated to me.

As soon as I conveyed the expressions of appreciation, Chou En-lai's face gleamed brightly and he thanked me. But, to my amazement, Sukarno, who was listening to the conversation, reacted emotionally saying: 'What about us? We have also been supporting the Palestinian cause.' I later told him that we took Indonesia's support, as a brotherly Islamic country, for granted, and so this did not need any commendation.

Having said that, I wondered to myself how even great men cannot contain or control such basic instincts as jealousy and invidious comparisons. It seems that everybody needs a pat on the back.

I held several positions during this eventful decade. The king at one stage appointed me minister of the royal court, a special advisor and representative of the monarch. During the 1962 session of the United Nations, and following Algeria's admission to membership of it, I had asked our mission in New York to arrange for me to visit Maurice Couve de Murville, a distinguished foreign minister of France. He welcomed me at his hotel suite in New York with utmost kindness and courtesy.

I told him that King Hussein, the government, and the people of Jordan wished to express their deep appreciation to General Charles de Gaulle for his courageous and farsighted action in support of Algerian independence. I added that Jordan would be happy to restore diplomatic relations with France which had been severed during the Suez war against Egypt in 1956. The French foreign minister was instantly forthcoming and reciprocated the overture.

Jordan thus became the first Arab country in the eastern part of the region to restore diplomatic relations with France. Less than a year later, the king paid a semi-official visit to France, during which General de Gaulle gave a luncheon banquet. The French leader spoke with his usual largesse and historical perspective about France's relations with the Hashemite dynasty. He declared, addressing the king directly, and I am quoting his words as best as I can remember them: 'I wish to apologise on behalf of France for the historic injustice which our country perpetrated against the Hashemites.' General de Gaulle was referring, without saying so, to France's overthrow of King Faisal I from the throne of Damascus in the immediate aftermath of World War I. In accordance with the secret Anglo-French Sykes-Picot Agreement, geographic Syria was partitioned, with Syria and Lebanon being placed under a French mandatory regime, while Palestine and Jordan were Britain's share of the booty. The Arab revolutionary forces, which had courageously fought on the side of the Allies against the Ottomans during the war and were unaware of the unholy agreement to carve up their country, had installed King Faisal as king of Syria. In a one-sided battle at Maysaloun in July 1920 the French triumphed and overthrew the kingdom. But the British were ready to pick up the pieces and immediately installed Faisal to the throne of Iraq as King Faisal I.

During my stay in Paris, Sherif Hussein bin Nasser, prime minister and uncle of the king, and myself held talks with Georges Pompidou, who later became president of France. The talks dealt mainly with economic relations and the avenues for cooperation between the two countries. Several French companies were interested in investing in Jordan, in telecommunications, the construction of an international airport and other related fields. I briefed him on Jordan's development programme and the areas in which France might be of assistance. A year later, King Hussein and Princess Muna were invited to make an official visit, with all the additional pomp and ceremony that characterise such occasions, including the cavalry phalanxes which parade at the forefront of the official carriages. I was not in the delegation which accompanied the king on this visit. But my colleague Nassuh al-Taher, vice president of the Development Board was. He told me later that General de Gaulle, after a few opening remarks, asked the king about the projects which Jordan had requested France to be involved with and why it was that his country had not followed up on the request after France had agreed to finance and implement the schemes. The king was evidently embarrassed and promised to inquire about the status of these agreements. The French are paternalistic in furthering and promoting the interests of French companies and enterprises at the highest levels.

There was a similar retraction on a request for the purchase of 50 Mirage fighter planes from France. An Arab summit had allocated specific sums toward Jordan's purchase of these fighters. The king instructed me to seek the approval of the French government for this transaction. On my way to attend a conference of Third World countries, comprising 80 states, at Algiers in 1965, I stopped in Paris where I met Couve de Murville at the Foreign Ministry, accompanied by my colleague Abdullah Salah, Jordan's Ambassador to France. The foreign minister indicated that France would give favourable consideration to this request and he would inform me of his government's final decision upon my return from the conference to Paris on my way home.

While in Algiers, where dozens of foreign ministers from Asia, Africa and Latin America were assembled at one of the major hotels in the city, we saw hundreds of youths skirmishing with Algerian security forces. News began to filter through that a military coup d'état had taken place and that President Ben Bella had been overthrown. Many foreign ministers, at a loss to determine what had happened, rushed to see me, hoping that, being an Arab foreign minister, I would be in a better position to assess the situation. But in all truthfulness I was as much in the dark as they were. The conference, which was to have been held at a new impressive conference hall amidst a newly constructed village to accommodate the various delegations, was postponed for several months, after which it reconvened in a more normal atmosphere.

Back in Paris, meanwhile, I met again with the minister for foreign affairs who informed me that his government had approved Jordan's request for 50 Mirages. I thanked the minister, without going into further details.

To obviate any misunderstanding, or as it seemed, and to confirm that this deal was a sale and not a grant, the foreign minister explained, somewhat apologetically, that there were costs involved in manufacturing the aircraft. To dispel his apprehensions I told him that I understood fully that my government would be paying for this purchase.

The reason why I mention this banal fact is that over many decades, huge transactions of armament sales, involving literally billions and billions of dollars, have been transacted with the countries of the Middle East through arms dealers and intermediaries. The latter have taken cuts, not only for themselves but also for the original purchasers, the rulers of the client countries. In such devious deals, all kinds of considerations have to be factored in, including double accountancy and under-the-table deals of every sort.

During my tenure of service, such wheeling and dealing did not exist, and if it did it would have been a rare and conspicuous exception, rather than the rule. Once an international businessman hinted that, according to his briefings in Washington, a five percent commission in the Middle East was the norm. I warned him that even if this were true elsewhere, it was not the case in Jordan and if he tried it he would be disqualifying himself.

In the 1960s, we in government had the highest and most impeccable standards of integrity. We never touched a penny or a *fils* of dirty money, thank God. I cannot vouch for succeeding generations, but I assume that each would be judged by his record, and nothing can be hidden in the present age of transparency and information.

As Ambassador Salah was accompanying me to Paris airport on my way home, Prince Hassan, younger brother of King Hussein who was spending a year in France before enrolling in university because he was too young to begin higher education, showed us an item in a secret intelligence report. This said that fierce competition was in progress regarding which aircraft Jordan would purchase from the sum allocated by the Arab summit. British Lightning fighters were zooming over Amman at their lightning speed, while F-4 American fighters, dubbed by some observers as the 'flying coffins', were also displaying their prowess over the Jordanian capital. Ambassador Salah, in genuine distress at the news, said to Prince Hassan: 'But we have just obtained the agreement of the French government for the purchase of the Mirage. How am I, as an ambassador, going to face the French government when it finds that we either reneged or were wavering over the deal agreed with them?' Prince Hassan, who was then 17, could only say that Dr Nusseibeh was returning to Amman and would have ample opportunity to explain the situation to the king.

During this period, in 1963 to be precise, I also paid a visit to the Soviet Union. On a Friday morning, the weekend in Amman, Prime Minister Sherif Hussein bin Nasser rang me up at home and invited me for a coffee. I went to his house, which is nearby in Jabal Amman, at the assigned time and without much ado he said to me: '*Sayyidna* (the king) wants to send you on a mission. Guess where?' I said I had no idea – perhaps London, Washington, Paris? As I continued to guess, he interrupted and said: 'Would you like to go to Moscow?' I said that, of course, I would go wherever the king wanted me to go. At that, he went on to say that the king would tell me all about the mission the following day, adding that only the three of us knew about it.

On Saturday, at the palace, where my office was as minister of the royal court, the king told me that the purpose of the trip to Moscow was to sign the Partial Test Ban Treaty, concluded between Washington and Moscow, with international application. Under the agreement, the acceding states were required to sign this document in both Washington and Moscow. While Jordan's Ambassador to the United States would sign in Washington, Jordan had no diplomatic relations with the Soviet Union. Indeed, when King Hussein addressed the General Assembly of the United Nations in October 1960, he went out of his way to criticise not only communism but also the Soviet Union itself, and to blame it for the death of Prime Minister Hazza al-Majali in that fatal explosion on 6 August 1960 which wrecked the building housing the prime minister's office. No less a person than President Nikita Khrushchev was representing the Soviet Union at that session, remembered as the occasion when he banged his shoe on the table in front of him.

I was in New York in 1960, coming from Washington where I had been attending a meeting of the International Bank for Reconstruction and Development, as a vice president representing Jordan. I had witnessed frantic efforts made by various Arab delegations, including Prince Hassan (later King Hassan) of Morocco to dissuade the king from giving his speech in its original form which contained a blistering attack against the Soviet Union. But King Hussein refused to budge. He had been shocked by the violent death of Prime Minister al-Majali, and had been constantly challenged since his accession to the throne by extreme leftist movements which had caused much turbulence and instability to Jordan. Indeed, one of the reasons for the king's dismissal of the national-left coalition cabinet of Prime Minister Suleiman Nabulsi was its insistence on establishing diplomatic relations with the Soviet Union.

It came, therefore, as something of a surprise, when King Hussein instructed me to explore the possibilities of establishing diplomatic relations with Moscow. I signed the Partial Test Ban Treaty, in a ceremony at the Kremlin. This was followed by a meeting with Minister of Foreign Affairs Andrei Gromyko. In my introductory remarks, I tried to present the foreign minister with a portrait of Jordan as it was, along with its hopes and aspirations for the future, taking into consideration that this was the first official contact between the two countries. Mr Gromyko, thinking that I was attempting to sell Jordan as a progressive state, which it was, but not in the Soviet sense, interrupted to say that the Soviet Union was interested in maintaining friendly relations with all other states, regardless of their ideologies or political systems. At this point I suggested the establishment of full diplomatic relations, and a communiqué was drafted jointly in English to this effect. Both sides in the talks then made a translation of the communiqué into Arabic, and I was impressed with the proficiency in Arabic of the draft made by the Russians, which almost dovetailed with my own version. The foreign minister gave a sumptuous official luncheon to celebrate this occasion, and my next step was to relay the text of the communiqué to the attention of the king for his approval.

My few days in Moscow were otherwise barren and uneventful. Accompanied by the king's military aide, Anwar Muhammad, I stayed at the huge Moscow Hotel opposite the Kremlin. It was spacious, but rundown and sparsely furnished. There was a small black-and-white television set in my room which I hardly used because of the lack of attractive programmes, at least from my viewpoint. There were no magazines or newspapers in English or Arabic at the hotel's bookstore. At dinner, an orchestra played, with long intervals between one tune and another. At 10pm sharp, members of the orchestra stopped playing, covered the musical instruments with white sheets and departed. Before I left Amman, two or three Western embassies in Amman had proposed that their missions in Moscow invite me over during my stay, but I thanked them and declined the invitations because it was difficult to foresee what schedule might be laid down for the visit.

The head of the Soviet Foreign Ministry's Middle East department came over in the mornings for talks, and on two occasions showed me the grand, aristocratic palaces on the outskirts of Moscow and the forests which surround them in the rain-drenched country. But from noon onwards I would be alone, with nothing else to do. My colleague, Anwar Muhammad, was a Circassian. There is a large Circassian community in Jordan, part and parcel of the country's ethnic fabric. Being a Circassian he was not afraid to venture into the streets of Moscow because he was sure to come across Circassian compatriots with whom he could communicate. But for me, it would have been a reckless and unwise venture, more so as I could not even read the alphabet. My loneliness was compounded by the fact that there was no Jordanian embassy or consulate.

I was, therefore, eager to finalise my assignment in order to return home. Because there was no telephone link between the Soviet Union and Jordan, the Soviet Foreign Ministry officials, at my request, put me in touch by phone with the Jordanian Ambassador to Damascus, Akram Zuaiter, a Palestinian leader, a renowned historian of the Palestine national movement and one of three accomplished orators in the Arabic language. I was relieved to hear his voice clearly at the other end. I asked him to pass on the joint communiqué to the palace, including the agreement on a simultaneous announcement at such and such an hour.

In less than half an hour all was set. The king had approved the agreement, and I made a booking on the first flight leaving for Vienna via Kiev.

Landing in Vienna after almost a week of hermetic seclusion the contrast was spectacular. The hustle and bustle of people, the bright lights, the commotion and tempo of life were in sharp contrast to what seemed to me the aridity, conformity and drabness of life in Moscow.

I spent the evening in Vienna wandering through the People's Garden where men and women of all ages sang, danced, listened to music, ate, drank and simply enjoyed life, past midnight. The Russian people, highly gifted and advanced, and with a great middle class, surely deserved a more active and liberal life, consisting of more than simply being a cog in a machine, no matter how sophisticated that machine might be. *Glasnost* and *Perestroika* came as the timely answer, even if the price was heavy, with the loss of superpower status and the dissolution of the Soviet Union. But this is a matter for the Russian people to judge.

This was not the end of the Moscow chapter. For when I returned home and settled back into my office, the United States charge d'affaires rang me, requesting a meeting. At the meeting he expressed deep anger at not having been informed about the establishment of diplomatic relations with the Soviet Union, prior to my trip to Moscow. The diplomat had asked me about the visit when he heard about it on the radio. I had told him that I would be signing the Partial Test Ban Treaty. About diplomatic relations, I had answered that all depended on whether or not I found a propitious atmosphere, which was true. Besides, I said in our meeting on my return, this was a confidential trip, which only King Hussein and the prime minister were privy to, and I was not ready to give away a state secret with which I had been entrusted. The United States charge d'affaires was later reassigned to another post.

In 1964, King Hussein made a 14-day official visit to India which was extremely interesting and enjoyable. One of its strategic aims was to counterbalance the impression that Jordan was aligned to Pakistan, to the detriment of India. True enough, there had been close relations between Pakistani and Jordanian leaders, and particularly in the field of military cooperation. Many Jordanian army officers had received their advanced training at staff colleges in Pakistan, in addition to those in Britain. And only a few years earlier Pakistan was to have been one of the main pillars of the pro-Western Baghdad Pact which India opposed, being a founder and a pillar of the Non-Aligned Movement, to which Jordan was admitted after some hesitation.

But the climax of the visit was the meeting of two leaders, each great in his own way. One, Jawaharlal Nehru represented the sprawling sub-continent of India with its massive multi-ethnic, multi-religious, multi-strata population. The other, King Hussein, a man of charisma, charm and modesty, was leader of one of the smallest and poorest countries in the world, and yet he was a man who had put his country on the geopolitical map with his statesmanship and balanced policies.

As royal court minister I attended that historic meeting between Nehru and King Hussein. One could not but be impressed by the sheer presence of a man of Nehru's stature. Many years earlier I had read his books, in particular his autobiography, written in the course of his long imprisonment.

They radiated wisdom, confidence, poise, temperance, unflinching determination, and a conspicuous absence of what would have been justifiable rancour. Such is the metal of great men.

The visit came in the immediate aftermath of the war between China and India over the Himalayan mountains border. China had the better of India in that encounter. Nehru explained to King Hussein, in his lucid, objective and honest language, the reasons for India's setback. I remember him saying that, among other things, the Chinese troops were better fed than the Indian ones. The talks were animated, friendly and sincere. Nehru talked about the war with China without feeling the need to provide excuses for the outcome or to put the blame onto someone else, as we Arabs are prone to do.

The president of India, in honour of the king, gave a state dinner. He read a written speech which was warm and generous. But I must say I was deeply impressed by the impromptu reply of King Hussein who, I discovered, had great powers of concentration whenever he faced a challenge. I was a speech writer for King Hussein and had prepared a number of speeches which he delivered at universities, institutions, public functions, etc. There is always a bit of affectation in prepared speeches, and I remember telling the king after hearing his impromptu speech at the state dinner in India that it was far more effective than a formal written one. He performed equally effectively when we landed at the lawn of the White House and replied to President Johnson's speech of welcome. It is always easier, of course, to have the luxury of prepared speeches because it does not require any mental effort under the strain of the moment. But there are some who are elevated by strain to higher levels of performance, and this was the case with King Hussein.

With the formalities over in New Delhi, the capital, a packed programme had been meticulously arranged to show the king and his accompanying delegation the great variety which India encompasses. Out-of-this-world Maharaja Palaces, with the most exquisite lawns and gardens, are set against a background of dire poverty, if not destitution. The only place we were not shown were some quarters in Calcutta, where we were told some people actually sleep on pavements.

The programme, as busy as any, even by US standards, had us constantly getting on and off planes and trains in order to cover the full length and breadth of India in a relatively short period of 14 days. Travelling by train, we could see the huge countryside which was, by and large, green and beautiful, but revealing at the same time the abject poverty of the masses which inhabited it. We were shown model schools, universities, large modern factories and dam sites.

At one site where a dam was under construction there were literally thousands of workers, and when they saw our motorcade coming they rushed to welcome the king and his companions. But our Indian hosts, fearing a stampede that might get out of control, directed the motorcade to depart. So we greeted the workers from a safe distance.

We were shown many impressive temples and mosques. But a highlight of those great monuments was the Taj Mahal which, at close range, is even more beautiful than it is in pictures.

We were also hosted by universities, institutions and associations. Islamic societies, which are quite prominent in big cities like Bombay, invited the king to special public gatherings where he was warmly welcomed. Although India is predominantly Hindu, there is a substantial Muslim population, in the range of 150 million, as large as the population of Pakistan or Bangladesh, both of which had originally been parts of united India.

The Gir national park in Gujarat province is one of the richer wild life reservations in the world. A special show was staged for us involving 25 lions and lionesses, big and small. They were packed in a small enclosure the size of a tennis court. We were made to stand a mere few metres distance from the lions, with only a light wire fence for protection. We were told to be silent as a buffalo was brought into the enclosure. The senior lion, unchallenged and alone, devoured the buffalo, piece by piece until little was left for the other 24 inferior lions and lionesses. For dessert, a young goat was paraded round the enclosure, but the lion king was sufficiently satisfied, so refrained from touching it. When this had been completed, the lions and lionesses helped themselves to the remnants of the buffalo, not much really for this big crowd of hungry animals.

While we were visiting the game reserve, Indian army sharpshooters were deployed up in trees overlooking the enclosure. Their gaze never wavered or shifted from the scene, in case of an emergency. General Akkash Zaben, King Hussein's aide-de-camp, kept his hand firmly on the revolver at his side, as he was prone to do in the course of carrying out his duty. About 10 metres away from where we stood, was an iron cage, 10 metres by five, and we were told by our Indian colleagues that it had been erected in the 1930s, after a visit by the Prince of Wales who had faced mortal danger when the lions, during a similar display, became agitated.

Later in the evening, at dinner, Ambassador Shupra, India's envoy to Jordan, expressed to me his displeasure at General Zaben's behaviour during this nerve-wracking live show. What, he asked, did General Zaben mean by gripping his revolver in that way? Did he think that if anything were to happen his revolver would save the king? Did he not realise that an enraged attacking lion would devour both his revolver and his leg? Evidently Ambassador Shupra interpreted General Zaben's attitude as a slight and an expression of no-confidence in the elaborate security measures put in place by the host government. I assured Ambassador Shupra that General Zaben did not mean anything of the sort, but because of the tight bunching together of the onlookers he automatically held on firmly to his gun. And that settled the matter.

On our way back to Jordan, the king and the accompanying entourage stayed three days in Tehran as guests of the Shah of Iran. We spent three relaxed days in the capital, shopping at its old market where the most beautiful works of artistic excellence are to be found, including Persian rugs, and fine silver and copper goods. It is exhilarating just to spend time watching such masterly craftsmanship, which has no parallel anywhere else in the world. Each member of the delegation bought a Persian rug as a memento of the visit.

A decade and a half later I was Ambassador of Jordan to the United Nations in New York, and I watched some of the student demonstrations against the Shah. But the most distressing part of the episode was the refusal of the United States government, the Shah's erstwhile closest ally, to permit him to remain in the country to receive treatment for cancer. He was given temporary refuge in Panama where he was exploited financially. Finally the chivalry of President Anwar

Sadat, no particular friend of his, enabled him to spend the rest of his life, in dignity, in Egypt.

CHAPTER 11

Drift Towards a Second Catastrophe: 1967

The debacle of 1948, a seminal event, exposed the fundamental weaknesses of Arab societies. The initial scapegoats were Arab heads of state – kings, princes and presidents – several of whom were subsequently deposed. But accompanying such upheavals was a growing realisation that the malaise went far deeper than the failures, decrepitude, or even treason of individual rulers. There were elements of backwardness in our civilisation which had pervaded the many aspects of national life over successive centuries of moribund existence.

The atrophy was the more glaring as it coincided with Europe's greatest leap forward. From the 9th to the 12th century, the Arabs were at the forefront of progress in the world. By 1492, when the last bastion of Arab Spain fell, the Arabs were in decline, and Europe was on the rise. Europe experienced the Renaissance, the Reformation, the Industrial Revolution and the seafaring enterprises which enabled it to discover new trade routes and continents, the Americas, Australia and New Zealand. The evolution of democratic liberal reforms expanded equality and, no less importantly, the flourishing of intellectual and artistic activity ensured society's dynamic buoyancy and continuity.

The first recognition of backwardness came with the Napoleonic invasion of the Middle East in the late 18th century, and the rise of Muhammad Ali's reformism in Egypt in the middle of the following century. It roughly coincided with the rise of Japan from its isolation, but in the Egyptian case the process met obstacles and fell short of what the Japanese managed to achieve.

In any event, since the second part of the 19th century there have been widespread calls for reform in the Arab and Islamic worlds, emanating from succeeding generations of reformers, religious as well as secular. In the main, they opposed despotic rule and favoured liberal democracy. Indeed, the constitutions which the Arab countries promulgated upon achieving independence were based on Western models, in some cases completely. Therefore, those advocating democratic reforms in first quarter of the 21st century are continuing with a process that is well rooted in Arab contemporary history. Military coups, under the pretext of saving or liberating Palestine, stunted the march of liberalism and democracy during the last half of the 20th century. But the catastrophes that befell the Palestinians and the neighbouring Arab states in 1967 proved that despotic regimes were certainly not the panacea for the Arab nation's ills.

The White Paper, issued by Jordan's Ministry of Foreign Affairs in 1962, which I drafted, comprised an analysis of the Arab state affairs from the viewpoint of their societies. It may seem strange that a state, or a government through its foreign ministry, would tackle issues which seemingly fall outside of its jurisdiction. But Jordan and other Arab states during the 1960s had been locked in an ideological dialogue that claimed to be progressive and egalitarian. Certain states were stigmatised, unjustly, as reactionary, while in today's common parlance they would be classified as conservative. The issue, therefore, was as much internal as it was seemingly external. Egypt had produced an important document called the Socialist Covenant, which advocated the nationalisation of almost all important means of production and distribution, including banking, heavy industries, land ownership, and the media. Egypt, over centuries, had been in the grip of a merciless feudal system and needed drastic remedial action. This was not the case in Palestine and Jordan where the middle classes constituted a majority.

In the introduction, the White Paper identified the main challenges confronting Arab societies as follows:

The cumulative legacy of many centuries of backwardness and sterility has kept Arab societies behind the advance of world civilisation. This backwardness has encompassed all walks of life, social, economic, educational, and scientific, as well as patterns of thought and behaviour.

Parts of the Arab world were under foreign rule and their resources were exploited by outside powers. This referred primarily to the Arab Gulf states which, at the time of writing the White Paper, were under foreign rule, and only gained independence in the early 1970s.

Another factor was the carving up of the Arab world into a motley collection of small and medium-sized states (in succession to the erstwhile all-embracing Ottoman Empire) without meaningful political and economic coordination amongst them; save within the League of Arab States, which itself has been handicapped by inter-Arab conflicts. This *status quo* ran counter to the deeply cherished aspirations of the Arab masses for some form of effective unity or union, federal or confederal; or at least integration along the lines of the European Union.

An important point highlighted by the White Paper was the emphasis on gradualism and peaceful means for achieving desired goals. This was a very important and relevant call, when judged against a background of violence, tyrannies, revolutions and military takeovers which characterised the landscape of the Arab world in the aftermath of the Palestinian catastrophes of 1948 and 1967. A new factor since then has been the rise of radical Islamic movements. Jordan has always argued that violent change is largely self-defeating, for it merely destroys the fabric and institutions of civil society, leading to counter-violence. The means, the White Paper argued, must be commensurate and compatible with the ends, if individual Arab citizens were to preserve their human dignity, self-confidence and civil peace.

In retrospect, although I have always been a staunch believer in Arab unity I have come to recognise the value of devolution, decentralisation and even independence of Arab states, within an overall unity. Would Amman have developed into the prosperous capital of 2 million inhabitants if it had remained a backwater of Damascus or, for that matter, if today's Damascus of 5 million had remained a backwater of Istanbul? There is a great deal to be said in favour of devolution, provided it does not lead to separation and hostility. The same guideline applies to provinces within each state where we find major population centres mushrooming and ever-expanding, while regions lag behind.

The aforementioned discussions were not intellectual exercises but involved real issues which manifested themselves in inter-Arab struggles, revolutions and wars. Thus we witnessed a union of Egypt and Syria; a union between Iraq and Jordan; Iraq's disastrous invasion of Kuwait which eventually led to the former's own undoing; the conflict between Morocco and Algeria over the Western Sahara; and many other border disputes.

In retrospect also, the Palestine plan (turned into the White Paper), although a theoretical framework and originally disparaged by President Nasser as unrealistic, was soon enough taken up by Arab summits.

The plan made the Palestinian question the priority once more, rather than, for example, the conflict in Yemen. The unity of Arab action in support of the Palestinian cause was symbolised by the creation of a unified Arab command and the mobilisation of Arab resources, military, financial, political, organizational and informational, behind this cause. These steps were made necessary because of Israel's unilateral diversion of the River Jordan which put the Arab states on the spot. And yet the implementation of these measures may have hastened the anticipated showdown with Israel, and thereby may have unwittingly contributed to the 1967 war, resulting in the total occupation of the rest of Palestine, including East Jerusalem. In 1948, Israel occupied 78 percent of Palestine's geographic territory; in 1967, it occupied the remaining 22 percent, along with Sinai and the Golan Heights.

Was the outbreak of the 1967 war inevitable? Not necessarily, except in the sense that there was still no solution to the question of Palestine, which had been deadlocked since the failure of the Palestine Conciliation Commission to obtain approval for its plan worked out in Lausanne in 1949. But the timing and the cause of its outbreak, over a relatively peripheral issue about the right of Israeli ships to pass through the Straits of Tiran in the Gulf of Aqaba, were not accidental. Rather, Israel launched a premeditated and pre-emptive strike to abort any possibility of a peaceful solution on the basis of international legitimacy and United Nation resolutions.

The question weighing heavily on Arab decision-makers then was whether or not the Arab states confronting Israel would have the time to prepare themselves militarily before Israel launched a surprise attack against them. The second question, facing Jordan in particular, was whether to admit Arab military forces, particularly Iraqi ones, into the kingdom before Israel launched an attack; or whether, as was the case, not to admit outside forces, thus denying Israel a pretext to attack. After the outbreak of war, Iraqi forces did come all the way from Kurdistan in northern Iraq, weary and out of shape, only to face Israeli aerial bombardment along the way. In any event, their arrival came too late.

The third challenge was how to stop the infiltration of Palestinian commandos into Israel, lest such actions provided a pretext for retaliation. At Arab conferences and in the press, Jordan found itself subjected to virulent attacks on grounds that it was standing in the way of the liberation of Palestine. The Unified Arab Command, realising full well the consequences of any rash or premature action, invariably came out on the side of Jordan in advocating reticence. The Command, having surveyed the military situation in the West Bank, described it as 'militarily naked', which it was. Israel's bloody attack against the village of as-Samu, south of Hebron on 13 November

1966, in which dozens were killed and wounded and all the houses demolished, demonstrated the total vulnerability of the West Bank.

Instead of extending assistance to Jordan, in face of this mortal danger, Egypt, Syria, and the PLO accused Jordan of failure to defend as-Samu, while Jordan accused the Unified Arab Command of failing to come to its aid. Clearly relations between Jordan on the one hand, Egypt, Syria, and the PLO on the other, had reached a nadir.

Counter-attacking in these verbal exchanges, Jordan accused Egypt of hiding behind the United Nations Emergency Force (UNEF) which had been stationed at key points separating Egyptian and Israeli forces. These included a UN position on the Straits of Tiran, set up in the aftermath of the 1956 Suez war to keep the waterway open to international shipping. Egypt was very sensitive to such an accusation and its hasty decision to demand the withdrawal of UNEF by 21 May 1967 is evidence of this. The United States, under President Johnson, had been tightening the economic noose around Egypt's neck, and demanding that it repay the debt it owed. Washington had apparently come to the conclusion that by advocating common Arab action, Egypt would become, sooner or later, a threat to Israel. At the same time, relations between Egypt and Saudi Arabia had been worsening in consequence of the prolonged conflict over Yemen.

On 7 April 1967, the Israeli and Syrian air forces engaged in a large-scale aerial combat. The Syrians incurred heavy losses. The battle was judged as an acid test of the merits or otherwise of Eastern and Western bloc armaments, and the outcome from the viewpoint of the Arab camp was disheartening. On 15 May 1967, the 19th anniversary of the establishment of Israel as a state, Egyptian Defence Minister Abdul Hakim Amer boasted that Egypt possessed the strongest attacking air force in the Middle East. On the same occasion, Israel organised a large-scale military parade in West Jerusalem, in stark violation of the Armistice Agreement, which prohibited the display of heavy armaments in the city.

In the middle of May, the Soviet Union passed on to Egypt and Syria intelligence reports that Israel had deployed its military forces in the Galilee and Tiberias areas in preparation for aggression against Syria. The information proved to have been fake or, possibly deliberate disinformation. What interest did the Soviet Union have in passing on such intelligence? No matter what the motivation was, it achieved its desired effect. In response to it, Egypt placed its armed forces on the highest alert and carried out large-scale manoeuvres in Sinai in support of Syria. Egypt also sent its Chief of Staff, General Muhammad Fawzi, to Damascus to coordinate military action between the two countries.

On 18 May, Egypt requested UN Secretary-General U Thant to order the partial withdrawal of UNEF forces from the Gaza Strip and parts of Sinai in order to make possible the deployment of Egyptian forces along the front. The secretary-general agreed to a total rather than a partial withdrawal, thus leaving the adversaries face-to-face, particularly at the Straits of Tiran.

Secretary-General U Thant may have had logistical reasons for not agreeing to a partial withdrawal because of the dangers that UN forces would face in the event of the outbreak of war. But this decision rendered a war inevitable. President Nasser, amidst the torrent of emotions which had been generated and galvanised by the crisis, could not retract his request for withdrawal of UN forces, nor could he, in that highly charged atmosphere, allow Israeli shipping to pass through the straits. Thus the Straits of Tiran were closed. It was now up to the major powers to act or react. The attitude of the Soviet Union was ambivalent, having passed on that alleged intelligence information about Israeli troop deployments for an attack on Syria. The major Western powers were insisting on freedom of navigation through international waterways as a basic principle of international law. But all the while the United States, the most important power of all, was colluding with Israel, as subsequent evidence has shown beyond any doubt. President Johnson was bent on bringing about the downfall of the Egyptian regime. The military experts at the Pentagon were fully convinced that a war would result in an Arab military defeat. President Johnson was reputed to have told Israeli Foreign Minister Abba Eban on 26 May, after a meeting of the National Security Council: 'What are you waiting for? Matters are all going your way.'

I had resigned from the government of Wasfi Tal on 13 September 1966 over the government's over-reaction in its policies towards the West Bank because of the tensions generated by the activities there of the PLO. The West Bank leadership had been summoned to the royal palace to receive a reprimand over the situation, a move which I considered unjustified, because they were not to blame for excesses committed by other groups or individuals. At any rate, in hindsight I am glad that I was not a part of a government that was stigmatised by being in power when the catastrophe of the loss of Jerusalem and the West Bank occurred. In fairness, it did not take place during Wasfi Tal's government either, which resigned on 4 March 1967, but during that of Saad Jumaa, formed on 23 April 1967. Jumaa had asked me to join his cabinet but I declined. I mention this in order to give credit where it is due. When his government resigned, Wasfi Tal was appointed chief of the royal court. On the morning when the war broke out, he implored the king not to join it because he knew from his extensive readings and experience, as well as intelligence reports, that the Arabs would be defeated and consequently Jordan would lose half its territory. Wasfi was a staff officer who had attended a British military staff college in Sarafand, in central Palestine, in the 1940s during World War II. And because of Jordan's obligations under the Common Arab Defence Treaty and the king's commitment to it, Wasfi suggested, as a compromise, that entry into the war be postponed until the evening in order to see how things would turn out. In fact, Jordan entered the war at 10am, one hour after it had effectively ended because of the destruction of the Egyptian air force.

Early the next day – Tuesday morning – orders were issued to the Jordanian armed forces to withdraw to the East Bank, which they did under heavy fire.

Abdul Munim al-Rifai, former minister of foreign affairs, Akef al-Fayez, speaker of the Lower House of Parliament and I used to meet every day and follow closely political developments. Ten days before the outbreak of the war, Richard Murphy, then counsellor at the US embassy (later assistant secretary of state) visited al-Rifai in his house in Luweibdeh, and I was present. In the course of the discussions he asked why we did not advise the king to patch up his differences with Nasser. This might seem to have been innocuous advice, considering that we were all in favour of a unified Arab front. So in a sense he was preaching to the converted. But in his position he must have known better and could have given us wiser advice, as the US Ambassador in Amman, Findley Burns, did. Seated together at a dinner in his residence, a few days before the war, he said to me in confidence: 'Be careful, for our president can be quite mean.' He was a man of great integrity and patriotism, deeply concerned about his country's national interest and a graduate of Princeton. I did not pass on to the king either piece of advice.

In the few days leading to the outbreak of war, the royal court had its hands full and was a hive of political and diplomatic activity. Ministers, ambassadors, commanders and public figures of all persuasions were tripping over one another in their visitations, passing on information or receiving it. I asked for an audience with the king on Sunday, just the day before Israel launched its attack on Egypt. I said: '*Sayyidna*, the Old City of Jerusalem is a precious 1-square kilometre living museum, a treasure house. If, as result of the fighting, it should suffer destruction – the Aqsa mosque, the Dome of the Rock, the Holy Sepulchre, the churches, the historic monuments – the loss would be irreparable and somehow or other we would be blamed. Why not declare the Old City an open city, outside of the fighting zone? If the Israelis refuse, then the world will blame them.' The king listened intently to the suggestion and said: 'I will give it careful consideration, but the military must be consulted first.' Within less than 24 hours the war had begun and nothing came of my suggestion.

Egypt had planned, with the agreement of the Johnson administration, to send Vice President Zakariya Muhieddin to Washington, in an effort to defuse the crisis. It was no accident that on the very day of his scheduled trip, Monday 5 June 1967, Israel struck and aborted any possibility of a peaceful solution.

In the meantime, a psychological campaign was being waged by the mass media in the Arab world. The emotive songs of Um Kulthum, the most famous and popular singer in the Arab world, and the words of orators, and poets all extolled the return to Palestine by force of arms, thus stifling any objective reasoning or rational calculation. It did not, evidently, occur to those hotheads that we were actually in possession of Holy Jerusalem and the rest of the West Bank, and the Gaza Strip. If they had been aware of the imbalance in the military strengths of the two sides then they surely would not have gambled with a war that placed Jerusalem and Palestinian land in mortal danger – all over the issue of free passage in the Straits of Tiran which hardly anyone had heard of. But again, false or exaggerated information concerning the Arabs' military preparedness galvanised public opinion and made people believe in something that turned out to be false.

I was at my home in Jerusalem on Friday 2 June, as I was every weekend after our move to Amman. The drive from Amman to Jerusalem, a mere 83 kilometres, would take 50 minutes. We always had family gatherings on a Friday, with a sumptuous meal prepared under the expert direction of my mother. Over a small drink before luncheon, and in a jovial and serene atmosphere, I saw clearly through binoculars the face of an Israeli sergeant, stocky and well built, standing a few hundred metres away behind a piece of artillery aimed, as it seemed, directly at our house. I said to my brothers: 'There is no doubt that this house of ours will be the first casualty of the war. It will be destroyed if war should break out.' But I added that, for the sake of Palestine, no price was too high. One of my brothers, Dr Ahmad, tried to make light of the situation by saying: 'I hope we won't be communicating with each other via the Red Cross, should war break out.' But he realised, as he was speaking, that it was a hollow joke. After 1948 and the dispersal of the Palestinians, one of the most popular programmes on all broadcasting services was one in which refugees sent messages to their absent families. It seemed to us inconceivable that such a fate could befall us once again after less than 20 years. Yet, alas, it did within a few days.

My concern at that time was both for my family and Jerusalem. I was always enthralled by the unique beauty of the Old City and would make a point of walking its narrow streets from end to end, from the Damascus Gate to Jaffa Gate (*Bab al-Khalil*), past the Holy Sepulchre and thence to the Christian quarter. There are more monasteries, churches and Christian sites of every denomination in this area than in Rome, or indeed anywhere else. The Orthodox, Latins, Greeks, Syrians, Copts and Abyssinians vie with one another, and squabble over control of various areas of the Church of the Holy Sepulchre. The Nusseibeh family have, over centuries, arbitrated in disputes between the contending denominations, in recognition of its judicious neutrality as a Muslim family.

On that Friday 2 June – may I be excused if I call it metaphorically the last Friday – the Old City was overflowing with tens of thousands of pilgrims, visitors and citizens, bumping into one another. In the years leading to 1967, literally hundreds, if not thousands of cars, buses, and military vehicles would park in long lines from Ras el-Amud, near the Tur quarter on the Mount of Olives overlooking the old city, to Damascus Gate and other entrances to the walled city. They came from Amman and other cities and towns, in the East and West Banks, and from as far as Damascus, for Friday prayers at the Aqsa mosque, regarded as equal in sanctity to Mecca and

Medina. Driving up from Amman that Friday I could also see Turkish pilgrims on their return from performing the '*Umra* (the minor Haj) and the pilgrimage itself in Mecca, going to Jerusalem to sanctify their pilgrimage. At the same times the city was packed with throngs of Christian pilgrims tramping along the stone-paved streets of the Old City and overflowing out into the adjacent new city, beyond the seven gates.

Close to 100,000 Muslims were estimated to have said their prayers on that Friday, and PLO Chairman Ahmad al-Shuqairi, who had returned from Cairo with King Hussein after making amends with the king at the urging of President Nasser, was at the Aqsa mosque for Friday prayers. He was one of the foremost orators in Arabic, and perhaps equally fluent in English, as his contemporaries at the United Nations would testify. The tension reached its peak when Ahmad al-Shuqairi addressed 15,000 demonstrators coming out of the mosque, demanding that they be issued with arms in order to participate in the defence of their city. In the melee, he lost his shoes and a new pair was quickly brought to enable him to leave. A mere 150 rifles were eventually issued to the citizens by the governor of Jerusalem, Anwar al-Khatib, but only after the outbreak of war, on the morning of Monday 5 June. Israeli aircraft, I was told by one recipient from Issawiya village near the Hebrew University on Mount Scopus, tracked them down and put them out of action.

I had returned to Amman and continued, like everyone else, following the news broadcasts and commentaries which had reached an even higher pitch of both excitement and incitement. On Monday morning I was accompanying my youngest son, six-year-old Khalid, for physiotherapy treatment with a Miss Prior at the main Amman hospital at Jabal Al-

Ashrafiya, for a tragic ailment which saddened Qadar and me more than anything else in our life. A male nurse, from Bethlehem, rushed in to inform us, with a great deal of excitement that war had broken out. Miss Prior, a devoted and highly skilled British nurse, reacted angrily to what seemed to her a callous reaction to the outbreak of war. She scolded the male nurse for his gullibility and reminded him that war meant death and destruction, which she had witnessed in her younger years. I tried to pacify her, explaining that the Bethlehem man was merely transmitting the news and that it was the Israeli side and not our side which had triggered the war.

Returning from hospital to my house in Jabal Amman was an arduous and a dangerous journey. Israeli aircraft, having raided Amman's military airport and rendered it unusable by creating huge craters on the runway, were flying so low over Amman that I could almost see the faces of the pilots. The planes flew over my house, adjacent to Zahran Palace of Queen Mother Zain, and across the street opposite the French embassy. The roar of Jordanian anti-aircraft guns made the atmosphere even more menacing. Almost everyone left the streets and took refuge in the nearest building, whatever it was. Hospitality was a public spirited gesture, to which all citizens subscribed. I should mention here that Amman had no air raid shelters, private or public.

My wife, Qadar, donated to the Red Crescent all the blankets in the house, in addition to dozens of sheets and other articles which could be of use in time of war. She and other ladies volunteered to serve with the Red Crescent. We had reckoned that there would be a war involving numerous casualties and extending over a period of time. This was our impression of wars, as we read about them, and this had been my experience during the 1947-48 war which continued, intermittently, up to the Armistice of 1949. But to our surprise and deep chagrin the war ended even before it had really started, with devastating results.

The earliest inklings of disaster came, somewhat ironically, with news broadcasts from Egypt announcing brashly the successful downing of astronomical numbers of Israeli aircraft by anti-aircraft fire. A group of retired Jordanian army officers, knowledgeable in the arts of war, had set up a mock operations room to follow war developments. It struck them as strange that all the claimed enemy aircraft had been downed by anti-aircraft fire. And, regardless of the excessive claims, they started asking themselves, with the dispassionate voice of hard-headed military experts, what had happened to the 500-plus aircrafts of the Egyptian air force. Why was there no news of air-to-air combat? They started pondering these and other questions, and gloom descended on them, at a time when the vast masses throughout the Arab world were rejoicing over what soon transpired to be fictitious claims of victory.

Needless to say, the battlefield was basically in Jerusalem and not Amman. The frontline was, of all places, a few hundred metres from my family house. My mother's love and concern for her loved ones is legendary. These noble characteristics were demonstrated most clearly of all towards the end of that fateful Monday, the first day of the war. At 6pm, the telephone rang in my house in Amman. At the other end in Jerusalem was my mother's voice, concerned but clear, inquiring about our safety instead of the other way round. The telephone lines were still functioning at that point, but soon they were to be cut for good.

A Jordanian army platoon, consisting of 120 officers and men, had been stationed in a house bought by the military in 1955. It lay amidst my family houses along the frontline, established by the Armistice Agreement in 1949. The only armaments in the possession of the military contingent were rifles and a few machine guns. They received no reinforcements of men or armaments after the war started, even though they were destined to bear the brunt of the onslaught. The commanding officer came to the house of my elder brother, Anwar, who had served as defence minister in 1955, at 8.30pm and asked him to move the family to another house, a few hundred metres away. The officer told him that a fierce battle was expected to flare up later in the evening right around the house. Nuzha, my sister-in-law, informed me later on that the commanding officer had intimated to them that there was an ammunition shortage. She wondered how this could be the case when the war had hardly begun. Anyway, my brother's family, and mother and brothers and sisters, all of whom were facing Israeli gun emplacements, moved to Dar at-Tifil al-Arabi, a stout stone building 100 metres away, housing a Palestinian orphanage founded by social philanthropist Hind al-Husseini. The building backs onto the American Colony Hotel at the southern end. The group, around 25 in number, were lodged in the basement of the building, as artillery and heavy fire echoed thunderously in the stillness of the night. The Israelis used heavy artillery against the Jordanian army and civilian positions, destroying gun emplacements and homes. All but one of the defenders were killed.

Then Israeli forces advanced across the street, in the face of heavy fire, and at 2am reached Dar at-Tifil al-Arabi building where my family had taken refuge. The attacking force lobbed hand grenades inside the building. My brother, fearing the worst, shouted to the soldiers that all the people in the basement were civilians. The soldiers occupied the building, sent over reserves to control it, and continued their advance eastward. By noon on Tuesday, they were in effective control of all of East Jerusalem, except for the Old City, because there were no other lines of defence, and civilians were totally unarmed. The fate of our family house was, as in 1948, to suffer extensive damage. Israeli helicopters lobbed napalm incendiary bombs into the house, which burnt the roof and the entire upper floor. Only a washing machine miraculously escaped the liquid fire because of a fault in the floor of the room which housed it. When fighting ceased altogether on Thursday, a team of Israeli army engineers advanced towards the house carrying explosives. They were bent on razing it to the ground. My sister, Sama, a strong and fearless woman, shouted at them to stop. She told them that it was a civilian house, and after heated exchanges dissuaded them from blowing it up. In the course of the argument, they claimed that firing from it had killed 83 of their soldiers. Such a number may have been killed, but the firing would have come from the adjacent house, occupied by the army unit from which only that one soldier survived. My sister-in-law saw what she thought were the bodies of two Jordanian soldiers in her garden. When she came closer, she noticed a movement in one of them. It turned out that he was dazed but alive, and had been pretending to be dead. He was provided with civilian clothing which enabled him to blend in with the crowds. Many Jerusalem families, particularly in the

Old City, took similar action to help soldiers escape death or captivity. This was the least they could do for their brethren in uniform who had put their lives on the line to defend them. Most of the soldiers died fighting valiantly against great odds and vastly greater fire power. There is a monument in Anwar's house commemorating the fallen soldiers. Similar monuments were erected in other locations in Jerusalem, where Jordanian soldiers and Palestinian National Guard died fighting.

Zaki, the eldest son of Anwar and Nuzha, had just graduated from Cambridge University when Jerusalem was occupied. He is my son-in-law, married to my eldest daughter, Laila. He was so saddened by the fall of Jerusalem and so ashamed of the manner in which the Arab armies were defeated that he stayed in his room in the United Kingdom for a whole month. Subsequently, he travelled to Jerusalem via Amman, before forking the River Jordan at a spot near Wadi al-Yabess. From there, he travelled by bus to Nablus and thence to Ramallah. My sister, Hala, was also in Amman on a visit when Jerusalem fell. Both of them went to great pains to smuggle themselves to Jerusalem, disguised and with no papers to present at the various checkpoints. Luckily, they arrived in Jerusalem where they joined their family. Anwar, when serving as Jordan's ambassador in London in 1966, had established ties of friendship with Sheikh Zayed bin Sultan Al Nahayan, ruler of Abu Dhabi, later president of the United Arab Emirates, an outstanding man in his own right. He advised Zaki to work in Abu Dhabi, where he eventually became a counsellor to the Amir until the latter's death in 2004.

In Amman, we were all glued to our radios, moving from one station to another. Our wishful thinking, or perhaps our escape mechanism, made us switch to Arab stations that were still audaciously proclaiming victory. We heard a report that the Governor of Jerusalem, Anwar al-Khatib; a venerable judge and former Foreign Minister Anton Attallah; the Director of the Police Department Muhammad al-Sareef; the Sheikh of the Holy Sanctuary Sheikh Saad Eddin al-Alami; and other dignitaries had been detained by Israeli occupation forces and interviewed live on Israeli radio. We later learned that they had been made to kneel for hours under the scorching June sun. I felt deep sadness as I heard about what had become of those distinguished personages who had served with distinction in the highest positions of the state. I recalled the dignified presence of Anton Attallah, as foreign minister, a mere two years earlier when we both were in the Oval Office at the White House, presenting our viewpoints on the Palestine question to President Johnson. But war is a ruthless enterprise, and its consequences are incalculable in human life and human dignity. It is the kind of humiliation and brutality which international instruments, such as The Hague Convention of 1907 or the Fourth Geneva Convention of 1949 had tried to mitigate, but to no avail. Occupation is the ultimate humiliation of human dignity, and the longer it lasts, the greater is the indignity.

In Amman, contradictory information began to seep in. Whispers of Israeli occupation of our holiest shrines on the one hand, and rumours of valiant feats, victories and sacrifices on the other.

Our closest neighbouring house was that of Prince Zaid bin Shaker and his wife Nawzat, an AUB alumnus and a lady of distinguished social standing. Her husband, Sherif, later Prince Zaid, had been commanding an armoured brigade in the West Bank. The news reports from various sources spoke of Jordanian armoured formations and infantry being subjected to a relentless hammering from the air in Jenin, Nablus, and the Jordan Valley which had destroyed or disabled almost all their vehicles.

They were totally vulnerable, operating or withdrawing without any air cover. Jordan had been promised air cover from the Egyptian air force before it was destroyed. Nawzat was in a state of frenzy, fearful, and justly so, that her husband might not survive the aerial bombardment, which included napalm incendiary bombs and took a heavy toll among escaping civilian refugees. For two or three days we tried to comfort her, until finally news came that her husband had arrived safely and unscathed. She broke into heart-rending tears of joy, and we empathised with her emotions.

On Thursday, the fourth day of the war, news was disseminated, possibly by the intelligence services, that the Jordanian army had been virtually annihilated, with dead and wounded reaching 30,000-40,000. The news was taken at face value, even in the well-informed councils of former Prime Minister Suleiman Nabulsi and highly placed officials. There was no way of confirming or refuting such staggering figures. The political trio of Abdul Munim al-Rifai, Akef al-Fayez and I arranged our schedules in a way which would enable us to visit and console as many of the homes of fallen martyrs as we could. We met day after day, awaiting information about names until finally we discovered that only a very few people we knew in the army had indeed been killed. It seems, in hindsight, that the news was designed to mitigate the shock of losing Jerusalem and the West Bank by spreading equally shocking news about the martyrdom of the army. In fact, the Jordanian army had received instructions on the Tuesday morning to withdraw to the East Bank, and the withdrawal had been accomplished with minimal casualties. The army was disbanded in its withdrawal, and it took some weeks before it was fully reassembled.

Even the police disappeared from the streets of Amman in the aftermath of the war. Captain Amin al-Husseini, a top-notch pilot and a resident of Jabal Amman, took it upon himself to organise a civil defence force to guard residential areas, pending the re-instatement of the regular police force.

Many books have been written on the 1967 war and the second catastrophe which befell the Palestinians, in particular, and the Arab world in general. There is no point, therefore, in elaborating further. King Hussein wrote a comprehensive account of what happened in his book, *Our War with Israel*. Besides, it would be outside of the scope of these Jerusalem reminiscences. But I think I would subscribe to what my good friend Adnan Pachachi, a former Iraqi foreign minister and one of the ablest ambassadors to the United Nations, said in New York when the full magnitude of the Arab defeat in 1967 became clear. He was at a loss when it came to explaining what happened, who should be blamed, or how one might justify in any meaningful way the outcome. He summed it all up in one sentence. It was, he said, a reflection of the civilisation gap between the enemy and us.

Two days after the occupation of the West Bank, Ahmad Tuqan, Jordanian Minister of Foreign Affairs, invited four former foreign ministers, Akram Zuaiter, Muhammad Adeeb al-Amiri, Abdullah Salah and me, to his ministry to seek our advice on how best to handle the situation. He assigned a special room for our meetings. At the first meeting he expressed concern about the presence of an Israeli armoured brigade near Suweimeh Bridge in the Jordan Valley which, he feared, was poised for a further advance towards Amman. I was the first to speak. I expressed the view that his fears were far-fetched, considering that Israeli forces had just occupied the whole of the West Bank, Egyptian Sinai and the Syrian Golan Heights. I added that my first priority was to close the bridges between the West Bank and the East Bank in order to avert a repetition of the disastrous exodus of the Palestinian people from their homeland. I stressed that military deployments here and there were temporary and could be contained by diplomatic action. But what would be of lasting consequence, judging by our sorry experience in 1948, would be if our people in the West Bank and Gaza were scared by the Israelis into starting a massive and irrational flight, with a lasting impact. Minister Tuqan wanted our advice on the kind of diplomatic steps which the government should take to save the situation. But while I agreed that diplomatic moves were very important I stuck to my argument that the paramount goal should be to prevent a massive exodus, by closing the two bridges on the river Jordan: the King Hussein (formerly Allenby) Bridge, and Prince Muhammad Bridge further north. My argument carried weight, in light of the fact that already 200,000 refugees who had been residing in camps in the Jericho area since 1949 had crossed the bridges into the East Bank, without restrictions. After all, they were citizens of the state of Jordan and had every legal right to move from one part of the kingdom to another without hindrance. And, as citizens, they were classified as both 'displaced persons' and refugees, representing a new classification. Immediately after the termination of hostilities, the General Assembly of the United Nations passed a resolution calling for the 'immediate' and unconditional repatriation of those displaced to their former homes. As I write today, more than 40 years of 'supplemental' dispersal have passed without an end in sight. With these differing approaches and priorities the foreign ministers ended their consultations.

The question of whether to open or to close the bridges remained an active and live issue for a number of years, with heated discussions over its pros and cons. It must be remembered that we, at the decision-making level, were talking about our own kinsmen, brothers, sisters, fathers and mothers, giving the issue a very profound and intimate human dimension. And quite apart from the inherent rights of citizenship, it was not easy to adopt decisions which amounted to 'alienation' and rejection of our closest kin. Yet the massive exodus of the Palestinian people in 1947-48 had left an indelible impact on our innermost consciousness and minds, which blinded us to the human dimension.

Bahjat Talhouni formed a new cabinet towards the end of 1967, in which I served as Minister of Reconstruction and Development, in charge of the affairs of the refugees and the newly-arriving displaced. It was a frenetic life, dealing with the plight and livelihood of hundreds of thousands of newly-arriving refugees. I took charge of supplying basic rations and shelter – mainly those ugly yellow tents which brought back memories of the mid-1950s when I was undersecretary of the same ministry and we had attempted to replace them with a more enduring abode, made from cement and asbestos. The supply of drinking water was a problem, let alone water for washing and other sanitary uses. Then there were the many human problems to deal with: a girl requesting financial assistance to join her family abroad; and students in all grades stranded without education. My job involved dealing with endless crowds, having multitudes of problems requiring immediate remedial action. To give feel of the situation, I might mention how we, at the Ministry of Reconstruction, put to good use a marquee tent, a gift from the Papal See. We used it to house upwards of 50 students at a makeshift secondary school at the Baqaa refugee camp about 10 miles north of Amman. This was just one example of the considerable assistance we received, primarily from Arab countries, but also from all over the world. Arab women donated their personal jewellery for support of the victims of the war. The Eisenhower Foundation sent a special envoy carrying a cheque for $10 million and he wanted to hand it to me in a formal and public way, with media coverage. I must confess that, at first, I balked at the idea, not for of lack of appreciation or respect but because it represented to me a case of *déjà vu*, a repeat of what we thought we had overcome in the aftermath of the 1948 war. It was just too stark a reminder of what we had again fallen into. But the picture-taking ceremony went ahead because I reckoned the donors back home would wish to see where their money went.

The phenomenon of the displaced needs to be accorded further attention and analysis. Unlike 1948, there were no massacres like that at Deir Yassin village. But there is little doubt that the inhabitants of the occupied territories were subjected to a great deal of harassment and terror, aimed at inducing them to emigrate. An eyewitness from the Palestinian Red Crescent Society testified that at one refugee camp Israeli soldiers fired at the homes of the occupants for days on end. He also saw children suffering physical effects caused by fright and sleeplessness.

As a minister, I received daily reports from the police and intelligence personnel stationed at the bridges to monitor the movement of people across the bridges. At one point, they observed that the numbers crossing from the Gaza Strip were exceeding their counterparts from the West Bank. They interrogated some of the passengers from Gaza and one of them disclosed that General Moshe Dayan was planning the emigration of the entire al-Shati refugee camp in Gaza, housing around 80,000 people. Special air-conditioned buses were prepared for the journey and each refugee received 100 Israeli liras for travel expenses.

On the day I heard this report there was a council of ministers meeting in the evening, and King Hussein made a surprise visit, as he was in the habit of doing every once in a while. He inquired from me about the movement of people across the bridges and I informed him and the council about the message which I had received. It was decided at that meeting to give instructions to the army units at the bridges to fire at the tyres of any of the scheduled buses carrying those refugees, and to turn them back, by force if need be. This was done and the buses never came back. Thus, the residents of al-Shati camp in Gaza were spared a further exodus.

Turning to international reaction to the 1967 war, hardly any UN resolution has been so widely quoted and discussed over so many years as Security Council Resolution 242, dated 22 November 1967. It was passed after extensive diplomatic efforts to deal with the consequences of the war. In its preamble, it asserted the principle of the inadmissibility of the acquisition of territory by force. In its key paragraph it called upon Israel to withdraw from the territories occupied in 1967, and asserted the right of every state to live in peace and security, within secure borders. The resolution made a passing reference to the question of the Palestinian refugees, calling for a just solution to their problem.

Although Security Council resolutions are mandatory, when it comes to 242 and Israel's reaction to it, the case is one of violation rather than observance. After more than 40 years, Israel still occupies the whole of the West Bank, including Arab Jerusalem, as well as the Syrian Golan heights. What is far more ominous is the fact that over this extended period, Israel has been sequestrating and colonising the occupied territories, to an extent which is rendering well-nigh impossible the arrival at a just and lasting solution to the question of Palestine and the Arab-Israeli conflict.

There is one anecdote which I feel is worth recording here, if only to show the deviousness of international diplomacy. When the resolution was passed, a discrepancy appeared between the English and French texts. I pointed this out to my colleague and friend Minister al-Rifai when he returned to Amman from New York. While the French text talks about withdrawal from 'the occupied territories', the English text speaks of withdrawal 'from occupied territories' without the definite article. I said that this discrepancy might be exploited by Israel to water down the mandatory withdrawal from all the territories. Minister Rif'i tried to minimise the difference between the two texts, by adding that the preamble of the resolution had made crystal clear the inadmissibility of the acquisition of territory by force.

The argument and the issue lingered on in my mind. When I became Ambassador of Jordan to the United Nations in 1976, Lord Caradon, a most able and amiable British diplomat, used to visit me at our mission at 866 UN Plaza, New York to discuss various aspects of this question. Lord Caradon, when he was Britain's Ambassador to the United Nations, had been the principal architect of resolution 242. He was nostalgic for Palestine, and in particular for the city of Nablus where, in his younger days, he had served as district commissioner during the British mandate. And on every visit, I would make a point of asking him how it was that there was this discrepancy between the English and the French texts. And on every occasion, Lord Caradon would play down the difference, asserting that both meant withdrawal from all the occupied territories. One day, when I insisted on hearing a definitive answer, Lord Caradon answered: 'Hazem, this was the most that we could get, in light of the consequences of the 1967 war.' The vagueness, therefore, was not inadvertent or the result of poor translation, but a deliberate choice.

The French had wanted an unequivocal withdrawal, the British, in their customary muddling (some would say meddling) way chose vagueness.

Photos

THE AUTHOR DELIVERING A SPEECH FROM THE PODIUM OF THE UN GENERAL ASSEMBLY IN THE MID-1960S.

A 19ᵀᴴ CENTURY PHOTOGRAPH OF MEMBERS OF THE NUSSEIBEH FAMILY, SEATED AT THE DIVAN AT THE LEFT SIDE OF THE ENTRANCE TO THE CHURCH OF THE HOLY SEPULCHRE. (HARVARD COLLECTION)

Photos

The author's father, Zaki, and mother, Fattuma, in 1929. The author is at the bottom left of the picture, with brothers Mahmoud to his left and Hisham behind on their fathers' lap.

Jerusalemites: A Living Memory

RAWDHA COLLEGE IN THE OLD CITY OF JERUSALEM IN 1930. SEATED AT THE CENTRE OF THE PHOTOGRAPH IS THE GRAND MUFTI OF JERUSALEM, HAJ AMIN AL-HUSSEINI, THE DIRECTOR OF RAWDHA COLLEGE, SHEIKH MUHAMMAD ESSALEH, AND OTHER TEACHERS AND STUDENTS. THE AUTHOR IS SEATED ON THE GROUND, EIGHTH FROM THE LEFT WITH A SILVER CUP IN FRONT OF HIM.

Photos

THE 1ST XI FOOTBALL TEAM AT VICTORIA COLLEGE, ALEXANDRIA IN 1938. THE AUTHOR IS STANDING, THE THIRD FROM THE LEFT.

THE AUTHOR STANDING BEHIND LADY TENNIS PLAYERS, MEMBERS OF THE JERUSALEM YMCA TEAM AGAINST HAIFA HADAR CARMEL TEAM, 1942.

Photos

PRESS AND BROADCASTING STAFF (ARAB, BRITISH AND JEWISH) IN JERUSALEM IN 1944. THE AUTHOR IS SEATED ON THE FLOOR, THE FIFTH FROM THE LEFT.

THE AUTHOR ADDRESSING A MEETING OF CHIEFS OF DELEGATIONS TO ARMISTICE COMMISSION IN DAMASCUS, SYRIA, 1955. CHAIRING OPENING MEETING WAS SABRI AL-ASSALI, PRIME MINISTER OF SYRIA (SEATED IN THE MIDDLE).

The author in London around 1960 with two of his brothers, Dr Ahmad to his right and Muhammad to his left. Both participated in, or saw fighting in 1947-48 and 1967.

Late King Faisal of Saudi Arabia in conversation with the author and the Sudanese and Syrian Ambassadors to UN in 1962. Also in the picture is Abdul Rahman Azzam Pasha, the first Secretary-General of Arab League.

The author in Moscow in 1963 at a ceremony for Jordan's signing of the partial Test Ban Treaty.

Jerusalemites: A Living Memory

THE LATE KING HUSSEIN RECEIVING THE CREDENTIALS OF AN AMBASSADOR AT ROYAL PALACE IN AMMAN IN 1964. TO KING'S LEFT ARE FOREIGN MINISTER ANTON ATTALLAH, CHIEF OF THE ROYAL CABINET BAHJAT TALHOUNI, CHIEF OF ROYAL AND THE AUTHOR (MINISTER OF THE ROYAL COURT).

Photos

Dean Rusk, US Secretary of State, greets the author at the State Department in Washington in 1965. Dr Muhammad al-Farra, Jordan's Ambassador to the United Nations, looks on.

Jerusalemites: A Living Memory

The author presenting his credentials to President Gamal Abdul Nasser, as Ambassador of Jordan to the Arab Republic of Egypt, 1969. To Nasser's right is Egyptian Foreign Minister Mahmoud Riyadh; to the author's left is the chief of Egyptian protocol.

Photos

PLO Chairman Yasser Arafat on the author's right at a press conference in Beijing. On Arafat's right is Jordanian Prime Minister Abdul Wahhab al-Majali. A joint Jordanian-Palestinian delegation was in China to promote a just solution to the Palestine problem.

The author talking with the late Pope John Paul II at a UN reception in October 1979. In the centre of the photograph is the UN's Chief of Protocol, Ali Taymour.

THE AUTHOR SHAKES HANDS WITH THE LATE KING HUSSEIN DURING A STATE VISIT TO WASHINGTON IN 1981.

The author and Kurt Waldheim, Secretary-General of the United Nations, at UN Headquarters in New York, 1982.

Photos

THE AUTHOR'S WIFE, QADAR, HAVING SHAKEN HANDS WITH QUEEN ELIZABETH OF BRITAIN IS GREETED BY THE DUKE OF EDINBURGH DURING A ROYAL VISIT TO JORDAN IN 1984.

KING HUSSEIN AND PRINCESS MUNA AT MARQA AIRPORT. AMMAN, WELCOMING A HEAD OF STATE. THE AUTHOR'S ELDEST DAUGHTER, LAILA, AND ELDEST SON, HAITHAM, ARE SEEN TALKING TO THE KING. LAILA IS CARRYING A BOUQUET FOR THE KING'S GUEST. ON THE FAR RIGHT IS LINA MUFTI.

Photos

On the occasion of the marriage of the author's eldest daughter, Laila, to her cousin, Zaki. From right to left: The author's elder brother, Anwar; his, sister Sama; Nuzha, wife of Anwar and mother of Zaki; Laila the bride and Zaki the bridegroom; Qadar; and the author.

Jerusalemites: A Living Memory

WAJEEH NUSSEIBEH, COUSIN OF THE AUTHOR, PERFORMS THE RITE OF OPENING THE CHURCH OF THE HOLY SEPULCHRE IN JERUSALEM. THE NUSSEIBEH FAMILY HAS BEEN ENTRUSTED OVER SEVERAL CENTURIES WITH THE DUTY OF UNLOCKING AND LOCKING THE CHURCH EVERY DAY.

THE AUTHOR'S COUSIN, WAJEEH NUSSEIBEH (LEFT), JOINING CELEBRATIONS AT THE HOLY SEPULCHRE, MARKING THE CROWNING THE NEW LATIN PATRIARCH OF JERUSALEM, PALESTINE AND JORDAN, FUAD TWAL IN JUNE 2008.

THE AUTHOR AT THE SECURITY COUNCIL IN 1982. TO HIS RIGHT IS THE AMBASSADOR OF JAPAN.

CHAPTER 12

FROM POLITICS TO DIPLOMACY

The United Nations appointed a distinguished Ambassador from Sweden, Gunnar Jarring, as special representative, with the task of mediating and facilitating implementation of Security Council Resolution 242, calling for the withdrawal of Israeli occupation forces from Jerusalem and the rest of the West Bank. Ambassador Jarring engaged in this mission with utmost zeal and dedication. He conducted shuttle diplomacy between Tel Aviv and the Arab states whose territories had been occupied, Egypt, Syria and, above all, Jordan which had lost half its people and territory to occupation. It was a painful and fruitless mission, a dialogue of the deaf and an exercise in futility that Jarring and the Arab states concerned had to endure for years on end. I saw Ambassador Jarring, accidentally, at the United Nations in 1972 and asked him what had come of his mission and he replied: 'I was going to ask you the same question.'

We had all assumed that a Security Council decision would be binding on all states; that occupation of the territories of other states was totally inadmissible; and that the occupation would be terminated by a peace treaty, as in the case of all other wars. Immediately after the occupation of Jerusalem and the West Bank, a colleague suggested that it might take six months for the occupation to end, and I was so infuriated by the suggestion that I exploded in front of him in anger. I had had an experience of almost two years at the Mixed Jordanian-Israeli Armistice Commission, where a violation of the other side's territory was promptly rectified and where the Security Council, the highest executive organ of the UN, firmly insisted on observance of the UN charter.

In one of my meetings with King Hussein, he showed me a letter from President Johnson in which the latter gave assurances that Israel would withdraw from the occupied territories. It was an unconditional and unequivocal commitment covering all the occupied territories. And yet, Ambassador Jarring, in his shuttle diplomacy, could not report an inch of progress because the Israelis found a way of bogging him down with irrelevant procedural matters. All this recalled to me the mission of one of Jarring's most eminent countrymen, Ambassador Count Folke Bernadotte, as UN mediator some 20 years earlier. He was assassinated, at close range and in cold blood, by members of the militant Zionist Stern Gang in the streets of West Jerusalem in September 1948. He was killed in order to derail the serious efforts he was making aimed at solving the Palestine problem on the basis of international legitimacy. He had insisted that there could be no just solution without first repatriating the Palestinian refugees to their homes. One year after the cessation of hostilities the towns, villages and homes of the Palestinian refugees were still standing, awaiting the return of their legitimate owners. This was before the Israeli destruction of close to 450 Palestinian villages all over Palestine.

Count Bernadotte had been visiting Ramallah on the day of his assassination, and a luncheon had been given in his honour by Brigadier Norman Lash, commander of the Jordan army division (*al-Firqa*) operating in the West Bank. It was headquartered in an olive grove in the village of Bitounya, near Ramallah. Count Bernadotte, a man of outstanding qualities and impeccable character, was wearing an elegant white uniform and shorts, and looked as grand as befits a cousin of the king of Sweden. He was also in jovial mood when I discussed his mission with him, on the look-out for material that I might use in one of the political commentaries which I was giving in English and Arabic at the Palestine Broadcasting Service. It was destined to be a farewell meeting with one of the most distinguished personages and diplomats of our age. He told his hosts that he was planning to cross to the other side, to West Jerusalem, for a meeting with the Israeli government, and the time then was after 4pm. I do not remember the exact time of his departure.

I was in my office at the broadcasting station in Ramallah preparing the 6pm news bulletins when, at 5.30, the telephone rang. The caller was Taher Shihabi, our correspondent in Jerusalem. He said in an agitated voice that he had bad and ominous news to tell me: that Count Bernadotte had been murdered on the streets of Jerusalem, together with his French aide-de-camp. I told Shihabi that only an hour or so earlier we had been having lunch with Count Bernadotte and he had been relaxed and in the best of health. I expressed the hope that the news of this vile murder would prove to be untrue, to which he assured me that his source was no less than the British Consulate in Jerusalem. His cousin worked as a wireless operator there and had sent a message about the assassination to London.

The news of the killing was exclusive to us for quite a while, but we had too much respect for Count Bernadotte to rush into broadcasting breaking news that might have turned out to be untrue. So I held back from broadcasting the news in Arabic, and only put it on the air in the English news bulletin at 7.30pm, edited and broadcast by our colleague, Naseeb Bulos. By this time, the killing of the count was public knowledge.

I remembered this sad episode as I talked to Ambassador Jarring but did not refer to it since to have done so would have been in bad taste and might have served as an ill omen. But many years later I received confidential information that Ambassador Jarring himself had received intimations that he could face the same fate if he did not desist from pursuing his assigned mission. In any event, he handed his resignation to the secretary-general in 1972, leaving a political vacuum until the October 1973 Arab-Israeli war. On 22 October, the Security Council passed Resolution 338, calling both for an end to the fighting and the implementation of Resolution 242. The futility of this multi-national effort was matched by a no less futile effort made by the United States in 1970, which carried the name of the Rogers Plan, as I shall explain in due course.

In the meantime, back in 1967, the government of Jordan was confronted with a novel and uncharted situation. Half of its population in Jerusalem and the West Bank had, overnight, come under occupation. The government needed to decide, as a matter of the utmost urgency, what to do and what role to play in the occupied territories. It was decided to keep all the government structures and functions in place, as though there was no occupation. The government in Amman continued to pay full salaries and allowances to thousands of teachers, doctors, engineers, and other civil servants in all West Bank towns, including Jerusalem. I was also a member of a ministerial committee which supervised the monthly transfer of assistance, small and symbolic as it was, to all governorates, in proportion to the populations of each of them. The paying of salaries in this way and provision of assistance continued uninterrupted until 1989 when King Hussein decided on a plan to disengage from the Palestinian territories. The idea, it was declared, was to hand over responsibility to the Palestinians themselves, whose sole and legitimate representative was the PLO. The only responsibility retained by Jordan was the role of administering and safeguarding the Muslim holy places in Jerusalem.

Many leading Palestinians in Amman including myself were staunchly against the disengagement plan and sent a memorandum to the government protesting against the move and declaring it to be illegal because only parliament could dissolve the unity, according to the constitution. Besides, it created a legal vacuum because there was no Palestinian authority in the West Bank to assume the responsibility of governing the territories. A governing structure did not emerge until 1993 with the Oslo Agreement, and even then only at the level of local government.

I resigned from the cabinet at the end of 1968 and was vacationing with my wife and children in Beirut (our favoured vacation resort) when I received a telephone call from Amman. The caller was Foreign Minister Ahmad Tuqan. He said that I should return to Amman immediately because His Majesty wanted me to be Ambassador to the United Arab

Republic (Egypt). I had disengaged from the cabinet a few days earlier because of misgivings about the government which I still felt. But Ahmad Tuqan was insistent. I agreed tentatively, contingent on my wife's agreement. Qadar had visited Cairo in her younger years and had loved it, so readily agreed. The agreement of a wife in ambassadorial appointments or those to any more junior posts in the diplomatic service is a condition precedent because it involves the uprooting of the whole family from their normal residences and routines, including schools, neighbourhoods, friends, clubs, and all the other attachments and amenities of life. Many diplomatic families have suffered, including their children, in consequence of unanticipated transfers, or moves to countries where the school curricula, and even the languages of teaching, pose problems. Substitute international schools are not always adequate compensation for the change.

It is normal for an ambassador who performs well at his job and has the right political connections to be promoted eventually to the post of minister of foreign affairs. Madeleine Albright is a good recent example, moving from the post of America's UN ambassador to secretary of state. But it is rare for someone to move the other way, from foreign minister to ambassador, unless there is a strong reason. In my case, it was argued that a Jordanian ambassador to Egypt had a pivotal coordinating role to play at that particular moment when both countries were locked into a fierce diplomatic and military campaign with the same goal of retrieving lost lands.

Having taken up my post in Cairo I remember clearly a series of meetings at the Egyptian Foreign Ministry, in which Foreign Minister Mahmoud Riyadh, his assistant Muhammad Riyadh, Jordanian Foreign Minister Abdul Munim al-Rifai and I, as ambassador to Cairo, worked for hours as a team. We were drafting a joint answer to a list of around 14 questions which Ambassador Jarring had addressed to the four countries concerned, pertaining to the various aspects of the Palestine question and the all-encompassing Arab-Israeli conflict. One of the cardinal questions was: what does your government conceive a final solution to the Palestine question to be? I said, and all present concurred, that the only standing and internationally valid solution would be one based on Resolution 181, adopted by the UN General Assembly on 29 November 1947, calling for the establishment of two states, Arab and Israeli, with greater Jerusalem and its environs as an international *corpus seperatum* for 10 years, subsequent to which the citizens would be asked to determine their future.

Putting international diplomacy to one side for a moment, let me say that Cairo is an extremely captivating city which has charmed, and continues to charm, generation after generation of citizens and visitors in equal measure, notwithstanding the overcrowding, the noise pollution, the shabby pavements, and other urban ills. But one can feel in the air an inherent richness which reflects the immense age and maturity of this cradle of civilisation, with the pyramids dating back over five millennia. At the same time, the 1,000 tall minarets remind one, if any reminder were needed, that Egypt is the accepted leader of the Arab world and the undoubted citadel of Arab and Islamic scholarship, with al-Azhar Mosque and University acting as the ultimate reference, in matters Godly and mundane.

Many people are unaware that Alexandria, where I spent my teenage years at Victoria College, was also historically a major centre of Hellenic thought and philosophy, where neo-

Platonism flourished. It is in recognition of this precious legacy that the famous Alexandria Library has been reconstructed at its original location, at the initiative of the Egyptian state and with generous international assistance, to pay a debt of gratitude to those Egyptian and Hellenic sages who enlightened the world with their logic, temperance, and wisdom. Sheikh Zayed bin Sultan Al Nahayan, late president of the United Arab Emirates and ruler of Abu Dhabi, stands out as the most generous single benefactor, with a donation of $100 million. In 2002, Victoria College celebrated the centenary of its founding, and I had the pleasure of attending the celebration. One of the highlights of the event was a tour of the newly reborn Alexandria Library. And while on this subject, I wish to reassert what has been confirmed by the world of scholarship that the burning down of the ancient library pre-dated by centuries the Arab habitation of Egypt.

Longevity has many advantages which I fully utilised during the centenary celebrations. I must have been the oldest person there, and I narrated to successive generations of Old Victorians attending the occasion, the names of the headmasters and teachers of the 1930s and 40s. I also shared memories of all kinds of goings on then that brought Victoria College to life – ghost stories, rumours of love affairs, victories and defeats in football, tennis and cricket, and so on. The younger Old Victorians enjoyed the experience as much as I did and promised to post my reminiscences on the old boys' website.

Returning to Egypt of 1969, in early September I presented my credentials to President Gamal Abdul Nasser, the legendary leader of Egypt and object of adoration for the vast masses of the Arab world, notwithstanding the seemingly incredible defeat of Egypt a year and a half earlier in the 1967 war. The defeat was blamed on his lieutenants and, primarily, on Abdul Hakim Amer, Minister of Defence who had established for himself a redoubtable power centre which was beyond even President Nasser's reach. The president received me cordially and, after finishing the formalities of handing over the credentials, he invited me to a private audience, in a small office adjacent to the main hall. President Nasser had a towering, natural personality with piercing, sharp eyes and a ready power of perception. He was not a superman, even if there ever was such a thing; but there is no doubt that in his presence one could feel the charisma of a great leader whose every utterance resounded across the Arab world, the Third World, and much of the rest of the globe, as far afield as Latin America. And, regardless of whether he was loved or hated, he was highly respected. Nasser was genuine and well meaning, believing from the depth of his heart that the backwardness, feudalism, and injustices of Egyptian society must be swept away by drastic and speedy action. The per capita income in Egypt in the 1960s was hovering around $50, below all criteria of poverty levels. He was determined to change the face of Egypt by revolution, not evolution, because the latter was too slow.

I am a staunch believer in freedom, private enterprise and initiative, and am averse, instinctively, to central planning and all other forms of authoritarian governance. I am also against any highhandedness or cruelty in dealing with citizens. But the socialist charter, drawn up in 1961 after the dissolution of unity between Egypt and Syria, rendered the interference of the machinery of state in the life of its citizens inevitable. Hence the nationalisations, the trials of members of the old regime, and the setting up of intelligence agencies that pervaded and poisoned national life. I wonder sometimes whether this revolutionary approach, quite apart from all its collateral damage, is the most efficient and speediest method of achieving the goal of lifting up the downtrodden segments of society. There is always the danger that instead of helping the latter, revolutionary action merely brings down to their levels and impoverishes the middle class. This is what was happening in Egypt when I took up my ambassadorial post. I could see, at close range, the suffering and despair of those who had once been prosperous and active. They had become dependent on a small salary, dished out by the state, for running what was once their own factory or business.

Another and more efficient way might be to create an expanding economy, with high rates of growth, say 6-8 percent per annum as is the case at present in India and China. Expanding prosperity would inevitably, if slowly, filter down and uplift the deprived masses. India has a robust middle class of over 250 million people, a magnet to outside investments, and China has an even more robust economy, now one of the major ones in the world. There is, admittedly, socialist control; but the real engine of change is the entrepreneurship of its business people.

In the course of the 10-to-15 minute talk with President Nasser, in his private office, he went out of his way to emphasise that top priority must be given to the deliverance of Jerusalem and the Went Bank because, he said, they were the national home of the Palestinian people. The Sinai Peninsula could remain occupied for 100 years, but would eventually be won back with the minimum of cost. But not so the West Bank where, he feared, Israel had geographic and demographic designs.

President Nasser was aware of the danger of colonisation, even before Israel had built any settlements on the occupied Palestinian lands, with the exception of the Eshkol residential settlement in Sheikh Jarrah in 1968, and the demolition of the *Maghariba* (Moroccan) quarter adjacent to the Western Wall immediately after the occupation in 1967.

In the course of that short discussion I felt compelled to mention to him the dangers inherent in Israel's monopoly of nuclear power. I had raised this issue with the US secretary of state and there was no harm, I felt, in raising it at this meeting. It may have been poor judgment on my part to have done so with a president who hardly knew me before except perhaps, I hoped, through reading my book on Arab nationalism. I had presented a copy to him and King Hussein when it was first published by Cornell University Press in 1956. But the nuclear issue was a strategic one that could be discussed only *in camera* and in full confidence. I hope I did not give him the impression that I had been trying to extract secrets from him, which I certainly was not doing. To me it was a matter of public concern. President Nasser made no comment one way or the other and steered the discussion towards something else.

The Cairo ambassadorial post kept me fully occupied, and I felt that I was in the hub of events and decision-making. It conveyed a feeling of satisfaction, the like of which I experienced only when I subsequently served as ambassador to the United Nations.

Delegation after delegation, parliamentary, military and others, came to Cairo at a dizzying rate, representing every sector of pubic life and pursuit. An ambassador was duty-bound, or at least expected, to receive such delegations at the airport, together with a high-ranking official representing the host country. And as if this were not enough, he was also expected to wine and dine those dignitaries, along with their Egyptian counterparts. The highlight came when the king was on a visit to Egypt and I obtained the agreement of President Nasser's office to fete the president and the king for dinner at the residence of the ambassador.

The residence was one of those beautifully located and elegantly built villas on the banks of the Nile in Giza, opposite the Cairo Zoo and adjacent to the villa of Ahmad Shawqi, acknowledged in Egypt and the Arab world as the *Amir al-Shuara*, prince of poets. It had a spacious garden containing tall and highly productive mango trees of the best variety. We had an excellent cook, by the name of Arafa who, with one or two helping hands, could prepare a sumptuous meal for 30 or 40 guests at short notice. Eventually we could not retain his service with the kind of salary we were paying and we certainly could not compete with the salary and terms that a prominent Saudi prince had offered him.

Hosting President Nasser was not a casual or easy matter. For a couple of days preceding the dinner the secret service agents were ubiquitous and conspicuous around the residence, and particularly the kitchen, even though they made every effort not to disturb us or be visible. At the set hour, 7.30pm, the roofs of the neighbourhood were filled with cheering and enthusiastic crowds, while the roof of the embassy itself was crowded with Jordanian women whom we had invited. They were all excited to see President Nasser at such close range and they cheered loudly, even hysterically, when the president's motorcade approached the gates of the residence. All went well, and it was an evening to remember for a long time to come for everyone in the neighbourhood.

President Nasser was frugal in his eating habits for health reasons. Most of the time, we were told, his dinner would consist of bread and white cheese, which he loved. Indeed, some food was brought to the residence, presumably to cater to the president's needs.

The most important events during this period were the quarterly meetings of the heads of state of Egypt, Jordan, Syria and Iraq, the so-called confrontation states, with occasional attendance by a Sudanese delegation. The main focus was on the military, as the objective was to appraise the military preparedness of each of the participating countries towards what was assumed to be a common effort to liberate the occupied lands. The central figure was General Muhammad Fawzi, a highly professional and stern commander-in-chief of the Egyptian army. Like a paternal teacher, he would quiz every delegation on what it had achieved or failed to achieve in carrying out the assignments given to it by the combined Arab military command. He was equally tough and exacting in quizzing the Egyptian delegation, even though President Nasser had personally taken command of all branches of military preparedness, even to the extent of inquiring persistently about the digging of trench emplacements to house aerial defence missiles.

In 1969, King Hussein and his accompanying delegation visited President Nasser at his summer residence on the Mediterranean shore at Maamura, Alexandria. The president said at the meeting that because of the depressing experience of 1967 he had lost faith in depending on assistants to perform tasks. He added that wireless equipment had been installed on the second floor of the villa to enable direct communications with each of the 14 commands, including the air force, air defence units and intelligence, as well as civilian institutions impacting on military preparedness. The motto raised during this interim period of military preparedness was 'No voice shall be higher than the voice of battle', and its message permeated all walks of life, draining public funds. As a result, the streets of Cairo had become dilapidated for lack of maintenance, the telephone system was dysfunctional and commonly described as 'lacking in heat' (*mafeesh harara*), water and sewerage infrastructure was in a state of disrepair, and the Egyptian people as a whole had been subjected to a regime of unbridled deprivation and austerity, unprecedented in the country's history. A box of apples in those days was considered a generous present.

During one of the quarterly meetings of the confrontation states, as the conferees were earnestly discussing the issues on the agenda, an assistant to President Nasser quietly walked in and handed him a small piece of paper. We all looked, in curiosity, at the president, but he read the note to himself, said nothing and allowed the discussion to continue. Then, after two minutes, he told the meeting that, a military coup d'état had taken place in Tripoli, Libya, and King Idriss al-Sanussi, a patriarchal old man, had been deposed. The leader of the military coup was a young officer by the name of Qadhafi. There were no further comments or inquiries from any of those present, and the conferees refocused on their agenda. Colonel Mu'ammar Qadhafi became a staunch admirer of President Nasser and his pan-Arab platform. He visited Egypt twice while I was there and considered himself the legitimate heir to Nasser when the latter passed away.

A few days later I received a message from King Hussein, instructing me to visit King Idriss, in exile in Cairo, and inform him that Jordan would be happy to offer any assistance he might need. King Idriss had a great liking for Egypt and had lived for years in Alexandria (as have many Libyans) before he ascended the throne. He had developed a close friendship with King Hussein when they both attended the second Arab summit in Alexandria in September 1964.

I decided to inform a senior figure in Egypt's ruling circle in order to avoid any misunderstanding concerning my mission. I knew perfectly well that my impending visit to King Idriss would be carefully watched and it was only prudent that I should obtain prior clearance from the government to which I was accredited.

I rang up Dr Hassan Sabri al-Khawli, one of President Nasser's close assistants and his 'contact man'. His office was in *Misr al-Gadida* (New Cairo-Heliopolis) close to the international airport. I told Dr Khawli of my instructions and my intention to visit king Idriss at his Cairo residence in Duqqi quarter. Dr Hassan replied excitedly: 'Mr Ambassador, you do not need permission to visit King Idriss, for he is our honoured guest in Cairo, and all his expenses are being met. But I want to tell you a secret which only a few know. In the aftermath of 1967, Egypt emerged in dire straits, with no money even to replenish the rifles which it had lost in Sinai. The president sent me on a secret mission to Tripoli to meet King Idriss and seek his assistance. King Idriss promptly responded with a cheque for the sum of £25 million Sterling. His only condition was to keep the matter in total confidence for fear that the powers hostile to Egypt might react to this assistance. How can we forget King Idriss' assistance in the hour of our most dire need?'

Qadar and I made a point of visiting King Idriss and his family every once in a while. My wife befriended the queen and her secretary, a highly educated Palestinian girl from a well-known family, Hala al-Yiouli. King Idriss was a tall figure with a white beard and tranquil face. He was serene, scholarly and fatherly, radiating goodness of heart that bore no ill. He immersed himself in classical religious works. He was also head of the al-Sanussi Sufi movement, to which the people of Cyrenaica, the eastern province of Libya, belong. He sat behind a reading stand on which he placed his books. Reading in this way was evidently his main occupation in retirement. With this sublimeness of character, it is hardly surprising that the power-hungry and indiscriminate young officers deposed this angelic character so easily. There were widespread rumours that Britain or the United States was behind his dethronement, but I have no comment to make, one way or the other, because I simply do not know. There are always conspiracy theories seeking to explain every occurrence, particularly in the Middle East; but a layman can not know if they are true or not.

On the international diplomacy front, meanwhile, a new initiative aimed at resolving the Middle East crisis, the Rogers Plan, emerged.

One of King Hussein's routine visits to Cairo coincided with what appeared to be a serious and substantive initiative by William Rogers, secretary of state of the United States during the Richard Nixon presidency in 1970. The secretary, a distinguished lawyer, was a man of integrity and patriotism. He formulated a proposed solution to the Arab-Israeli conflict based on the provisions of Security Council Resolution 242, in all its aspects. At the airport to welcome King Hussein, was President Nasser. After words of welcome, the two leaders sat side-by-side on a couch for coffee. President Nasser asked the king whether he had studied the Rogers Plan, which had been communicated the day before. The king, perhaps not wishing to commit himself so early, replied that he had had a cursory look at it. He then stopped to hear President Nasser's reaction. The president said that he looked favourably on the plan and was ready to accept it. The plan would at least, return our occupied territories and, this being the case, we could sell it to our people. The king nodded in agreement.

Not everyone was happy with the plan. Both the Palestinians and the Israelis, each side for its own reasons, were unhappy.

The Palestinians had always taken the position that Security Council Resolution 242 was relevant primarily to the Arab states concerned and to Israel, in as much as it had been adopted to deal with the consequences of the war of 1967, mandating withdrawal from the occupied territories in exchange for peace. The Palestinian question had its own set of resolutions, primarily 181 on partition and the two-state solution, and 194 on the repatriation of the Palestinian refugees to their homes and homeland. The Security Council had only made a passing reference to the latter and had diluted the main substance of the earlier UN resolutions pertaining to the refugees. Thus the Rogers Plan had created a dichotomy between the urgent need of the Arab states for an Israeli withdrawal from the occupied lands, on the one hand, and the Palestinian rights and aspirations for statehood and repatriation to their homeland, on the other. The Popular Front for the Liberation of Palestine went to the extent of mocking President Nasser in a cartoon, showing him riding a donkey back-to-front. Nasser was extremely sensitive about his public image and felt particularly hurt because the criticism had come from the Palestinians themselves, whose cause he had always championed and to which he had been dedicated.

In any case, President Nasser had first and foremost to sell the plan to the Egyptian people. A conference, bringing together close to 3,000 politicians, university professors, intellectuals, party and labour leaders, and other weighty figures, was held in the main auditorium of Cairo University. The conference, with President Nasser in the chair, lasted for three days, and the discussions were often animated, if not heated. Just before the end of the conference, a university professor stood up and addressed the following question: 'What guarantee, Mr President, do we have that if we were to approve the Rogers plan it would be implemented?' To which President Nasser replied that he had none. But he added that even if there was only a 1 percent chance that it might be implemented, it was still an opportunity worth taking. On this note the conference ended.

In Washington, however, the initiative was stifled by internal machinations and discord. The Rogers plan had been formulated without the knowledge or counsel of Henry Kissinger, the National Security advisor to President Nixon, as the former narrated in his memoirs. He was piqued at having been deliberately excluded from its formulation, and succeeded not only in torpedoing the entire plan, but also in bringing about the resignation of the secretary of state himself. Rogers was not the first, nor would he be the last, to be sacrificed at the altar of the Arab-Israeli conflict. Preceding him were luminaries like James Forestall, secretary of defence in the late 1940s, and Governor William Scranton, former US Ambassador to the UN. In 1968, when he was the US' Special

Envoy to the Middle East, Scranton said after returning from the region that his country's policy there should be 'more even-handed'. Those words cost him his political career, just like similar words and policies cost many others.

But while internal power struggles in Washington are relatively easily overcome by the rise and fall of politicians, the ramifications of such struggles upon the world, and particularly the countries concerned, can be lethal and devastating. One can visualise how different the Middle East might have been if the Rogers Plan had been implemented. There would not have been a 1973 war, in which tens of thousands lost their lives on both sides; there would not have been two bloody civil wars, one in Jordan and the other, lasting for 15 years, in Lebanon. One might have avoided three Israeli invasions of Lebanon, one in 1978, the second in 1982, and the third in 2006, where the devastation was horrific. I was president of the Security Council for the month of October 1982 when the second invasion took place and I know the full magnitude of the suffering and destruction. Thirst had become a priority concern to the Council because of the destruction of the water systems in Beirut. Hunger had also been a concern because of the destruction, or total dislocation of the distribution system in a populous city under siege. I was in constant consultations with members of the Security Council, day and night. I remember once calling the ambassador of China at midnight, asking whether it was agreeable to meet at once because of the gravity of the situation.

The ambassador in question, who was duty-bound as the representative of one of the permanent members of the Security Council, to safeguard peace and security, asked, almost apologetically and imploringly, whether the meeting could not wait until the following morning. As for events in Lebanon itself, President Ronald Reagan found it necessary to intervene with the Israeli government when its air, sea, and land bombardment of Beirut had exceeded seventeen hours on end without a let-up.

Such are the dire consequences of failures of policies, or inaction, particularly when emanating from a superpower. In June 1972, when I was ambassador in Rome, my government instructed me to travel at once to New York to handle a delicate political issue. Dr Ahmad Hassan al-Zayyat, Egypt's Minister of Foreign Affairs, had arrived in New York with the purpose of calling for a Security Council meeting to consider the grave situation resulting from the political stalemate in the Middle East. The Rogers Plan had been discarded and there was nothing else to fill the vacuum. I had become accustomed to visiting New York in the middle or third week of September to attend the annual plenary sessions of the UN General Assembly. Autumn in the northeastern United States is heavenly and exhilarating. The falling leaves are brown, golden, yellow, orange and other exquisite colours, combining to make a harmonious combination of beauty, unmatched anywhere. My visit in June, therefore, showed me a different New York, murky, hot, sticky and humid. Apparently Dr Zayyat, in his presentation to the Security Council, had made outlandish references to a Palestinian state, which Jordan considered to have impinged on the unity between the East and the West Bank of Jordan. As a former ambassador to Cairo with close and friendly links to Egypt's establishment, it was felt by my friend and colleague Ambassador Abdul Hamid Sharaf, Jordan's permanent representative, with the concurrence of our government, that I could help to mend the rift that had developed and clear up any misunderstandings. Dr Zayyat was staying at the Pierre Hotel, one of the most luxurious in New York. I had a lengthy talk with him, putting the issue of the Palestinian state in its proper context and thus closing the rift. I attended a meeting of the Security Council with Ambassador Sharaf at which Dr Zayyat, in the face of Security Council inaction, inertia, indifference or even helplessness, declared, and his words, after more than three decades, still ring in my ears: 'I shall be going back to Egypt. What shall I tell my people?'

With its words unheeded, Egypt, along with Syria, provided its own answer in the form of the October War of 1973. The answer was loud and clear. And while on this point, I wish to narrate an episode which occurred in October that year, a mere 24 hours before the outbreak of the war and in which the indomitable Henry Kissinger was involved. As I mentioned elsewhere, the United States secretary of state would meet at the General Assembly as many delegations as time would allow from countries considered friendly or important. Jordan's Foreign Minister was Zuhair Mufti, and the delegation included me, Prime Minister Zeid al-Rifai, who was then ambassador to London, Abdullah Salah, a former foreign minister and ambassador to Washington, and, naturally, Ambassador Sharaf. We assembled in the lounge of the US mission, located opposite United Nations Headquarters to await the meeting. At the set time, Henry Kissinger bounded into the room with his usual energy. He shook hands with each one of us while the TV cameras recorded the greetings. He made a joke, which we thought was overtly facetious, when he said: 'It is nice to be in the company of such famous people.' His remark prompted the television people to film us. Anyway, we took his remark in good spirits and waited for him to open the discussion. He started by asking Ambassador al-Rifai, who had been his student at Harvard University, about King Hussein's health. Then he added, thinking aloud, that he was planning to meet the king around the 20th of the month. Secretary Kissinger, having finished these niceties, then plunged into the serious matters of the day. He said it was time to start doing something about peace because the situation was deadlocked. He then wondered aloud: 'What does it matter to Israel if it remains entrenched along the Suez Canal for the next 10 years?' Secretary Kissinger was implying that the dislodgement of Israeli forces from Suez was beyond Egypt's military power and, therefore, some peaceful initiative must be pursued.

In retrospect, I find it strange that the secretary, meeting with a delegation representing the occupied West Bank, including Jerusalem, as well as the East Bank, did not find any soothing words to say concerning this very central issue. It almost indicated a connivance with a state of occupation, so blatant and so fraught with danger, and yet it was then and still is the core issue of the conflict. What gives credence to my impression was that in the aftermath of the 1973 war, when Kissinger embarked on his 'shuttle diplomacy', he arbitrarily and nonchalantly excluded Jordan from any disengagement agreements, such as he had been arranging between Egypt and Syria, on the one hand, and Israel, on the other. His contacts with Jordan were with no less a leader than King Hussein himself, and Prime Minister Zeid al-Rifai, his erstwhile student. Jordan had requested a disengagement agreement, even partial to Jericho, but the request had been turned down.

After the October 1973 meeting with Kissinger I returned

to my room at the Waldorf Astoria Hotel for the night and woke up early in the morning, as I was often prone to do when travelling. I always brought along a small radio set to hear news, music or even some interesting talk shows, which are on the air in the early hours of the morning for the benefit of those who suffer from insomnia. Some of those talks can be very interesting and absorbing. But that morning the programme was interrupted by news flashes, sketchy and unconfirmed at first, but gradually becoming more definite. The breaking news said that troop movements had been observed all along the Egyptian and Syrian fronts. The news accelerated by the minute, and I felt that I should call my colleagues to wake them up and to inform them of the news, and in particular Ambassador Sharaf, the permanent delegate to the UN. Soon enough, the breaking news became public knowledge, filling all the airwaves with a vast inflow of information and comment, the way the prodigious US media does at times of war.

The Jordan delegation met in open-ended sessions to follow developments, as these were bound to impact on Jordan, directly and possibly decisively, so our opinions would be sought. Should Jordan take the plunge, side-by-side with Egypt and Syria, to retrieve its own occupied territory, the West Bank, including Jerusalem? This would be a unique opportunity as Israel's hands were full fighting off the advancing Egyptian and Syrian armies. After the war, my elder brother, Anwar, a former minister of defence who never left Jerusalem, told me that an Israeli named Farhi, an Arabist and advisor to the Israeli military governor, would visit him every day in his house to inquire anxiously whether Jordan would or would not join the war. Anwar became irritated with such persistence and told Farhi: 'How am I to know? You know better.'

Our people in the occupied territories reported that there were no Israeli troops at all in the whole of the West Bank and that if the Jordanian army were to move in, there would be no-one to stop it. At our end in New York, we had a more panoramic perspective of developments. In addition to the prolific volume of news and learned commentaries, we at the Jordan mission were receiving conflicting reports from Amman on the progress of fighting. During the first week or so, Egypt and Syria achieved brilliant military feats: Egypt dislodged the Israelis from the presumed impregnable Bar Lev line on the Suez Canal, while Syrian armour had almost retaken the occupied Golan Heights and had reached the shores of Lake Tiberias, the original armistice line. Whether we should or should not join in was the crucial question on our minds, and there were heated discussions amongst us on this matter. But then news began to reach the mission from Amman that Syria had been seeking Jordan's involvement in the war, on an urgent basis, and that the latter had responded by sending its crack 4th armoured brigade to the Syrian front to engage the Israeli forces. Two Iraqi divisions had also been despatched to take part in the defence of Damascus. Ominous developments seemed to have taken place at the front which made us all very subdued and nervous. Hardly five years had lapsed since we had lost an entire precious country, and now there would be no fall-back position if, by rash and impulsive action, we gambled with the fate of what remained. I was walking in the delegates' lounge in the United Nations, when Syria's permanent delegate, General Haitham Kailani, a military strategist, stopped to tell me, while slapping his forehead in an expression of despair, that Syrian armoured forces had suffered a disastrous encounter, losing 1,000 tanks. I inquired from him how this could have happened, and he said Israel had deployed its anti-armour forces armed with TOW (tube-launched optically-tracked wire-to-command) anti-tank missiles which, on impact, destroy the tank. The Syrians, we subsequently learned, had failed to replace their armour with infantry to consolidate their hold on the liberated territories, thus leaving their tanks exposed, like sitting ducks, at the mercy of Israeli anti-tank missiles. Israel also had the additional advantage of superior air power.

Meanwhile, television stations in the United States were showing pictures of top-of-the-line American tanks being loaded onto huge transport planes and ships bound for Israel, in an undisguised move to impact on the situation. Some of this brand new armour arrived a few hours later at al-Arish airport, on the doorstep of the Sinai battlefield, to replace the substantial losses which Israel had suffered in the opening weeks of the war. All the Arab foreign ministers and their delegations present in New York met on a daily basis to discuss the developing situation. The meetings would begin by the Egyptian ambassador to the UN, later foreign minister and secretary-general of the Arab League Ismat Abdul Majid, reading with great emotion, on the first day with tears in his eyes, the military communiqués detailing Egyptian victories on the battlefield. The day after seeing the arms shipments to Israel, the Arab foreign ministers decided to request a meeting with the president of the United States to protest against this open alignment with Israel, against Arab countries which, after all, had been fighting to liberate their own occupied soil. The Minister of Foreign Affairs of Kuwait, Sheikh Sabah Ahmad al-Sabah (now the Amir of Kuwait), Saudi Foreign Minister Mustapha al-Saqqaf, and the Foreign Minister of Morocco met with President Nixon to convey the message. This was the first in a series of steps which culminated in the imposition of the famed oil embargo against the United States, and other countries which had sided with Israel against a united Arab world. All 50 African states, without exception, severed diplomatic relations with Israel in an act of solidarity with Egypt, a sisterly African state.

With fierce fighting under way, news began to filter in that Israeli forces had succeeded in establishing a bridgehead behind Egyptian lines. This development was at first regarded complacently by Egypt as little more than a pocket which would soon be liquidated. But as the days passed the so-called pocket had expanded to a degree which endangered Egypt's Third Army. It later became known that American satellites images had guided Israeli forces, led by General Ariel Sharon, as they drove a wedge between Egyptian forces; and Israel exploited the wedge to the full.

I shall not go into the intricacies of this military development because I am not qualified to give an informed opinion one way or the other. But as this story was developing, I received a telephone call from my colleague and friend, Ismat Abdul Majid, Egypt's Ambassador to the UN, inviting me to go at once to the Pierre Hotel for urgent discussions with Egypt's foreign minister, Dr Zayyat. I went there immediately and was received by Dr Zayyat and the ambassador. They informed me that they had also invited the foreign ministers of India and Yugoslavia, two pillars of the Non-Aligned Movement, and Khaled Mansour, Foreign Minister of Sudan. Dr Zayyat and Ambassador Abdul Majid briefed me on the purpose of the meeting before the others arrived in order to secure at least my understanding, if not my agreement. When we all assembled,

Egypt's foreign minister told us in a controlled voice that he had received instructions from Cairo to arrange with friendly countries for an immediate convening of the Security Council in order to seek a ceasefire. The foreign ministers present heard this request with disbelief and dismay. India's foreign minister argued, as I had earlier, before the arrival of the others, that Egypt had not achieved any of its declared goals. Dr Zayyat replied that the Third Army had been encircled and it was a matter of utmost urgency to break the siege in order to supply it with essential needs. The foreign minister of Yugoslavia inquired about the First Army, stationed in Cairo, and asked: 'Why does it not launch a counter-attack to liquidate the Israeli wedge?' Dr Zayyat had strict instructions to convene the Security Council and was in no mood to argue strategy. The two Non-Aligned foreign ministers present, though taken aback, stressed that their instructions were to carry out Egypt's bidding. They would, therefore, at once start consultations with members of the council, to arrange for a meeting.

This was a classic example of the overriding importance of dovetailing true facts with the decision-making process. For the layman, as I am sure for the overwhelming majority of people in the Arab world, the request for a ceasefire before at least some military objectives had been achieved must have caused a terrible shock. Conspiracy theories circulated widely that the whole purpose of the war had not been liberation but the initiation of peace talks. In Arabic, the words were *Tarik Al Tahrir*. The Jordanian delegation, as mentioned earlier, had met Henry Kissinger on the day preceding the outbreak of the war and there was not the slightest indication that he had been anticipating a conflict, let alone that he was conniving in one. On the contrary, his remarks were predicated on the assumption that the existing stalemate could go on and on, and that only a peace process, rather than a war, could undo it. Yet, conspiracy theories abounded that Kissinger had somehow contrived this war in order to restore to Egypt its pride, and make it easier for it to come to terms with Israel. Such a theory is not only farfetched but also historically untrue. Furthermore, it denigrates the heroism and sacrifice of tens of thousands of officers and men who were killed in the attempt to liberate their lands. When the British Empire was the superpower in the world, the same James Bond-like fairy tales were attributed to its alleged intrigues, as I remember as a young boy in the company of elders, in their *diwans* (open councils) in Jerusalem in the 1930s and 40s.

Over and above the general political and military coordination between Egypt and Jordan, during my tenure of service as ambassador to Cairo I also had to deal with a few stormy situations arising from the ambivalent and inextricable relationship between, on the one hand, the Palestinian people, with their numerous categories and affiliations, and, on the other hand, the Jordanian state and people. The dispersal and diffusion of the Palestinian people had made them speak with multiple voices, reflecting their different situations, affiliations, social backgrounds, and authorities. The spectrum is large, extending from over 1 million Palestinians who acquired Israeli citizenship with the creation of Israel, to over 3 million Palestinian Jordanians, and 3.5 million in Jerusalem, the West Bank and Gaza. In addition, there are close to 1 million refugees in Syria, Lebanon, Iraq, Egypt and elsewhere.

The PLO, created in Jerusalem in 1964 under the aegis of Jordan, had evolved to the point where it laid claim to be the sole legitimate representative of the Palestinian people, regardless of their other situations. This had created a sharp schism which exploded into full-fledged violence in September 1970. After the fall of the West Bank in 1967 it was inevitable that there would be resistance to the occupation, as had been the case throughout history. In fact, foreign journalists in 1967 taunted the Palestinians in Jordan for what they regarded as the docility of the Palestinian people under occupation. I remember answering one of them, saying that it took time for occupied people to recover from the shock, to catch their breath and then organise resistance. And this was what happened, not only in the occupied West Bank but, even more forcefully, in the East Bank where arms could be more easily acquired.

A dozen or so resistance organisations sprang up in Amman and the rest of Jordan, representing the different parties and facets of Palestinian-Jordanian society. Fatah was by far the largest and most important, and it was genuinely Palestinian in loyalty, outlook and objectives. Others had different platforms, reflecting varying party and ideological commitments, including the different types of 'isms'.

Thousands of people, Palestinian and Jordanian, joined the ranks of the resistance, without prior checks on who they were. Gradually the controls over such motley multitudes began to weaken. The result was chaos, violence and lawlessness, presenting a challenge to the authority of the land. The Palestinian groups had become a state within a state, with all the dire consequences which accrue from such duality. The Jordanian army itself became restless, seeing its monopoly on military power challenged by insurgency. Indeed, there were signs that insubordination, if not mutiny, might break out within the army unless the king acted quickly to curb the lawlessness.

The king made a visit to Egypt to consult with President Nasser and possibly seek his help. He was accompanied by a high-level delegation which comprised several former prime ministers, including Suleiman Nabulsi, the acknowledge leader of the opposition whose stature President Nasser would recognize, as a friend of Egypt. President Nasser was vacationing in *Maamura*, his summer beach resort in Alexandria, and had asked a number of his vice presidents to partake in the impending talks. The king and his entourage were lodged in Ras al-Tin Palace, the most prestigious of Egypt's erstwhile royal palaces, an honour bestowed only once or twice before on a visiting dignitary. It is from this palace that King Farouk was dispatched to exile by ship in 1952 after an official farewell in which he was saluted by a guard of honour.

President Nasser opened the discussion by welcoming King Hussein and the accompanying delegation. He added: 'On behalf of Egypt, and here with me is the top leadership, I wish to express to you Egypt's gratitude for your honourable stand with us in our hour of need in 1967. I wish to assure you that Egypt will stand by Jordan and provide whatever assistance it may be in need of.'

King Hussein thanked President Nasser for his expressions of support and then detailed his complaints against the armed Palestinian organisations which had wreaked such havoc with the peace and stability of Jordan. The king also expressed his fears concerning the Iraqi army units in Jordan and the danger that they would collude with the Palestinian resistance.

President Nasser told the king that Egypt had access to centres of power within the ranks of the Iraqi army and if there was any foul play against Jordan, Egypt would come to the rescue. Therefore the king should have no worries on this score. As for the Palestinian resistance organisations, Nasser advised the king to be patient with them, adding that they had subjected him to a campaign of calumny when he endorsed the Rogers Plan. He added that the people in question had lost their homeland and had to be dealt with patiently. Nasser also promised to do all that was in his power to ameliorate the situation.

The meeting ended on a friendly note, and our delegation retired to its headquarters at Ras al-Tin palace for a rest and lunch. Each member of the delegation gave his assessment of the meeting. Mudhar Badran, who was chief of the royal cabinet and, subsequently, prime minister, said that Nasser's response was positive and cooperative, and I concurred with his view adding: 'What else did we expect of him? To declare war on the Palestinians, or on Iraq?' But Zeid al-Rifai, also subsequently prime minister and speaker of the Jordanian Senate, expressed the view that the delegation had not obtained the support from President Nasser which the meeting had sought.

The Americans and Russians do not have a monopoly on eavesdropping, and the Egyptians are no strangers to it. No sooner had we finished lunch than Dr Hassan Sabri al-Khawli appeared on the scene, purporting to ask if we were satisfied with the outcome of the meeting. He evidently must have heard the misgivings expressed by Zeid al-Rifai, which the latter repeated. Dr Khawli said he would arrange a one-to-one meeting between the president and the king so they could freely exchange views. Heads of states have a tradition of meeting alone before the plenary meetings of their delegations in order not to be constrained by the latters' presence. Who knows what secrets or strong opinions might be divulged by any one member of either delegation which could cause considerable embarrassment to one or other head of state? At any rate, the king and the president had a private meeting in the evening and I have no way of knowing what transpired. On our side, I have a feeling that my esteemed friend and colleague, Zeid al-Rifai, being a close confidant of the king, would be the only one to have known.

I have elaborated on this point, because when Jordan clamped down on the Palestinian resistance on 17 September 1970, reports or rumours had been circulating that maybe at the private meeting between the king and the president the latter had given the green light to the king to curb the excesses and unruliness of Palestinian resistance, provided it was done quickly and efficiently. This reminds me very much of Lady Macbeth's utterance to her husband in William Shakespeare's *Macbeth* (Scene 7 Act 1): 'If it were done when 'tis done, then t'were well, It were done quickly'.

Less than three months later, the Jordanian army, using full force, clamped down on the Palestinian resistance and, in spite of heavy fighting and heavy odds in having to conduct urban warfare among the sturdy buildings of Amman, the army eventually succeeded in dismantling organised resistance. A day prior to the clampdown the king had appointed a military government consisting of serving or former army officers and intelligence personnel, with Brigadier Muhammad Daoud as prime minister. Muhammad Daoud, from Eizariya village directly overlooking Jerusalem, had been one of my military assistants in 1955 when I served as chairman of the Jordan delegation to the Jordanian-Israeli Mixed Armistice Commission. He was a very amiable, disciplined, unassuming man, faithful to his job and scrupulous in carrying out his orders. He was also personally brave and would rush with the international observers serving with UNTSO, without fear or hesitation, to any location on the armistice lines wherever and whenever fighting flared up. But while recognising all his good qualities, I believe in retrospect that he had been unfairly assigned a task which exacted from him far more than his physical or psychological constitution could endure, as I shall explain in due course.

The fighting in Amman and other Jordanian cities continued unabated for longer than had been anticipated, or was politically tolerable throughout the Arab world. During the first few days, the Egyptian press confined itself primarily to news coverage of the fighting and casualty figures, inflated though they were. But as the conflict dragged on the mood in Cairo darkened, with the press and public opinion becoming more and more agitated and hostile. Public opinion against Jordan was inflamed to boiling point when Sudanese President Jaafar Nimeiri returned to Cairo from Amman. He had been on a mission to arrange safe passage for PLO Chairman Yasser Arafat. The latter had been under siege, hiding in the house of Muhammad al-Huneidi, a Palestinian from Lydda, in Jabal al-Hussein in Amman. The Sudanese president felt humiliated during his visit to Amman, and had to endure heavy fire when he was at the Egyptian ambassador's residence in Jabal Amman. In Cairo, he addressed large gatherings in Tahrir Square where he inflamed the masses by describing wild scenes of massacre of the Palestinian people at the hands of the Jordanian army. The media were talking in terms of tens of thousands of dead and wounded, which subsequently proved to be far off the mark. But the harm had already been done.

Personally, I was so worked-up by the news that I seriously thought of resigning my post. But calmer counsel advised me to await further authentication of the reports. Civilian and military emissaries coming from Amman assured me that the high figures of dead and wounded and the reports of whole quarters being destroyed on top of their residents were largely exaggerated and without foundation. I attempted to publish corrections in *al-Ahram* newspaper, where I had influential friends, but the paper insisted politely that its reports were correct.

My Palestinian identity and humanistic instincts and convictions had been sorely tested without in any way compromising my integrity or my oath of office to serve my government in full faithfulness. I had resigned from the government twice in protest against measures which I reckoned had been unfriendly, punitive or drastic towards the Palestinian people, during the years of unity in the mid-1960s. And on this occasion my protests, addressed to the highest officials of government, were very harsh indeed. This did not mean that I thought the government was all wrong and the resistance was right, for I had witnessed at first hand the indefensible behaviour of many of those resistance organisations which alienated Jordanians and Palestinians alike. But still, the military clampdown in which civilians were suffering even more than the resistance was galling by any standards. Amman's civilian population was on the frontline.

On the sixth day of the on-going war, Sami Sharaf, personal assistant to President Nasser and chief of his communications office, located opposite the residence of the president, invited me to see him. He handed me a message addressed to the Royal Court in Amman in which the president expressed his profound concern over the bloody developments in Jordan. This was followed by a second and a third message, culminating in a decision to convene an Arab summit conference in Cairo to deal with the grave situation in Jordan. But prior to that, the Prime Minister of the military government, Muhammad Daoud, had arrived in Cairo, accompanied by the Chief of Jordanian Intelligence, Ahmad Ubaidat, who became prime minister in 1984-85. The prime minister had a grim and sad countenance, and his speech was short and circumspect. When we reached the Nile Hilton Hotel, where reservations had been made, he said he wanted to talk to me alone on the veranda of his suite. As soon as we stepped out onto the veranda he wept openly and said to me: 'You know me very well. Did you ever get the impression that I was a traitor?' 'Of course not, Abu Daoud,' I said. 'I always appreciated your patriotism and your sense of duty.' To which he replied, with tears flowing from his eyes: 'Have you listened to *Radio Kuwait*? Did you hear my daughter on it calling me a traitor and asking me to resign?' I said that I had not heard it and advised him to calm down.

The next morning, two members of Libya's Revolutionary Council arrived at the hotel and began talks with the prime minister in his suite. They introduced themselves to me and invited me to join their meeting. I suspected that there must be something fishy and unbecoming about this surprise meeting and I declined to join, not withstanding that the prime minister himself had invited me to do so. If I had a more inquisitive character and more of a taste for intrigue, then I might have joined them so that at least I could have learnt what went on. But I could not allow myself to get involved, as an ambassador of Jordan, in talks adversely affecting the country.

After the meeting, Muhammad Daoud informed me that he had decided to resign his office, and promised to deposit his resignation letter at my residence by 5pm.

Ahmad Tarawneh, chief of the royal court and a legal authority in his own right, was upset because the resigning prime minister had not, as yet, delivered his resignation in writing. According to the Jordanian constitution, resignations must be submitted in writing, whereupon the king entrusts another political leader with the task of forming a new government. Ahmad Tarawneh was greatly relieved when I handed him Daoud's letter of resignation in the evening.

The meeting of the Arab summit was tumultuous, with heads of state trading calumnies. One accused the other of being hysterical and requiring treatment at a mental infirmary. King Faisal of Saudi Arabia, in an effort to calm the exchanges, said that perhaps all of us needed such treatment. The whole atmosphere was charged, and some heads of state had taken security precautions, with their military aides-de-camp gripping their personal weapons. The conference ended with a number of resolutions, requiring the dispatch of a mediation commission, ceasefire observers and the like.

The heads of state began their return journeys, with President Nasser himself bidding them farewell at Cairo's international airport. The head of state before last to depart was King Hussein. I was standing between the president and the king when Nasser, in what must have been some of his last utterances, said to the king that even prime ministers had a right to resign and to return to their country. Whereupon the king answered that he agreed, and that he had directed me to get in touch with Muhammad Daoud in order to offer him, on behalf of the king, any post that he might wish to take up upon his return. The king also assured President Nasser that Daoud's rights as a citizen, including his pension rights, were completely safeguarded. I promised to communicate this message to Daoud soonest. Regretfully, Muhammad Daoud died a few months later in exile, saddened and ravaged by an ordeal which fate had thrust upon him and for which he had neither the disposition nor the stamina to endure. I regarded him as a good and sincere friend.

I had never seen President Nasser's face so dark and greenish, signalling, perhaps, a blood circulation problem. Normally, he would walk the 15-to-20 metres across the tarmac to his limousine, but on this occasion the car was signalled to move towards where he stood. After bidding the king farewell, the president and the rest of us went home. President Nasser returned to the airport around 3pm to bid farewell to the ruler of Kuwait.

At 5pm I turned on the radio at the residence to hear the news, only to find the station giving non-stop recitations from the Quran. In the Arab and Islamic worlds these readings, at unassigned times, signal the passing away of an important leader, much the same as classical music is played, to the exclusion of other less serious entertainment programmes, in the Western world to mark such occasions. We caught our breath, and telephone calls began pouring in, sensing that something ominous must have happened. A short time later, crowds of Cairenes began filling the streets in a state of uncontrolled shock and sorrow. The bereaved masses improvised slogans, gushing eulogies, and melancholy songs as they bade farewell to their beloved leader. 'O Gamal, beloved of the masses', was the predominant chant.

The next day, all the Arab heads of state who had been in Cairo a mere 24 hours earlier streamed back to participate in the funeral ceremonies. Dignitaries and other heads of state from all over the world also arrived in the capital. Cairenes packed the main thoroughfares, squares and rooftops in their millions. Cairo had a population then of 10 million, and it was estimated that close to 4 million had taken to the streets, in a state of acute agitation. We all feared a breakdown of law and order as we observed scenes of frenzy and uncontrollable emotions, permeating even some of the special forces, who were responsible for the maintenance of security.

King Hussein and his entourage occupied a whole wing at the Nile Hilton in preparation for the funeral. Amidst the excitement and the comings and goings in the hotel, against a background of thunderous howling masses, I looked around, ready to join the king and his entourage, but I could not find them. I was told later that the king and his aides had been whisked away by security agents by boat to the opposite bank of the river, to a relatively secure spot. National delegations marched across the Qasr al-Nil bridge, with the country's flag at the front. The Jordanian delegation consisted of me alone, plus the flag bearer. Three journalists from *al-Ahram*, whom I knew well, saw my predicament. They feared that the pent-up feelings of the crowds against Jordan, instigated by the media and, a few days earlier, by President Nimeiri of Sudan might find expression in mauling the flag and the tiny Jordan delegation. So they rushed over to me and said that they would like to join me in the march, in the hope of affording anonymity as Egyptians. I deeply appreciated their gesture, because mob psychology which, as I mentioned in an earlier chapter, William McDougall analysed so succinctly and ably, could turn into an uncontrollable monster, at the slightest instigation, resulting in collective madness.

The world delegations assembled in front of the building where Nasser's body lay in state, once the headquarters of Egypt's Revolutionary Command Council. When the cortege started, with 60 heads of state and government leading the march, I was next to the former Amir of Kuwait Sabah Salem al-Sabah whom I had befriended when he was foreign minister. I had been the only Arab foreign minister to attend Kuwait's first celebration of independence. It was a hot June summer, and he advised me to stay put with him under a shady tree where we had been standing. He had good advice for me, too, in Cairo on the day of Nasser's funeral. The heads of state walking serenely in the funeral procession, he said, would in a few minutes be scrambling back to safety, lest they be crushed under the weight of the stampeding crowds. He was correct in his prediction. The funeral march descended into chaos, and it fell to the security forces to extricate the VIPs from the menacing crowds.

I remained Jordan's ambassador to Cairo, for a few months during the presidency of Anwar Sadat who, for the historical record, was one of the friendliest, most affable people that I have known. He was polite to the point of shyness, and his character gave no hint that, when he was younger, he was once an army officer and a revolutionary. I had the pleasure of visiting him several times at his homes, on the road to the pyramids and on the Nile in Giza, close to the Jordanian ambassador's residence. His wife, Jihan, an attractive and impressive personality, was a close friend of Qadar. Together with the wives of other Arab ambassadors they would meet frequently for social occasions, and to help with social service projects to which Jihan was dedicated. She had several projects in her name and would enlist the help of Arab ambassadors and their wives, as well as Egyptian socialites, to further their progress. One of the highlights of their joint social activities was attending the monthly performances of the celebrated Egyptian singer Um Kulthum, lasting into the early hours of the morning.

The Jordanian government eventually informed me that it had decided to transfer me to another posting. My wife and I made our round of farewells and gave a farewell party in the garden of the embassy for all our colleagues and friends. I visited President Sadat to bid farewell, and he handed me Egypt's highest award *Wissam al-Jumhurriya*, the medal of the republic, as an expression of appreciation for my efforts to strengthen the ties of friendship between Jordan and Egypt, in spite of the period of chequered relations they had recently experienced. But, more importantly, he gave me rough indications as to the timing of Egypt's plans to recapture the occupied territories. When I returned to Amman, I reported Sadat's conversation with me to Wasfi Tal, who had once again assumed the premiership. Dr Abdul Salam Majali, a minister in Wasfi's government and subsequently prime minister, was present. Both were incredulous of what he had said, and thought that he was merely posturing. When Egypt did, in fact, launch the 1973 war of liberation, they remembered what I had told them and conceded their error in not taking his words seriously.

Back in Jordan, Jordanian-Palestinian relations had suffered a serious battering which impacted on every facet of national life. Politicians and public figures, Jordanian as well as Palestinian, did not emerge unscathed. When the king returned to Cairo for the funeral of President Nasser I felt that he wanted to blurt out some of his pent-up feelings. He said that he wanted to talk to me alone, while resting on his bed suffering palpitations and pain in his heart. He explained that he had been through a great deal over the previous three years: insurgency, violence, insubordination and conspiracies. Above all, he considered that he had been let down by the 'old guard' around him. He felt betrayed and abandoned to fight the battle of survival alone, but for a few of his faithful followers.

At the Nile Hilton Hotel he listened to the chants of the howling crowds below and had heard his name being mentioned: 'Oh Hussein, why did you make Abdul Nasser leave us?' They evidently felt that the Jordanian crisis had exacted an exorbitant price – Nasser's life. In fact, Nasser's health towards the end of his life had become so poor that his doctors had advised him to take a vacation, which he did. But he had decided to interrupt it when the situation exploded in Jordan.

The king walked to the balcony to hear more clearly the words being chanted. He came back inside, only to walk back again as the noise of the crowds became more vociferous and virulent. I was standing with him as he re-entered the suite and said: 'Damn you, Nimeiri, for what you have done.'

The king, reflecting on the difficulties which he had encountered in forming a national government to deal with the insurgency said: 'I looked around for all those politicians to whom I had entrusted responsibility all those years, but they walked away when I needed them most.' The king went on to say that he would never entrust responsibility to them again, and he was as true as his word. It is not fair for me to mention the names of those politicians whom the king had in mind because they are all dead and are in no position to defend themselves. I certainly was not one of them because I was in the diplomatic service and not at home to be put to the test. But my opposition to the violent clampdown, which I had expressed vigorously and loudly, was not outside the purview of the king. My remarks, spiced up, I suspect, had placed a regrettable strain on my close relationship, even friendship, with the king. The previous trust and loyalty did not survive the ordeal of what had been, virtually, a civil war.

I was reassigned to Amman, pending a government decision on a future assignment. The king offered me the ambassadorship to Japan but, challenging as it was, I declined it because of the schooling requirements of my children. Laila, Haitham, Lina, and Khaled were in secondary and primary classes, a critical phase which could only be disrupted at a cost. The king then offered me the ambassadorship to Turkey, and I remember remarking to him in jest: 'Do you want to send me to Turkey to help recreate the glory of the Ottoman Empire?' The king smiled and said: 'Well, take this assignment as an interim vacation for the time being.' Thus, I became Ambassador to Ankara. I sensed in my heart that the king had been disconcerted by my aversion towards the turn of events in Jordan and the military clampdown. I had made no effort to conceal my innermost feelings, and had expressed them in deeds as well as words. I declined to receive at the airport a high-level delegation headed by Saeed al-Mufti, speaker of the Senate (and a former colleague in the cabinet of Samir al-Rifai) which came to Egypt to explain the events in Jordan and dispel the grave misgivings felt in Cairo towards them.

There are not many leaders in the world endowed with the kind of lofty instincts of forbearance, magnanimity and understanding that King Hussein possessed. Some other leader in his position, with a vengeful and rancorous disposition, would probably have placed me on premature retirement, if not worse (in some Middle East countries possibly in jail). But not so King Hussein. He always put himself in the other person's shoes in order to better understand and thereby forgive his behaviour. He knew my feelings pretty well, as a dedicated Palestinian who would not forsake his country of birth and his countrymen. Consequently, the king acted with laudable self-control under the circumstances. A decade later, he restored me to the cabinet of Zeid al-Rifai, with the same staunch support which I had experienced from him in the past.

CHAPTER 13

TURKEY: HOME OF TWO GREAT EMPIRES

Turkey looms large on the map, a huge country of 780,000 square kilometres linking Asia and Europe, not only geographically but culturally as well. It has over 8,000 kilometres of coastline laced with bays. Inland it boasts lakes, year-round summer resorts, and plenty of areas with deep snow. Its 65 million people have undergone far-reaching transformations since the Kemalist revolution of the 1920s and 30s, and more particularly in the post-World War II era, during which they have achieved substantial progress in the development of industry, agriculture and tourism. During the past 25 years alone, the value of Turkey's annual exports rose from a mere $5 billion when I was ambassador there in the early 1970s to around $80 billion in 2005, with the total volume of trade worth $200 billion. The number of tourists has risen from less than 2 million a year to around 20 million. It appears that the only limitation is the speed with which Turkey is able to build sufficient hotel accommodation to house the exponentially expanding tourist inflow.

Turkey has benefited greatly from its close proximity to Europe, where millions of its citizens have had the opportunity to learn the skills of industrialisation at the source, in the factories and plants of Europe. A few million have opted to remain in Europe, while many others have returned to their country of origin, where they participate in all fields of industrialisation. This is modern Turkey which has made great strides towards modernisation and secularism, and is now struggling to deepen its democratic roots at the prompting of the European Union, the membership of which it aspires to attain.

But Turkey also loomed large in the consciousness of my generation which had been nurtured by their parents and grandparents in the ways of Ottomanism, good and bad. With the exception of Morocco, the entire Arab world belonged to the Ottoman Empire as full citizens for four centuries after the fall of Cairo and the transfer of the sultanate to Istanbul in the early 16th century.

My father, as I mentioned earlier, served as director of finance in Jerusalem during World War I. I can cite names of family members – and this applies to other Palestinian families – who served in the Ottoman army, in the Balkans and elsewhere. A first cousin, Umar, was a companion officer with Kemal Ataturk at the ferocious battle to defend the Dardanelles Strait at Gallipoli in 1915-16, in which the British fleet and army were forced to withdraw in defeat having suffered heavy casualties. Winston Churchill lost his job as secretary of the navy as a result.

There was also intermarriage between Arabs and Turks, and other ethnic groups, reflecting the universalism and unity in diversity of the Ottoman Empire. When the British and their allies, commanded by General Edmund Allenby, defeated the Ottoman army and took over Palestine in 1917, they retained many Ottoman customs and administrative practices. They also kept the uniforms of the Palestine police, with the Qalbaq headgear, and the *dunum* as the measurement of land (roughly 1,000 square metres). Furthermore, *Muharram*, the first month in the Muslim calendar, remained the month when the payment of rent on housing and real estate was due. Such matters would arise in the conversations of the retired elders at their daily meetings at the *diwan* of my grandfather in Jerusalem. They talked nostalgically and, more often than not, favourably about their Ottoman era experiences. So I did not take my assignment to Turkey lightly, nor did I feel that I was going to uncharted territory, to a strange land.

Indeed, one of the preoccupations of Arab ambassadors to Turkey was to seek permission from the office of the prime minister to access the voluminous archives of the Ottoman Empire in search of family records, title deeds, and documents throwing light on the history of their home countries. The archive is vast because the empire lasted for more than 400 years covering, at one time, all the territories from Algeria in the west to the Arab Gulf in the east. Historians, including Bernard Lewis and Amnon Cohen, have expressed admiration for the detailed accuracy of Ottoman records, including the population census which was carried out when the Turks occupied Jerusalem in the 16th century. And up to this day, the records preserved at the Shari' a courts in Jerusalem and the rest of Palestine provide the most authoritative reference on the history of the area over five centuries.

But modern-day Turkey to which I was heading was no longer the Ottoman Empire, not only in territorial terms but also, and perhaps this was most relevant to my assignment, in its cultural orientation. Even the Arabic alphabet, in which the vast legacy of Ottomanism was cast, had been changed to the Latin one because Ataturk had wanted a complete break with the past. This meant not only Turkey turning its back on the old bonds which had existed with the Arab and Muslim worlds, but also, no less importantly, the alienation of the Turkish people from their own great historical legacy and culture. This represented a gargantuan cultural separation, with few similar precedents in recorded history.

The Turkish people, nonetheless, are profoundly religious, and they are much more so in the vastness of the countryside than in urban Ankara, Izmir or Istanbul. Islam spread among the Turks primarily through the teachings and practices of mystics and ascetics, the most illustrious of whom was Jalaluddin al-Rumi. The first Islamic Turkish sovereign was Mahmoud of Ghazni, who invaded northern India in the early 11th century. By the end of the century, the Seljuqs had seized control of the Near East and Turkish rule extended to Anatolia. Finally, the Ottomans, taking over from the Seljuqs at the end of the 14th century, spread Islam more widely, and dedicated themselves to enhancing the new empire. It may well be that through an admixture of modernism and a profound religious heritage Turkey will set an example of liberal religiosity which is the real spirit of Islam, as I understand it, and not the Islam of some of the zealots who are unable to free themselves from the narrow-minded accretions that piled up over many centuries of retrogression and lethargy in the Muslim world. Islam is liberal and teaches temperance and moderation. It is also futuristic and advocates movement and creativity in understanding the universe and all that lies within it, terrestrial and cosmic. Islam's forward-looking and scientific spirit, however, is understood only by those who have studied in depth the faith as it was in its pure and simple genesis 15 centuries ago.

After presenting my credentials to the president, I made the established round of protocol visits. Foremost amongst them was to lay a wreath at the mausoleum of Kemal Ataturk with a formal military escort. The mausoleum is located in an imposing plaza, an impressive fusion of architectural design. There is a museum housing a wax statue of Ataturk, along with his writings, letters, artefacts and belongings, as well as photographs recording important moments in his life and that of the republic. Exhibited also is his 1920s Rolls Royce, and his sitting room, with a stand in the middle on which is displayed an open copy of the Quran. I was curious to know which *Sura* and verses of the Quran were displayed. One line caught my eye:

'O children of Israel we have favoured you over all nations.'

Every verse in the Quran is as authentic as any other but must be taken in context. This is a verse which praises the Israeli people when they were scrupulously observing the Torah and their religious commandments. But in another context, when they deviate from its precepts and its true path, they are deplored.

The apparent selectivity in displaying a particular verse in the Holy Book had drawn the attention of the Arab ambassadors, because of question marks regarding the role of *Donmes*, Turkish citizens who had converted to Islam from Judaism, but whose loyalty to their adopted faith was in doubt. Sultan Abdul Hamid, in a carefully calibrated message to one of Konya's celebrated Sufi figures in Turkey, accused them of playing a pivotal role in his dethronement through the revolutionary Young Turks because of his outright rejection of Theodor Herzl's proposal for the establishment of a Jewish national home in Palestine. Whether true or not, contemporary Turks do no more than whisper such suspicions concerning the *Donmes*.

An ambassador of a small country can only play a minor role, commensurate with the weight which his country represents. This is the case particularly when there are no outstanding issues between his country and the one to which he is accredited. At present, with the expansion of globalisation, there surely would be a greater scope for an ambassador's role in promoting commerce and trade, as well as cultural and multilateral exchanges. But in the early 1970s, this was not the case. Turkey was engaged in combating the leftist movements in the labour force, as well as in colleges and universities. The military had been watching such dissident movements closely (particularly with their Kurdish separatist overtones) and did not hesitate on several occasions to overthrow civilian governments because of their failure to abide by and safeguard the ethos of the Kemalist revolution. Islamic overtones were, likewise, closely watched and combated, and Prime Minister Adnan Menderes paid with his life for just such sympathies. He was hanged in 1961 after a military coup the previous year.

The language barrier can also be an impediment. This is not the case in contacts with officials. But they naturally impart their own version of events, to the exclusion of other opinions. Ambassadors of small and medium-sized countries in such situations tend to create their own world, closed social circles which are primarily centred on the diplomatic community. Regular meetings are arranged, including dinners and other social functions. As is only to be expected, news, information and gossip are exchanged, adding to every ambassador's pot of information in reporting to his government. At these social events personages representing various sectors of society, including the opposition, are invited, along with government officials.

Ambassador Samir Shihabi of Saudi Arabia was the *doyen* of the diplomatic corps in Ankara. A versatile diplomat and a member of a prominent Jerusalemite family, he served as Saudi Arabia's ambassador to several countries at times of crises such as Pakistan and Somalia. His last assignment was as permanent representative to the United Nations, where, in 1991, he was president of the General Assembly.

I discovered in my travels that ambassadors of Saudi Arabia have been the *doyens* of the diplomatic corps in a number of different countries. This is because they retain their ambassadors in countries to which they are accredited for long terms of service. Ambassador Hafiz Wahbeh served as his country's ambassador to London for almost 25 years in the first half of the 20th century. But even a sustained service of 10 years is a sufficiently long tenure to gain seniority and thus become *doyen* because the tenure of ambassadors from almost all other countries is a fixed four-year term.

Ankara is a modern, well-planned city which lies in the centre of Anatolia, at an altitude of 850 metres. It was an important cultural and trading centre in Roman times, and was an important trading centre on the caravan route to the east in the Ottoman era. It again became important, when Ataturk chose it as the base from which to direct the war of liberation against the Allies in the aftermath of World War I. In consequence of its role in the war and its strategic position, it was declared the capital of the republic in 1923. It does not have the grandeur or the magnificence of Istanbul, and any comparisons would be invidious. The founders of the modern republic which succeeded the defunct sultanate chose to distance Turkey from Istanbul's heavy, history-laden past, with which the country in general, and the city in particular, had been associated.

But the choice of Ankara, 500 kilometres away, was also a signal of disassociation with all that Istanbul embodies as a former capital of a sprawling Islamic world where the Sublime Porte was the equivalent, in today's parlance, to the White House, Downing Street, the Kremlin and the Elysée Palace. Every mosque, palace and mausoleum is a reminder of that great centrality, with Arabic and Turkish inscriptions in Arabic letters and numerals.

One negative feature of Ankara having been selected as the capital relates to the environment. The city is hemmed in by mountains which trap the air and prevent circulation. This is felt particularly acutely in winter when the temperature dips well below zero centigrade, making life untenable without sustained heating. During my stay in Ankara, coal of low quality was burnt in most houses to obtain heat and energy. Smog and a foul smell would blanket the city. As ambassadors, we met more than once to request our respective governments to grant us two periods of leave per year: the normal summer vacation and hardship leave in winter.

The Turkish government in the 1970s was considering several options to overcome the pollution problem. These included the installation of generating facilities far away from

Ankara, and the piping of gas into the city. In the course of writing these remembrances I visited the Turkish ambassador in Amman who informed me that the problem had been solved decisively by using clean gas for fuel instead of coal. Gas, he explained, was being imported in abundance through several routes: from the Middle East, Russia, Iran and Azerbaijan.

Society in Ankara is fairly liberal, without inhibitions or undue restrictions. Conservative women dress conservatively, covering their heads with scarves, while the more liberal and younger generations wear shorts in the summer. The two groups co-exist, and the decision to belong to one or the other is a personal choice, if not family influenced. What Turkey would, by law, disallow, and rightly so, would be the covering of women's faces. This practice is brutal, constraining and objectionable, and is unrelated to Islam in precepts or practice. Women in the early years of Islam participated in public life and, on occasions, fought side-by-side with men, as in the battle of Uhud in 625, under the command of the Prophet (peace be upon Him).

Ankara boasts a developed educational sector, with high quality colleges and universities, foremost being the Middle East University which excels in scientific and technical education. There are today upwards of 80 universities, and they attract students from Jordan and Palestine. And while on this subject, I am glad to state that in Jordan today there are 22 universities, and more are in the process of being established, while Palestine also has a university in almost every city.

Ankara is also a centre of culture, ancient and modern, and home to the opera, ballet, jazz and modern music, as well as home of the Presidential Symphony Orchestra. But Ankara is dwarfed by Istanbul as the metropolis of art and culture, Turkish and foreign. Istanbul is an exhilarating living museum, predominantly Islamic but with Roman and Byzantine features such as Ayia Sofia, which was originally a basilica but was subsequently turned into a mosque, and is now a museum for visitors to admire.

Istanbul stretches along the two shores of the Bosphorus that links the Sea of Marmara in the south with the Black Sea to the north. It is Turkey's largest city, with a population of close to 15 million. It has expanded exponentially over the past three decades, and is the heart of the economy of Turkey, together with the nearby industrial city of Izmet and other smaller towns. It is beyond the scope of this memoir to detail the magnificence of Istanbul, which we had visited, as a family, and with Subhi and Salwa Dajani and their children, several times in the 1960s.

But I can not ignore the magnificence of Istanbul's ancient palaces: Topkapi, where so many of the treasures of East and West are stored. Here one can see the gifts of foreign sovereigns to the successive sultans, the evolving customs of the rulers, the garment of the Prophet brought from Cairo after the fall of the last Abbasid caliph, along with exquisite Chinese and European tapestry: in short the fabulous legacy of a mighty empire. There are also the breathtaking modern palaces of Dolmabahçe, on the shores of the Bosphorus and Yildiz, residences of the last Ottoman sultans. According to one story, every afternoon beautiful damsels were made to swim in the pool at Yildiz Palace, and the sultan gazed eagerly on the scene before selecting his favourite.

As the Jordanian ambassador and a Jerusalemite, whose country and city had fallen under Israeli occupation a few year earlier, I could not help but feel a sense of quiet frustration, because the scope and volume of work were so limited. I have no doubt that the Turkish people as a whole, judging by conversations I had, are staunch in their emotional attachment to the Palestinian cause and their support for it. They have a particular sensitivity towards Jerusalem, and many went out of their way to express their profound feelings once they knew that I was from the city. The same could be said, I sense, at the government level.

But, and this is an important distinction, Turkey's government and many others feel a sense of helplessness and an inability to influence decision-making concerning the question of Palestine. I might add that even countries the size of Britain, France, Germany or Russia are similarly constrained, because they all desperately want a solution to the Arab-Israeli conflict but, apart from expressions of sympathy, find themselves unable to influence events. The height of the irony is that the superpower itself, the United States, is likewise constrained, by internal forces and pressures and finds substitutes in brave words and diversionary excuses to conceal its paralysis.

Whether in Turkey or subsequently in Rome and elsewhere, I would get the same feedback: the inability to influence events. I would be told that all the cards were in the hands of the United States of America, a frustrating and inhibiting state of affairs.

In the quiet circumstances I found myself in Ankara I read in my spare time a great many books in every field. I remember distinctly reading two novels which were particularly breathtaking: *The Day of the Jackal*, describing the plot hatched by the French-Algerian colonists to assassinate General de Gaulle; and *The Godfather*, describing the ways and world of the Mafia. The books were more thrilling than the movies produced on both.

I also utilised my spare time, to translate into Arabic D C Somervell's abridged version of Arnold J Toynbee's classic *A Study of History*. Somervell's work abbreviates in a most readable way the essence of Toynbee's elaborate 12 volumes on history and historiography. They are, in my opinion, the greatest single contribution to the study of history ever written. I translated almost one third of the book. But when I was transferred to Rome the manuscript was lost on the way, as were many other things. I am glad to say that the book has since been translated by others and published in Arabic.

There are no set rules in Jordan for the term of service of an ambassador, particularly a political, non-career one. I completed less than two years in Turkey, and the same in Italy – this time for political reasons which I shall have occasion to explain in the next chapter. In the meantime, I made my farewell rounds and departed to Amman for reassignment.

CHAPTER 14

Two Sovereign States in One

My next ambassadorial assignment, as I mentioned, was to Rome, this great city, the capital of two sovereign independent states and formerly the capital of the Roman Empire, which contributed to the world a great *corpus* of law, as well as a top-notch model administration. An ambassador to Rome can not be accredited simultaneously to the two sovereign states – the Republic of Italy and the Vatican State. They must be two separate ambassadors. This is in accordance with the concordat concluded between Italy and the Vatican in 1929. However, and this was an additional complication, while Italy had established diplomatic relations with Jordan, the Vatican had declined to do so, for reasons which I shall explain.

Having presented my credentials to the president, I settled down with my wife and children in an ancient villa at Via Casia Antica which, we were told, had once been a resting house for popes travelling from one part of Italy to another.

I received instructions from my government to visit the Vatican and propose the nomination of Ambassador Edmond Rock, a Palestinian leader from the city of Jaffa and formerly an ambassador of Jordan to Italy, for years. He was a distinguished ambassador and a distinguished figure by any standards, and had established a name for himself in both Rome itself and the Vatican. He belonged to the Latin Church, and this fact, my government reckoned, would be an added asset in support of his nomination. In fact, when I was foreign minister in the 1960s he used to get in touch with me by telephone or wireless, complaining that he felt embarrassed because while the Vatican was receiving regular reports from Jerusalem on all kinds of issues, the Jordanian government was keeping him in the dark, even though it was governing Jerusalem. His failure to receive information, he said, rendered him unable to answer the Vatican's questions. This was a failure on the part of the foreign ministry itself because the governors of Jerusalem were always accessible to the representative of the Holy See, and would have answered all requests and demarches with authority and speed.

    I made an appointment to visit Monsignor Agustin Cassarolli, the Vatican's Secretary of State, to present to him the candidacy of Ambassador Edmond Rock, who needed no introduction other than as a formality. When I had done so, Cardinal Cassarolli said the Vatican's relations with Jordan were as close as they could possibly be, adding that the Vatican had deeply appreciated the very warm welcome accorded to His Holiness Pope Paul VI when he visited Amman and Jerusalem in 1964. King Hussein devoted his entire time to checking that the visit was going smoothly and successfully throughout. As minister of the royal court, I was beside the king, together with the president of the Senate and the prime minister, at the steps of the plane carrying the pope. It was one of the coldest winters in years, five to six degrees below zero. And yet, out of respect for the pope, the king and the rest of us waited at the steps without overcoats, scarves or any other winter protection. Stamping on the tarmac was the only instinctive movement to counter the freezing cold. The pope descended, wearing white or off-white woollen clothes which seemed to afford him warmth and comfort in such brutal weather. When the pope was driven in a motorcade to Jerusalem the king was airborne in his helicopter to keep a watch on the convoy. The crowds welcoming the pope in the Old City of Jerusalem were so massive that the danger was from overcrowding and the ever-present threat of a stampede.

Cardinal Cassarolli explained that the Vatican would be more than happy to establish diplomatic relations with Jordan and to accept the accreditation of a Jordanian ambassador. But if the Vatican did that, then Israel would want to have formal relations, too, and this would complicate matters for both of us. I agreed with what he said and informed my government accordingly.

This did not mean that there were no relations or contacts between Jordan and the Vatican. On the contrary, there were regular informal contacts on every problem connected with Jerusalem and the Holy places. My driver would furl the flag on the front side of the embassy car upon entering the Vatican, and unfurl it again when we left.

The most important topic that I raised with the Vatican was its position on the future of Jerusalem. The reason for raising this question, to which I had requested an answer in writing, was to avoid any misunderstanding or breakdown in communication. When the United Nations adopted Resolution 181 on 29 November 1947 it stipulated, as I mentioned earlier, that Jerusalem should be an international *corpus seperatum* for 10 years, subsequent to which the inhabitants of greater Jerusalem would decide its future in a referendum or election. The Vatican was a staunch supporter of the internationalisation of Jerusalem, and this continued to be its position until the occupation of the Arab part of the city in 1967.

King Abdullah I had been against internationalisation, unless it was part and parcel of an overall final settlement, in accordance with Resolution 181. The Israelis were also against the internationalisation of greater Jerusalem, but supported the internationalisation of the Arab sector. What the Israelis had been saying was, effectively: 'What I have is mine, and what you have shall be shared.'

Israel's occupation of Arab Jerusalem created a whole new game. The Israelis were not as scrupulous in observing the existing *status quo* as the Ottomans, the British and, lastly, the Jordanians had been. Many Christian sites and churches, including the Holy Sepulchre, have been desecrated or vandalised at one time or another. Church properties have been sequestrated or bought from corrupt officials. Besides, internationalisation in the late 1940s would have given the predominant share of responsibility to Christian states, many of which would have been Latin American, because most of the rest of the Third World at that time was under different forms of tutelage or colonialism. But after the decade of de-colonisation, in the 1960s and 70s, membership of the world community increased greatly, leaving open the possibility that the choice of a new governor of Jerusalem might well have gone to a country with little religious or spiritual association with the three monotheistic faiths.

The gist of the answer to my question about internationalisation was that the Vatican was not concerned about the final political status of Jerusalem. Its only concern was to safeguard the religious and civil rights of all denominations. This represented a leap backwards towards political disengagement, amounting to indifference.

I forwarded this answer verbatim to my government where it stands on the record. A few years ago, Israel and the Vatican concluded a treaty enumerating the rights and properties of the Latin churches in Palestine, with a view to safeguarding and recognising their sanctity and inviolability. And even though the relations of Jordan, Palestine and other Arab states with the Vatican are close and friendly, and appreciative of its unwavering support for the Palestinian cause, many of us felt that the agreement prejudged and prejudiced the sovereign Palestinians' position *vis-à-vis* the holy places in Palestine. It was felt that it might have been advisable to postpone such a sweeping agreement, pending a final settlement of the Palestine issue, and the Arab-Israeli conflict.

Moreover, the agreement evidently did not take into account the enormous depletion of the Christian communities' presence in the Holy Land. The Christian Arabs of Jerusalem had been a sizeable portion of the inhabitants of the city and a very active constituent of the united Jerusalem during the British mandate. While Christians maintained a relatively sizeable presence in Arab East Jerusalem during the period when the West Bank and the East Bank were united, today is has dropped to a pitiable 4,000 or less, with the depletion ongoing. The Christian presence in West Jerusalem is zero.

There are multiple reasons for the drop in the number of Christians. No-one, if given an alternative, would wish to live under occupation, with all that that entails in the way of closures, curfews, imprisonment, economic strangulation, unemployment and, above all, the lack of a horizon for the future. Many such citizens have migrated to the Americas, Canada and Australia, while many others have settled in Jordan, along with their Muslim compatriots. In Amman and its adjacent townships today there are more than a quarter of a million Jerusalemites, whether from Jerusalem the city, or adjacent semi-urban villages, such as Ein Karem, Malha, Lifta, Rumeima, Kalonia, Eizariya, Tor and Silwan (two quarters of Jerusalem proper since the days of the British mandate), and many other quarters which can be seen on any town planning map of Jerusalem.

What all this means is that we face the prospect of a Jerusalem bereft of a viable Christian community. This would, to all intents and purposes, turn the Christian holy places in Jerusalem into empty museums for visitors and pilgrims, without a vibrant indigenous Christian presence. Perhaps the born-again evangelical movement in the United States will belatedly recognise that its all-out support for Israel, at the expense of the Palestinians, whether Christian or Muslim, is contributing to the extinction of the Christian presence in Jerusalem.

It is a distinct privilege to be afforded the opportunity of serving as ambassador to Rome. It is no exaggeration to state that Italy, by and large, is perhaps one of the most beautiful, exciting and challenging countries in the world. Apart from its physical beauty it also has a vast heritage of culture and history, which go back over two millennia. The Roman Empire ruled such disparate countries as England on the Atlantic and Syria, which included Palestine, Jordan and Lebanon, on the Mediterranean shores. There are as many

Roman remains in greater Syria as in Italy itself. Jerash, in Jordan, is the most complete Roman city in existence, and wherever one excavates there are Roman remains to be found – a water canal, an aqueduct, a road, a coin or a statue. From the era of the Eastern Roman Empire (Byzantium) one can unearth Christian artefacts. It is important to mention here that cultural, political and military exchanges between Rome and the East worked both ways. Syria, for example, gave a good deal to Rome, including four emperors, and its southern province, Hauran, was reputed to have been the granary of the Roman Empire. Greater Syria had a highly advanced civilisation in its own right. Ebla, in northern Syria, testifies to its great Syriac civilisation, and Jerusalem, in the south, was the birth place of Christianity.

There is a small Jordanian community in Italy, mainly students, for whom the embassy provides whatever help is needed. There are also comings and goings of Jordanian merchants and business people, reflecting the robust trading relationship between the two countries. During my tenure in the 1970s, the Arab ambassadors to Italy formed a committee to oversee the construction of a mosque and a cultural centre in Rome. This was considered a massive leap forward in Muslim-Christian relations and certainly without precedent at that time. Saudi Arabia, with its vast oil revenues, particularly after 1973, made a generous contribution towards this project, as did Kuwait and other oil-producing countries. But the financial factor was not the only or even primary one to be carefully considered. The architecture of the project, innately Islamic, had to be attuned to the architectural landscape of Rome. I did not serve long enough in Rome to see the completion of the centre which I hope has satisfied the requirement of harmony in this historic city.

My presence in Rome coincided with the great oil crisis and the embargo which followed the 1973 October War. The Arab oil-producing countries, at the initiation of King Faisal of Saudi Arabia and Sheikh Zayed bin Sultan Al Nahayan of the United Arab Emirates decided on a policy of rewarding countries which were supportive of the Arab cause and penalising those that had adopted a hostile attitude towards it. The Saudi Minister of Petroleum, Zaki al-Yamani, made a visit to Rome as a part of this sifting process, with a view to reporting back to his government on the compliance or otherwise of the various states targeted for the embargo. The Saudi Ambassador to Rome, Ahmad Abdul Jabbar, who had been my classmate at the AUB in the 1940s, gave a reception at the Saudi Embassy in Rome in honour of the visiting minister. Anybody who was anybody in Italy attended the reception, including ministers, public figures, business people, leaders of political parties, journalists and so on. Attending the reception, too, was the Kuwaiti ambassador to Rome. He watched the crowds of guests pushing in every direction and tripping over one another in an effort to reach Minister Yamani and shake hands with him. I was standing with the ambassador who commented with sarcasm: 'Last year, King Faisal of Saudi Arabia himself visited Rome and the visit assumed considerable visibility. The president of Italy gave a reception in honour of the king, and King Faisal wished to reciprocate. A reception was given at the same Saudi embassy, and the highest governmental official attending the reception was the chief of protocol. And now, because of petroleum, everyone in Italy is racing to shake hands with one of King Faisal's lieutenants.'

The duty of an ambassador is not only to conduct diplomatic efforts on behalf of his country but also to report to his government on the multifarious aspects of the country to which he is accredited. There are occasionally some 'extra-curricular' occurrences, meaning events which are beyond the routine. One such event happened during my term of service in Rome. An Arab national said he wanted to meet me urgently. During our meeting he conveyed to me truly frightening and seemingly authentic information about a plot being hatched to assassinate King Hussein. I asked him to write down the details of all the information in his possession, which he readily did. I put the report in a closed and sealed envelope and asked my number two at the embassy, Nayef al-Hadid – later a minister for parliamentary affairs – to take the first plane to Amman and deliver the report to the palace at the highest level because it appeared to be so serious and authentic. Nayef, upon his return, informed me that not even Prince Hassan, the Crown Prince at that time, wished to be the conduit for conveying such ominous news to the king. The report, of course, was given to the competent quarters to be followed up. Regrettably, the planned plot had a Libyan connection. I am talking about the early 1970s, before the world became aware, perhaps too consciously aware, of the phenomenon of international terrorism.

Such pieces of information, in relatively well-staffed, medium-sized and large embassies, are handled by a military or consular attaché. These days I imagine there would be a special section to handle terrorism and counter-terrorism activities. But in scantily-staffed embassies it is the duty of the ambassador and his small team to do what is incumbent upon them to the best of their ability.

Italy is also home to one of the world's most important international bodies, the Food and Agricultural Organization (FAO). Jordan had been an active participant in the work of the organisation, as the source of senior staff members and as the recipient of FAO's assistance to the Palestinian refugees, as well as in upgrading agricultural production in semi-arid areas of Jordan. Senior Jordanian staff or emissaries to the organisation included: Adnan Anabtawi; Dr Yahya Salah, FAO envoy to Egypt; Dr Sami Sunna, former director of Jordan's Agricultural Credit Corporation; and Salah Jumaa, a former Jordanian minister of agriculture. As Arab ambassadors, we had a significant voting weight, and we lobbied hard and successfully for the re-election of Edward Sauma of Lebanon for the post of director of FAO for another term in the 1970s.

Our stay in Rome was a most enjoyable experience, having on our doorstep the city's great treasures belonging to so many eras, from the ruins of the old world, which were continually being unearthed, to those of the medieval period, the Renaissance, the Age of Enlightenment, right up to the present day. Instead of trying to cram everything into a week or two in a mad rush and at great cost, as a tourist or pilgrim usually does, we had the keys of the city, so to speak. We could get to know Rome leisurely and with most expenses paid by the government during the duration of my service. This is what governments are duty-bound to do for their envoys plenipotentiary and ambassadors extraordinary, as the diplomatic jargon still describes an ambassador in the letter of credence that he presents to the head of state of the country to which he is accredited. These pompous descriptions are a relic of the past, when the journey of an ambassador to his destination would take weeks if not months at sea or over land, before the era of aviation.

Many names and places are imprinted in our memories of Rome and the surrounding area: the Coliseum; St Peter's Basilica and other renowned basilicas; Via Veneto's shops and restaurants; Piazza di Spagna, where youths assemble; and Piazza Navona, where talented artists and painters gather; Villa Borghese; Villa d'Este in Tivoli, surrounded by splendid terraced gardens, with fountains, statues and running water. While in Rome we moved the embassy residence to a spacious apartment at Parioli Street, an extremely busy thoroughfare where the whizzing of passing cars never stops. The unending noise can really drive one crazy, and I hope my successors in Rome have installed double-glazed windows to spare themselves and their successors the ordeal of the noise.

My familiarity with Italy and admiration for its breathtaking beauty and eternal heritage pre-dated my ambassadorship in Rome. In April 1950, Qadar and I spent our honeymoon in Austria and Italy, and I remember distinctly our train journey from Rome to Vienna. We looked out on large areas of land that were covered by flood water. I remember, too, the dense forests through which the train passed en route to Vienna.

Fregene beach is a mere half an hour's drive from Rome, and not much further away from the city is Castel Gondolfo, where the pope has his summer residence, looking directly down onto a beautiful lake. Also, in the environs of Rome is Lake Bracciano which surrounded by greenery.

Our honeymoon in 1950 took us to the incomparable city of Venice with the famous and monumental Piazza San Marcos, and the great basilica of San Marcos. As for the

Grand Canal, the beauty of this picturesque and famous waterway highway was captured in song some 50 years ago by Muhammad Abdul Wahab, the legendry Egyptian musician and singer. As soon as we arrived in Venice, at around 5 pm, we hired a gondola to take us for an hour's trip on the canal. It was a bitingly cold day and we were dressed in light clothing as the weather was spring-like in Jerusalem when we left. I communicated by word and gesture with the boatman, asking him to take us back to the shore, but he pretended not to understand. I offered to pay him double the agreed fare if he would cut the trip short, but to no avail. Finally, when he had completed the two-hour punishing cruise and returned us to shore I made a point of penalising him by paying for only one hour in consideration of the pain which his greed had inflicted on my stomach.

On several of our journeys across Italy we visited Milan, Bologna, the Isle of Capri, and Pisa with its leaning tower, about which we had learnt in childhood, regarding it as one of the Seven Wonders of the World. We also visited Naples and Florence, the latter rich in great monuments, including the famous Duomo (cathedral), Renaissance churches, and works by Michelangelo. We went to Como, on the shores of Lake Como, and several other cities and lakes in northern Italy, the names of which escape me. We visited Trieste, this cosmopolitan port city on the borders of former Yugoslavia, and Padua to the west of Venice with its academic tradition and universities. We travelled in our Mercedes towards this seaside city of Rimini on the Adriatic for two hours. At a crossroads we turned west, unthinkingly in the hope of reaching our desired destination. As a Jerusalemite, my orientation is that a coastal city must lie in a westerly direction from me, whether it be Jaffa,

Tel Aviv, Haifa, Gaza or Acre. This is where the Mediterranean Sea is, and so is Rome. But it had not occurred to me that the sea could lie in an easterly direction, which is the case with the Adriatic Sea. After driving for 10 minutes we realised that we were heading the wrong way, so changed course.

During my time in Italy in the diplomatic corps, the Sicily Chamber of Commerce invited the Arab ambassadors to Italy and the Vatican and their spouses to Palermo as guests of the city. Sicily is the largest island in the Mediterranean, separated from the mainland peninsula by the straits of Messina. The flight was bumpy as we came into land at Palermo. We were then taken by bus to a comfortable hotel in the centre of the city. As an amateur farmer, owning a citrus plantation in Kafrein in the Jordan Valley, I was highly impressed by the substantial citrus plantations which bordered the road. The citrus trees were dark green and healthy, attesting to good care and plenitude of irrigation water.

During this era, the 1970s, there was a good deal of talk and writings in the press about the power of the Mafia, its extensive and ubiquitous network, and its involvement in the murder of Italy's renowned and popular Prime Minister Aldo Moro. But the ambassadors assured themselves in jest that if the Mafia was so powerful then the government of Sicily would not have dared to invite us without their blessing. Therefore, we agreed, we must be in safe hands, which was indeed the case. We did not need escort – we were simply guests and tourists.

One of the highlights of the visit was to discover Sicily's Arab connection. The Arab era was described by one publication as the island's golden age. It states *inter alia*: 'Palermo is of Punic foundation, though it owes its name to the Greeks.' It adds: 'During the Island's period of Arab domination (9th-11th century)', when Sicily was transformed into the 'garden of the Mediterranean', Palermo became 'the most beautiful, the most prosperous of the entire known world. Traces of this golden age can still be found in modern-day Palermo in the particular pattern of the streets, in its historic centre and, is several of its buildings which, though erected long after the Norman conquest (1072), are still of evidently Arab influence.' Some chapels were built over Arab castles.

Taormina stands out as uniquely enchanting. The Arab ambassadors and their wives were crowded into a long coach and driven to this elevated location, with an historic market place right at top that reminded me of our old *suqs* in Jerusalem, Damascus, Cairo, Tunisia, Algeria and Morocco. The road was narrow and the climb was arduous, long and grinding, with constant changes of gear, to take the coach and it passengers higher and higher to the peak. We were all holding our breath because our safety was contingent on the power of the engine and the steadfastness of the brakes until the coach reached the top, around the last bend. This was a treacherous and very tight bend, with no way back. Although the driver was skilful, he did not succeed in getting the coach around the bend, and slammed on the brakes. There we were, dangling at this high altitude on a narrow, meandering road, waiting anxiously to see how the driver would deliver us from this scary suspense. The wives of the ambassadors suddenly screamed with one voice while we, the ambassadors, not supposed to show fright, confined ourselves to sweating it out. Finally, the driver, having chosen the right gear and the right angle on the road got the coach to the top. For an hour or so we strolled in the glittering, clean market. It is one to remember. We re-boarded the coach which started its descent slowly but surely. I remember remarking that long vehicles should never be used for such a narrow, steep and meandering ascent.

Italy's rich heritage and its exhilarating beauty are such that, only an expert in many fields could describe it adequately. My bird's-eye-view remarks and observations are simply remembrances – fleeting ones at that – because I did not record my impressions in any meaningful way at the time, so I may have overlooked some important points.

Aware, perhaps, that my mission in Rome, and previously in Ankara, did not fully occupy my time, my government in the first half of the 1970s would assign me to the Jordanian delegations attending the annual sessions of the General Assembly between September to November each year. My special task during those sessions was to represent the Jordanian and the Palestinian viewpoints on the many facets of the on-going question of Palestine, the oldest and the most inscrutable item on the agenda of the United Nations.

Knowing the ins and outs of this question, in the course of my services as permanent ambassador in 1976-82 I took many initiatives pertaining to it which I shall have occasion to narrate. But before this, in 1973, out of the blue, I drafted a General Assembly resolution to bring back to life the defunct UN Palestine Conciliation Commission which had attempted to solve the Palestine problem, on the basis of partition Resolution 181, and had almost succeeded in doing so. The protocol of Lausanne, which was initialled by both parties in 1949, lapsed because Israeli Prime Minister Ben-Gurion refused to endorse it.

A member of the US delegation asked why I wanted to recreate this commission, consisting of the United States,

France and Turkey. Because, I answered, the commission was the only entity empowered to act on the basis of the records, the title-deed and the dispositions which had been duly ordered and catalogued by the British mandatory government, and handed over to the custody of the United Nations, pending a resolution or settlement of the rights and outstanding issues relating to the Palestinian refugees. Few people had been aware of this dimension, and the resolution seemed innocuous enough, passing without argument or opposition. We asked that the commission should release these records to the quarters concerned. Two years later, in 1975, as I mentioned in an earlier chapter, I accompanied Ambassador Abdul Hamid Sharaf, permanent delegate to United Nations headquarters where we obtained a microfilm copies of all the records relating to land and property.

In addition to attending United Nations plenary sessions, I had the privilege of being present at Arab summit meetings, as part of the Jordanian delegation, and other international gatherings, such as Third World conferences and meetings of the Non-Aligned states. I would like to mention, in particular, one such summit meeting held in Algiers in November 1973, in the aftermath of the October War. I mention this summit because it represented a seismic change to the question of Palestine, with far-reaching ramifications for Jordan and Palestine alike.

There was a euphoric atmosphere at the summit because of what the Arab world regarded as catharsis, the settling of scores with Israel after the 1967 catastrophic humiliation. The triumph may not have been complete (thanks to the US's massive assistance to Israel) but still it had demonstrated Arab unity and resolve, as well as mastery in handling the tools of modern electronic warfare.

Prior to the meeting of the heads of state, the foreign ministers of the 22 Arab states, under the chairmanship of Abdul Aziz Bouteflika, foreign minister of Algeria, held preliminary talks. The purpose was to draw up an agenda for the summit, and prepare all the relevant draft resolutions. Jordan was represented by Abdul Munim al-Rifai, one of the most accomplished diplomats worldwide and a renowned figure in the halls of the United Nations. He was foreign minister at the said meeting, and I was sitting next to him when a proposal was tabled which stipulated that the PLO should be the sole representative of the Palestinian people. The proposal did not come as a total surprise, except in its sweeping assertion about the PLO's monolithic representation of the Palestinian people, to the exclusion of everyone else.

Considering that at least half the population of Jordan were Palestinians, and taking into account that Jerusalem and the rest of the West Bank were legally Jordanian occupied territories, on whose behalf the Security Council had passed Resolutions 242 and 338 ordering an Israeli withdrawal, Minister al-Rifai intervened in the discussion. He suggested that the PLO be designated the representative of the Palestinian people but not the 'sole' representative. Minister al-Rifai was silenced by his fellow ministers and accused of not knowing about or caring for the Palestinian cause. This wild accusation was made by ministers including Sheikh Sabah Ahmad al-Sabah, a wise and a most versatile foreign minister of Kuwait and a close friend of Minister al-Rifai. But, as I was to discover, even foreign ministers can sometimes, under certain circumstances, be stampeded into acting emotionally and irrationally at meetings. The Arab foreign ministers knew perfectly well that Minister al-Rifai had devoted his entire career to the service of the Palestinian cause. Indeed, as an outstanding poet, he had devoted a great deal of his poetry to the cause, and the lyrics of some of the foremost Palestinian nationalist songs were written by him. And, needless to say, he is a Palestinian himself.

The foreign ministers then decided to set up a subcommittee to draw up a draft resolution in this regard. Four countries were selected for the committee, together with Sayyid Noufal, the Arab League's Assistant Secretary-General. He was adept at drafting resolutions after seeing which way the wind was blowing, thus offering the most appropriate one in the circumstances. Although Jordan was deliberately excluded from membership of this committee, Minister al-Rifai urged me to try and influence the drafting of the resolution, in light of Jordan's reservations. I went straight to where the committee was working and reiterated to them Jordan's position. Representing the PLO at the committee was Said Kamal, a close family friend from Nablus and PLO representative to Cairo. He whispered to me not to waste my time and energy because, he confided to me, Egyptian intelligence was behind the adoption of the resolution, that ended my intervention.

The 'heroes' at the Algiers conference were Egypt and Syria, the major combatants in the war. Other Arab countries had made subsidiary but vital contributions: Jordan, its best mechanised brigade; Iraq, two divisions; Morocco, Algeria and other Arab countries, aircraft and small fighting units, but mostly towards the defence of Damascus, the capital. Jordan had not been consulted or briefed on the timing of the war and, therefore, could not be blamed for not participating. In hindsight, such participation would have involved untenable risks and might have ended badly, considering the final turn of events. But, as a non-participant on its own front, it stood vulnerable and politically disadvantaged at the summit. The result was the assignment of responsibility for the West Bank to the PLO, unwise as this may have been.

The following year, another Arab summit conference was held in Rabat, the capital of Morocco. I was not invited by my government to attend, but its overall ramifications impacted on me, both as a citizen of Jerusalem and as an ambassador of Jordan in Rome. King Hussein delivered to the conference a long, 25-page statement, one of the best-reasoned that he ever made from both the political and legal aspects.

The king outlined in definitive and crystal-clear terms the consequences which were bound to flow from withdrawing responsibility for the occupied territories from Jordan and assigning it prematurely to the PLO which had not, at that time, evolved into an internationally recognised political entity. He told the summit that such a step would create a legal void in the West Bank which could only be to the benefit of Israel. He asserted that the proposed re-assignment would turn the West Bank from an occupied territory to one disputed between the Palestinians and Israelis, and would thus undermine the potency of Security Council Resolution 242.

The Arab heads of state and government were, however, in no mood to listen to any reasoning, and were bent on pursuing this course of action, come what may. And if this were not enough, the king was subjected to a barrage of innuendos against Jordan and its role in the question of Palestine. The king returned to Amman anguished and bitterly angry. He wanted to show his colleagues, the Arab heads of state, what their decision would mean on the ground: a policy of de-politicisation in all walks of life, both in the West Bank as well as the East Bank. In the long run, if pursued, it was nothing less than withdrawing inalienable rights, privileges and duties from a major segment of the population.

It was 7.30am Rome time when the telephone rang in my residence. Speaking at the other end from Jerusalem was my youngest brother, Muhammad, who had been chief engineer for the West Bank until its fall in 1967. He offered me congratulations. I asked for what. He said I had been transferred back to Amman. I told him that I had not been informed. Muhammad said he had heard the news on the radio and television in Amman. This was not the first time, nor would it be the last, that I was to hear first via the media about my transfer, retirement or dismissal, rather than from the competent government quarter, before it became public knowledge. It is a faulty practice of which many governments stand guilty, and for which there is no excuse. Together with my name, was the name of Akram Zuaiter, a renowned Palestinian leader and a highly gifted orator, who had succeeded me as minister of foreign affairs in 1966, and who was serving as Jordan's ambassador to Lebanon. The powers-that-be in Amman wanted to send a message to the other Arab states to the effect that releasing Jordan from responsibility for the West Bank carried with it consequences that would affect an entire people. The choice of Akram Zuaiter and me in the first batch to be withdrawn was not personal, nor was it motivated by any ill-will. To the contrary, both of us had served loyally as ministers of the royal court, as well as ministers for foreign affairs. But it was precisely because we were Palestinian Jordanian public figures of renown that we had been chosen as scapegoats in this wretched conflict. I was requested to return promptly, but I needed a week or two to make essential arrangements, including placing my daughter, Lina, and my son, Khaled, who had been at American and British schools respectively in Rome, at alternative schools.

I took the first plane to London where, with the assistance of the embassy, I placed my son, Khaled, at a public school, Dover College in southern England. We took Khaled and his two heavy pieces of luggage literally to the door of the headmaster and left him. Upon my return to Amman, I placed my daughter, Lina, at the AUB, my own *alma mater*. Unfortunately a ferocious civil war broke out in Lebanon in 1975 which lasted for almost 15 years. Russian-made Grad rockets and other missile started falling on the campus or whistling over it. Lina barely completed the first year when the security situation in Beirut deteriorated to the point where her personal safety became the overriding consideration. We brought her back to Amman and, soon afterwards, I was offered the post of permanent delegate to the United Nations, in the heart of New York. Lina enrolled at New York University where she earned a BA and an MA.

A return to base invariably involves problems of adjustment, including finding a suitable house to live in. Our villa had been leased to the United States Embassy and, according to Jordanian Law, a tenant is protected, so it is not permissible or easy to retrieve a house, save with the consent of the tenant. I, therefore, rented a house, at the fifth circle in Jabal Amman and gradually settled down.

I had been retired more than once, in the whirlwind of shifting cabinets, but I never taken my retirement seriously, considering that my energies and mental capacities were still flourishing. But the problem with attaining the prestigious post of a cabinet minister, at a relatively early age, is that it deprives its holder of accepting lesser jobs in the prevalent social scale of values, even though they could be equally stimulating and rewarding. For example, in government service one cannot, after serving as a minister, accept the post of undersecretary which has greater permanence. It is just not done, for it very much smacks of demotion, which is always debilitating and demoralising.

This could well be a universally accepted norm, but it is a more particularly Arab characteristic. Arabs are strongly imbued with the culture of shame, which denigrates anything that detracts from what is conceived to be a person's dignity. There is an aversion, for example, to manual labour in specific areas in one's own country or society. But the same person would not mind doing a similar manual job if he were in Europe or the United States where nobody would recognise him.

In any event, my retreat into temporary retirement took me to the 400 *dunum* (100 acre) citrus and banana farm which I had started in 1959 in the Jordan Valley, about half an hour's drive from Amman. I do not know how I stumbled into this intractable, obdurate, highly enticing, but also highly demanding field. During a social evening back in the late 1950s, a friend of mine, Hisham Abdul Hadi, spoke fervently about a citrus farm which his father owned in the Jenin area of Palestine. This evoked in my mind childhood memories of a 1,000-*dunum* (250-acre) citrus farm that my grandfather on the maternal side, Jawdat Nashashibi, had owned in central Palestine, at a place called Mkalkha, near Wadi al-Sarar, a railway station between Jerusalem and Jaffa on the main Palestine-Egypt international railway line.

Once a week my grandfather's household would be busily immersed in the preparation of some of the most delicious Arabic dishes, including stuffed sheep and chicken, *kubeibet Arab*, a dish that is well known in the Jerusalem-Abu Ghosh area. It consists of round balls of minced meat, almost the size of a tennis ball, stuffed with ground meat, rice and walnuts, all cooked in onion sauce (like French onion soup, but not as thick), with rice on the side and yoghurt. This food was produced in abundance and was enough to last for a whole week. It would be placed in special saddles, to be ferried on horseback a few kilometres between the local railway junction and the farm at Mkalkha, close to Latroun in central Palestine. At the station to welcome my grandfather would be Abu al-'Abed of Moroccan origin, supervisor of the citrus farm and two assistant labourers. My grandfather would inspect the farm, spend a night at a small house built at an elevated spot called the *baydar* (threshing field), and the labourers at the farm would enjoy a sumptuous dinner as they told him about their work.

My grandmother, Um Umar, from Abu Ghosh, a few kilometres west of Jerusalem, was an expert in cooking, as is the tradition and reputation of the town. For centuries, the Abu Ghosh clans controlled the lands, villages and roads between Jerusalem and Jaffa, as Western travelers and consular officers have narrated. Most of the Abu Ghosh families have managed to remain in what became Israel. Thanks to the astuteness of their elders, they did not panic and join the ranks of their fellow Palestinian refugees.

My grandfather's house was the building that today is the American Consulate in East Jerusalem. He had to sell the house in the mid-1940s to cover losses incurred at the farm during World War II. As my generation knows the export of citrus to Britain and the rest of Europe ceased because of the war, with priority given to transporting war materials and other vital goods connected with the war effort. Managing such prioritisation was a Middle East Supply Council, and citrus was at the bottom of priorities. A sack of 25 kilos of select Jaffa oranges would sell along the roads in Palestine for a shilling or so, and losses of citrus groves were massive. The Director of Supply, G Walsh, was, as mentioned previously, one of those killed in the King David Hotel bombing in July 1946.

But everything has a price, including, of course, exquisite and delicious food. When I remember the long hours which my grandmother spent – albeit with servants – at a special kitchen in a corner of the garden, I feel strongly the injustice which she suffered. The cooking included even making from scratch the thin palette sheets of *goulash* and *kinafeh*, famous Arab sweets, all the way to the ready-to-eat stage. Added to this burden was my grandfather's predilection, to invite others to have dinner with him, as often as he could and with total disregard for the additional work and expense involved.

This immersion in the kitchen would not be tolerable in our contemporary societies and I could never imagine asking my wife to spend so many hours there. Even if I did, she would most certainly refuse, and rightly so. And for what? That food was truly delicious but this was largely because of the careless addition of edible fats and other unhealthy ingredients. Health consciousness, in addition to women's liberation, has delivered our womanhood from virtual servitude.

After 45 years of prosperous agriculture, and great fun practising it, I arrived at a parting of the ways for reasons beyond my control, foremost of which has been a serious draw-down in the water level from which I had been pumping my irrigation water, and at great cost. Salinity has also increased dramatically in the aquifers feeding the area of my farm, thus precluding banana planting which is the most lucrative, and degrading the quality of my citrus production. I have had to reduce the citrus farm by three-quarters and to stop, altogether, banana planting. But as an old-timer in farming, and a virtual addict, I cannot simply walk away. I have, therefore, embarked on a programme of replacing the entire farm with palm trees of top quality, which grow extremely well in the Jordan Valley. They endure salinity and their water requirement is containable. Already the farm is producing two varieties in commercial quantities: the Majoul and the Barhi. In the meantime, I have to drill deeper and deeper to get to a sustainable water supply, without which no farming can possibly survive, let alone prosper.

CHAPTER 15

FROM BINATIONAL TO MULTINATIONAL: THE GAME OF NATIONS

It was on a hot July afternoon that Ambassador Abdul Hamid Sharaf, former colleague and close friend, contacted me to tell me that *Sayyidna* [the King] was offering me the post of permanent Delegate of Jordan to the United Nations. I had been offered this post before, but because of family considerations (primarily schooling at critical junctures) I could not accept. Since my return from Rome, I had settled down reasonably well in Amman, and a highlight was the marriage of my eldest daughter, Laila, to my nephew, Zaki, in a ceremony which King Hussein was intending to attend in person, but could not at the last minute for overriding reasons. But he kindly delegated the Chief of the Royal Court, Mudhar Badran, to attend and to present on his behalf a precious wedding gift. King Hussein always regarded the citizens of Jordan as his own extended family, and met its exacting obligations meticulously. He would visit the sick, pay condolences to the family of the bereaved, attend wedding ceremonies of those around him in the service of the country and the state, and carry out many other related functions. Amman's population today is close to

2 million, and urbanisation has reached advanced levels which, perhaps, will weaken but not eradicate the close, neighbourly, easygoing paternal social system which had existed hitherto during his era.

Anyway, I was still in my early fifties, at the peak of my mental as well as physical energies, and grossly under-worked. My citrus farm was functioning smoothly and efficiently and did not require from me more than cursory attention. The occasional writing and lecturing I undertook were not sustained or structured, and I was far from being fully engaged. So, I accepted the offer conveyed by Ambassador Sharaf, promptly and without hesitation. My answer had to be quick because I would be replacing Ambassador Sharaf himself who was being transferred to Amman to serve as chief of the royal court. He subsequently became prime minister.

I made the necessary disengagements and arrangements in Amman, and was ready to leave in mid-August for New York to prepare for the heavy duties which every mission to the UN must undertake in preparation for the opening of a new session of the General Assembly. I was by no means venturing into uncharted territory, and my association with the work of the United Nations, in its manifold fields, had already been extensive. The association started with the Jordan-Israeli Mixed Armistice Commission in 1955-56. I then had close links with UNRWA in my capacity in 1957-59 as undersecretary of the Ministry of Reconstruction and Development, in charge of the affairs of the Palestinian refugees in Jordan. I was also the Jordanian representative to the UNRWA advisory council, consisting of representatives of donor countries as well as the host countries, Jordan, Egypt, Syria and Lebanon, at the ambassadorial level, and headquartered in Beirut. After that I was alternate governor of Jordan at the World Bank's annual meetings in 1959-60; and from 1962 to 1966 I served as foreign minister of Jordan, leading the country's delegation to the annual sessions of the General Assembly. And over and above these assignments, my government had delegated me to assist the Jordan delegations to the UN annual sessions in New York almost every year during the 1970s, up to 1976 when I became permanent ambassador to the UN. Indeed, I regarded the UN as my own turf.

Looking back, I have no hesitation in stating that it was the pinnacle of my diplomatic career, after which there could be no promotion. It was not an ambassadorship to one country, no matter how important that country may have been, but to the world community at large, represented during my term of duty by 150 states, but incessantly visualising and striving for universality. Today, the UN membership has reached 192, but to the international community's unforgivable shame; it has not accepted Palestine as a sovereign state, equal to others. This issue of Palestine, in its multiple manifestations, was to take up most of my time and energies for seven consecutive years, up to the end of 1982 when I was relocated to Amman.

The Jordan government had purchased a five-storey house at 126 East 72nd Street between Lexington and Park Avenue. The government should be grateful to Ambassador and Mrs Laila Sharaf, a prominent feminist and public affairs leader, for purchasing this sumptuous residence in the early 1970s at one of the best locations in New York for a very good price in the range of $0.75 million. At a social gathering, a vice president of City Bank approached me to pass on his thanks to the Jordanian government because the latter had paid the last instalment on the purchase of the residence. He said the bank would be glad to oblige on any other deal. This residence today must be worth millions of dollars.

The weeks leading up to the opening of a new session are extremely hectic. Quite apart from the heavy load of substantive work on the agenda, there is a heavy social programme. Just to give a feel of things at the social level, suffice it for me to say that every head of state, prime minister and foreign minister attending the session would want to give at least two-to-three parties – luncheons, dinners, or receptions – during his short sojourn in New York, averaging a couple of weeks. Even with the 150 member states in the mid-1970s, one can well imagine the jigsaw puzzle of sorting out, coordinating, and prioritizing literally hundreds of elegantly printed invitation cards requiring RSVP. This stage was reached after a mission, all missions, had secured attendance of invited guests to its own head of delegation parties. In the circumstances, some of these invitations have to be shared by the staffs of the missions – the ambassador and his principal aids.

In addition, the UN institution itself must also offer hospitality to its attending guests, and particularly at the level of head of state. The secretary-general usually gives a luncheon in honour of the head of state, at which cordial speeches are exchanged. A major party is given, in tandem, by the president of the General Assembly, and the president of the Security Council for the month of October at which all VIPs are invited. In October 1982, I was, by rotation, president of the Security Council and was seated at the elevated head table, reserved for the president of the Assembly, the president of the Security Council and the secretary-general, with scores of renowned foreign ministers, squeezed onto parallel tables below. Such is the power of protocol which is impersonal and tolerates no breach of its stringent rules. The notable exception was General Carlos P Rumolo of the Philippines, one of the founders of the UN, who persisted in showing up at every session, even while out of any office. He was given a place of honour next to the president. But anyone who is egotistic must swallow his pride. Another major reception is given annually at a revamped Delegates' Lounge by the president of the Assembly and the secretary-general.

The United Nations is, in word as well as in deed, second to none in its embrace of democratic ideals and practices. The charter speaks of equality of states, and I must testify that perhaps nowhere else can one witness democracy in action as at the UN. I am fully aware that some states are more equal than others; I am equally aware that the Security Council is inherently constituted, and realistically so, on the basis of recognising power, according the veto power to the five permanent members, with the potential for the number to increase. But democracy is manifestly present, even in the corridors of this supreme executive organ of the United Nations.

I have served on the Security Council as the representative of Jordan, the Arab group and the much larger Asian group, and on many occasions was able to get through the adoption of decisions, notwithstanding the displeasure of one major power or another. The United States often found itself isolated and in the uncomfortable position of choosing between exercising its veto power, unpopular and unethical as this was, or of letting a decision pass by a majority of 13 to 14 votes, with none against, and its own abstention.

But of no less importance are the manner and the methodology by which decisions are formulated, and repeatedly amended, even the minutest wordings and details. Behind closed doors, the draft resolution is circulated amongst the 15 members of the Council, subsequent to which every member state has a chance to make comments, suggest amendments or express reservations. The process is carried out in an informal, friendly, but business-like manner. The ambassadors of the major powers are in close liaison with their governments (some, more than others) on the minutest details, while the ambassadors of small and medium-sized countries exercise greater leeway.

But the main referral would be with the group or the area on whose behalf the member state was serving on the Security Council. In my own case, the initial liaison was with Zuhdi Tarazi, a fellow Jerusalemite and representative of the PLO to the United Nations. The PLO had only observer status but was the quarter most directly concerned, as representative of the Palestinian people. The next reference would be the Arab group, to which Jordan belongs. And finally, the group of the Non-Aligned countries representing 120 states, whose representatives at the council garner over six seats, from Asia, Africa and Latin America.

But there was an even greater manifestation of genuine democracy in the halls, corridors and lounges of the General Assembly, where the mighty and the weak, the big and the small, meet in conditions of natural, unaffected comradeship. Where else would one see the foreign minister of a major power chatting nonchalantly with his counterpart from a small country in some tiny corner of the Assembly's lounges over a cup of coffee, a lemonade, a beer or something even stronger, and concluding agreements without cumbersome visits to each other's country? There are no guards of honour, no national anthems, no constraining protocols, simply human-to-human contact and understanding. How many opportunities does an ambassador of a small country have to meet the foreign minister of the country to which he is accredited in normal circumstances? And yet here at the United Nations he is sought after eagerly, not least because his vote is equal to the vote of the high and the mighty in all matters on the UN agenda.

Not only is there manifest democracy but there is also a clear and staunch adherence to the principles of the charter and the norms of morality and justice. It is almost a collective will, natural and spontaneous, which reads through the lines and can clearly discern the right from the wrong in any issue. At every session there were scores of resolutions supporting the Palestinian cause, with overwhelming majorities. This was not because the Palestinians and their supporters had any lobbying clout, but simply because the world community, almost as one, recognised that the Palestinians were the underdog in the game of nations, and that their land had been cannibalised beyond recognition. Their detractors at the United Nations misread this universal support, calling it a mechanical majority. In fact, it radiated the fundamental goodness of men and women from various regions of the world, and their natural urge to redress a terrible wrong, to the best of their ability.

Although a relative newcomer, being in existence for a mere six decades, the United Nations has accumulated a body of traditions and practices, such as who speaks when at the opening of the session. The president of Brazil has traditionally been accorded the honour of being the first speaker, after the inaugural speech of the newly elected president of the Assembly, followed by the annual comprehensive report by the secretary-general on the major issues facing the world.

The president of the United States is the main speaker on the second day, and the first week or two are crowded with the speeches mainly of major powers, interlaced with those from energetic smaller countries, whose missions had learnt the rules of the game and had acted in accordance with them. There is no seniority system, nor is there an alphabetical order, to determine the list of speakers. Again democracy and equality of states reign supreme. Early in the morning of a specified date, according to an established schedule, an officer of the United Nations registers the names of states wishing to speak on a first-come-first-served basis. In preparing for one of those sessions I was informed that Crown Prince Hassan wished to address the General Assembly on behalf of Jordan. Knowing the diminished attendance of delegations at the hall of the Assembly after the first week or two, I decided to ensure that Prince Hassan would be among the earliest speakers. To do that, I instructed one of our local employees, Joe, a Philippine national, to go to where registration takes place in the early hours of the morning and stay there at the head of the line to register first. This is what he did and he was the first to register. This translated into Prince Hassan being the first speaker on one of the first three days in the general debate. The timing impinged on the customary turn of the Soviet Foreign Minister, Andrei Gromyko. The Soviet mission contacted me requesting a rescheduling; but I politely declined and the crown prince gave his speech on schedule.

    As the general debate winds up it attracts smaller and smaller attendance because of the lengthy, tediously long and repetitive speeches by most delegations – and the smaller the country, the longer the speech. When the debate is finally over, the substantive work of the Assembly begins in earnest, at five plenary committees, plus a special committee for perennial topics which include the question of Palestinian refugees. The assembly elects the chairman and vice-chairman of the committees early on in its procedural and organisational work, and states compete vigorously to get their candidates elected. I might mention in passing that before the advent of simultaneous translations, speeches, at least at the Security Council, had to be read aloud in the official languages, English, French, Russian, Spanish, and Chinese. One can well imagine the sheer boredom which must have afflicted all present, waiting until a speech had been read out loud in all those languages.

The question of recognising Arabic as one of the official languages of the Security Council had been floated several times prior to the 1970s, the first being during 1946, the founding year of the United Nations. But efforts to have Arabic recognised failed on technical grounds, such as the lack of availability of an extra translator's booth. When I became president of the Security Council, in October 1982, I had excellent relations with my colleagues there, so I decided that perhaps the time had come for it to act decisively on this issue. After brief consultations, I tabled a draft resolution to recognise Arabic as one of the official languages of the council. The council unanimously adopted the resolution, and I feel proud to have been instrumental in fulfilling this long-standing longing of the Arab and Islamic worlds to secure the international community's recognition of this great and ancient language. For we must not forget that our area of civilisation had given the world its greatest gift: the alphabet.

The agenda of every General Assembly session is loaded with items widely ranging from general disarmament (the first committee) to one whose intricacy I have never fully comprehended entitled 'outer-space and its proper uses' (special political committee). In between, are perennial but important economic and social issues (second and third committees), budgetary and legal issues (fourth committee) and the winding-up of the relics of a trusteeship system, bequeathed by the League of Nations to its successor, the UN, but which has lost much of its resonance and its *raison d'être* by massive, if not universal, decolonisation. Every delegation has highly qualified delegates to represent it on these committees, and the decisions of each are referred to a plenary meeting of the General Assembly for ratification.

These activities represent the international community's involvement in the social, economic and moral progress of its member states and many, if not all, of the decisions are eventually incorporated into the national legislation of every country. These efforts are aided by semi-autonomous institutions such as the Social and Economic Council, the High Commission for Human Rights, and the numerous other 'interventionist' activities of the United Nations. When a draft resolution was tabled at the General Assembly in the late 1970s for the creation of the post of high commissioner for human rights, the group of Arab states indicated that it would reject the resolution on the grounds that it could be used for interference in the affairs of member states. I dissented from the Arab group and am proud to state that I voted for the creation of this post. I was inspired by a higher moral imperative and a concern for human life and dignity, even if this were to lead to interference in the internal affairs of other states. There was a moral plateau that was higher than strict self-contained sovereignty, within whose bounds human degradation might occur, beyond the watchful eye and conscience of the world. I am happy to record that today almost all states recognise the importance of this watchful eye, aided and abetted by national chapters on human rights, whose mere existence should act as a deterrent against inhuman behaviour, from whatever source. It is these positive activities and institutions which constitute the ramparts of a world order anchored in humanity and justice. When the League of Nations ceased to exist after the outbreak of World War II, what remained were institutions like the International Labour Organization (ILO), which looks after the welfare of the working class throughout the world, regardless of country, race or political regimes.

There are occasional special sessions of the General Assembly to deal with particular issues that become part of an ever-evolving body of international law. A case in point was a succession of meetings in the 1970s over the Convention on the Law of the Sea, in which I participated. There are special sessions on disarmament, children's rights, the environment and many other worthy causes which have their countervailing pressure groups, represented by myriads of non-governmental organisations which constitute effective lobbies and power centres, supportive of these causes, in every civil society in the world.

There was a world movement, in the early 1950s of the last century, clamouring for the reconstitution of a world government (there are still remnants of this movement, and I received an invitation to attend one of their meetings years ago, but not knowing the participants, I did not). The movement may have been generations ahead of its time, but what we are witnessing today is a partial implementation of the thrust towards unity, represented by globalisation, free-trade areas, interventionism in good causes which we should accept, and in bad causes which we should reject, leading eventually to virtual unity. But this should be done without discarding the rich legacies of diversification, or the regimentation and remoteness of central control.

And quite independently, many of these causes are eventually taken up by the international Inter-Parliamentary Union (IPU) as items on its annual agenda, adding weight, credibility and implementability to these causes.

But by far the most ubiquitous, painful, acrimonious, and insoluble subject, on the agenda of the United Nation has been the question of Palestine. Since 1945 and up to this day, generation after generation of statesmen, politicians and diplomats from every corner of the world have found themselves grappling with it and its ramifications, but without success. What started on 29 November 1947 as the partition of Palestine, with crystal-clear borders down to the last metre between two states, Arab and Jewish, and a *de facto* demographic condition, with no refugees or displaced, has been snowballing over the decades into scores of items on the agenda of the General Assembly and the Security Council. In 1980, 15 separate items pertained to it. The ambassadors of the 22 Arab states, dismayed by the dwindling attendance of the member states at the lengthy and repetitive debates over these issues, came to the conclusion that such proliferation was counterproductive, dispersing efforts which could have been conserved for two or three major debates, with substantial participation at reasonably high levels ensuring effectiveness. To give an idea about the proliferation which I am referring to I will cite some of the titles of resolutions under which those items have been discussed, most of them year after year: the question of

Palestine – a special committee to investigate Israeli practices affecting the human rights of the population of the Occupied Territories (16 December 1976); affirmation that the Geneva Convention, Relative to the Protection of Civilian Persons in Time of War, of 12 August 1949, is applicable to all the Arab territories occupied by Israel since 1967, including Jerusalem; deploring illegal Israeli measures in the occupied Arab territories, designed to change the legal status, geographical nature and demographic composition of those territories (28 October 1977); the early convening of a Middle East Peace Conference under UN auspices (6 December 1979); calling on Israel to begin complete withdrawal by November 1980 from all Palestinian and other Arab territories, occupied since June 1967, including Jerusalem (29 July 1980); requesting the Committee on the Exercise of the Inalienable Rights of the Palestinian People to study the reasons for Israel's refusal to comply with relevant United Nations resolutions; grants and scholarships for higher education, including vocational training for Palestinian refugees (3 November 1980, at my own initiative); on the question of Palestine – reaffirming the right of the Palestinian people to return to its homes and property in Palestine and the right to establish its own independent sovereign state (15 December 1980); deep concern over the enactment of a 'Basic Law' in the Israeli Knesset, proclaiming a change in the character and status of the holy city of Jerusalem, and determines that all legislative and administrative measures and actions taken by Israel, the occupying power, which have altered, or purport to alter the character and status of the holy city of Jerusalem, and, in particular, the recent 'Basic Law' on Jerusalem and, the proclamation of Jerusalem as the capital of Israel, are null and void and must be rescinded forthwith

(1980); condemning Israel's aggression against Lebanon and the Palestinian people (16 December 1980); demanding that Israel desist immediately from all excavations and transformation of the historical, cultural and religious sites of Jerusalem, particularly beneath and around the Muslim holy sanctuary of Haram al-Sharif (al-Masjid al-Aqsa and the noble Dome of the Rock), the structures of which are in danger of collapse (28 October 1981); requesting that the United Nations assistance to the Palestinian people in the Arab host countries should be rendered through the specialised agencies and organs of the United Nations, in consultation with the parties concerned. (4 December 1981); again on the question of Palestine – reaffirming the General Assembly's rejection of those provisions of the Camp David Accords which ignore, infringe or deny the inalienable rights of the Palestinian people, including the right of return, the right of self-determination and the right to national independence and sovereignty in Palestine (10 December 1981); urging the establishment of a university in Jerusalem for Palestinian refugees (16 December 1981). I could go on and on citing General Assembly and Security Council decisions *ad infinitum*, but the point is clear: proliferation and repetitiveness have resulted from lack of implementation and the continuing collateral ramifications of occupation.

There are some interesting and seemingly confusing backgrounds to some of those resolutions. Take, for example, the last item just cited, concerning the establishment of the University of Jerusalem. I was the initiator of the resolution because, as a Jerusalemite, I was always conscious of the fact that whereas the Jews of Palestine, as far back as 1925, had established a highly renowned Hebrew University on Mount

Scopus, the Arab citizens of Jerusalem, in particular, and of Palestine, in general, had been deprived of a similar centre of learning, notwithstanding previous efforts to establish one. In 1948, one of the casualties of the war was the demise of just such a potential centre, the prestigious Arab College on Jabal al-Mukaber, overlooking Jerusalem and contiguous with the former Government House, today occupied by UNTSO. The Arab College had been the nucleus of a Palestinian Arab University and plans were well advanced to achieve this objective. But, unfortunately, it fell under *de facto* Israeli occupation, and the location became totally inaccessible to Palestinian students under the permanent Armistice Agreement of 1949.

I tabled the draft resolution for the university before the General Assembly and I was happy that it received widespread support. Israel, not unexpectedly, opposed the resolution, on the grounds that the Arabs had universities nearby, such as the universities of Bethlehem, south of Jerusalem, and Bir Zeit University, to the north, in Ramallah. I replied that Israel had many universities all over the country, so why should we be denied one in Jerusalem simply because we had universities elsewhere? Did Jerusalem not deserve one? It was a straightforward, classic confrontation, which I had prepared myself for. But I was truly saddened when I discovered that my colleague, the representative of the PLO, was also lobbying to defeat the resolution, along with the Arab group. Strange as it may sound, I found myself fighting on two fronts: Israeli and Arab. By some misguided logic the Arab group had been told that Israeli students would overwhelm the proposed university which, of course, is sheer nonsense because Israel had all the universities it needed and wanted. And in order to overcome the impasse, I had to agree to the incorporation of the few words indicating that the university was for Palestinian refugees. This was at a time when, quite apart from prestige and other moral imperatives, East Jerusalem had a population of almost a quarter of a million. It needed higher education in its own right and deserved to have it, as the capital of a future Palestinian state. Besides, the Palestinian people make no distinction between an indigenous resident and a refugee, because all belong to one Palestinian family, including those who became part of Israel in 1948, and who constitute 20 percent of the population. Today, the University of Jerusalem in Abu Dis, overlooking Jerusalem from the east, has a student body of over 7,000 from all segments of Palestinian society, regardless of geographic or political status.

By far the most serious dimension of the ever-evolving Palestinian question has been the policy of massive Israeli settlement and colonisation of Palestinian lands. Foreign occupation may come and go, leaving little more than an ephemeral memory, like the European colonialism of the 19th and early 20th centuries. But Israeli settlement and colonisation are fundamentally different and far more lethal, for they infringe upon the basic prerequisite of existence which is land, whether it is for personal family use or for the all-embracing national existence. If Shakespeare's soliloquy 'to be or not to be, that is the question' has relevance and application, it is most decidedly so in its application to Israel's sequestration and settlement of Palestinian lands and properties. This has been Israel's official policy since 1948, by virtue of which over 450 Palestinian villages have been obliterated and their lands seized, placed in the custody of the so-called custodian of enemy or absentee owners. The same policy of despoliation had been applied in scores of Palestinian cities and towns, without any prospect for restitution or recompense. What difference, if any, is there between this policy and highway robbery, one might legitimately ask? The Palestinians who became part of Israel in 1948 and suffered massive despoliation over decades have earmarked 'Land Day' as their most cherished national day. Not until after 1967 and the occupation of the West Bank did Israel lift military rule, under which Israeli Palestinians had been forced to live, to the extent that going from Nazareth to Haifa required a military permit.

The aforementioned policy should have been covered by the core United Nations Resolutions 181 on partition and 194 on the right of the Palestinian refugees to repatriation, and to compensation for those who may not wish to exercise this right. But these resolutions have been placed on the shelf to rot. Then in 1967 came Israel's occupation of the West Bank, including Jerusalem, and the Gaza Strip.

The occupation created a new situation, governed by a different set of rules and conventions. The occupied territories had been an integral part of an independent sovereign state, namely, the Hashemite Kingdom of Jordan, a member of the United Nations. The charter of the UN rejects outright the acquisition of territory by force, and this fundamental principle was embodied in Security Council Resolution 242 of 1967. This has become the most cited resolution in the annals of the UN, because for four decades it has pointed out how the Middle East crisis should be resolved.

In addition to the inadmissibility of the acquisition of territory by force, contained in the preamble to 242, there is the Geneva Convention Relative to the Protection of Civilian Persons in Time of War of 12 August 1949. In particular, Article 1: 'The High Contracting Parties undertake to respect and to ensure respect for the present convention in all circumstances'. I presume that Israel, like all other states in the world, has signed this document, and yet it has followed a systematic pattern of flouting the provisions in almost all of their facets, especially in regard to the settlement of occupied land and expulsion of its inhabitants.

As a permanent delegate to the UN, beginning in 1976, I had been receiving regular reports from my government on Israeli sequestration and colonisation of Palestinian lands under occupation. I would expeditiously send those reports to the office of the secretary-general, with a request that it be circulated to all member states as an official document of the United Nations. It became almost routine, with diminishing returns. On one occasion, an ambassador of one of the Western countries asked me whether the confiscation of 500 or 1,000 *dunums* here and there was worth all the commotion which I had been stirring over it. I replied that if such seemingly small parcels of land were put together they would constitute something like an avalanche.

Furthermore there had been a World Zionist Organization master plan for the development of settlements in the West Bank, including Jerusalem, for the period 1979-83 and a 20-year plan (1975-95), which was being implemented. These plans were prepared by Matitiyahu Drobles, and named after him. The introduction to the plan states *inter alia*:

> 'For some considerable time now, the lack has been felt of a comprehensive, well-founded and professional plan of settlement of Judea and Samaria (West Bank). Therefore, upon my assumption of the post of head of the Jewish Agency's land department, and head of the rural settlement department of the world Zionist department, I began with

the help of first-rate staff in the department, to seek out various possibilities for the consolidation of a general master plan in Judea and Samaria, whose implementation would extend, in the first stage, five years.' The plan adds that, after a comprehensive and systematic land survey, 'we shall plan for additional settlements to those proposed below.' The following principles guided the plan:

'Settlement throughout the entire land of Israel is for security and by right. A strip of settlements at strategic sites enhances both internal and external security alike, as well as making concrete and realizing our right to Eretz-Israel.

'The disposition of the settlements must be carried out not only "around" the settlements of the minorities [meaning the Palestinians], but also in between them. Therefore, the proposed settlement blocs are situated at a strip surrounding the Judea and Samaria ridge. Starting from its western slopes, from south to north both between the minorities' population and around it.'

One day in 1979, my government informed me that the scale of colonisation was accelerating out of control. It requested me to submit the entire question to the Security Council. The office of Crown Prince Hassan had been working diligently and methodically on the whole issue, assisted by experts in the field. When the study was finished, a thick dossier was sent to me, with a map marking where settlements had been established on Palestinian land, at times on state domain which is collectively owned by the people of the territories. The map was indescribably galling, and beyond even my worst fears. Like a widespread rash, marked in red ink, the map revealed how inundated Jerusalem and the West Bank had become with Israeli settlements. These covered almost 27 percent of Jerusalem and the West Bank, and their relentless expansion was continuing.

I rang up the US mission and arranged an urgent meeting with Ambassador Andrew Young, chief of mission. Ambassador Jim Leonard also attended the meeting. Both were amiable gentlemen and highly public-spirited and patriotic Americans. I showed them the map, which was self-explanatory, and explained that if Israel were to persist in the policy of devouring the occupied lands, then the prospects for the continued existence of the Palestinian people on their lands, let alone a peaceful resolution of the Arab-Israeli conflict, would be minimal.

I expressed the hope that the US mission would convey to Washington the gravity of the situation, adding that if I did not hear from the mission about concrete steps to deal with this grave issue, then in two weeks I would bring the matter promptly to the consideration of the Security Council. I knew full well that neither the mission, nor the powers-that-be in Washington would or could bring about a miracle, but at least by putting them in the picture, ahead of time, I would increase the chance of gaining their support, which was the case.

No sooner had the two weeks lapsed, without my hearing from the US mission, than I saw the president of the Security Council for the month of March and requested him to convene a meeting of the Council as soon as possible. The Council's agenda was clogged with other crises requiring its attention, so Jordan's request had had to wait for two weeks.

When the Council met on 20 March 1979 I made a 60-page presentation on the extensive settlement of occupied land, with maps clarifying the presentation placed on a board behind the Security Council and guided by an expert from a Palestinian research centre in Jerusalem. The evidence, presented in two consecutive sessions, was overwhelming. But not withstanding that, I had requested in the draft resolution that a commission, consisting of three members of the Security Council, be established by the president of the Council to further examine the situation relating to settlements in the Arab territories occupied since 1967, including Jerusalem. Resolution 446 of 22 March 1979 requested the commission to submit its report to the Council by 1 July 1979. The resolution passed, with three abstentions: Norway, the United Kingdom, and the United States.

On 20 July that year, the Security Council, taking note of the report and recommendations of the commission established under the previous resolution (446), deplored the lack of cooperation of Israel with the commission, accepted the report of the commission, and called upon the government and people of Israel to cease on an urgent basis the establishment, construction and planning of settlements in the Arab territories occupied in 1967, including Jerusalem. It further requested the commission, in view of the magnitude of the problem of settlements, to keep under close survey the implementation of the present resolution and report back to the Security Council before November 1979. The resolution passed with 14 votes in favour, none against and the United States abstaining.

These steps, reports and decisions culminated in Resolution 465 of 1 March 1980 which called upon Israel to dismantle the settlements in the occupied Arab territories, including Jerusalem. The all-embracing dimension of this resolution was part of a pattern established by the Security Council to deal with this grave issue. It also created a problem for the president of the United States. For the above reasons, I feel that it should be put on record in this context, in spite of its length:

The Security Council

Taking note of the reports of the commission of the Security Council, established under Resolution 446 (1979) to examine the situation relating to settlements in the Arab territories occupied since 1967, including Jerusalem, contained in documents S/1340 and S/13679.

Taking note also of letters from the permanent representative of Jordan (S/13801) and the permanent representative of Morocco, chairman of the Islamic group.

Strongly deploring the refusal by Israel to cooperate with the commission and regretting its formal rejection of resolution 446 (1979) and 452(1979).

Affirming once more that the Fourth Geneva Convention relative to the protection of civilian persons in time of war of 12 August 1949 is applicable to the territories occupied by Israel since 1967 including Jerusalem.

Deploring the decision of the government of Israel to officially support Israeli settlement in the Palestinian and other Arab territories occupied since 1967.

Deeply concerned over the practices of the Israeli authorities in implementing that settlement policy in the occupied Arab territories, including Jerusalem, and its consequences for the local Arab Palestinian population,

Taking into account the need to consider measures for the impartial protection of private and public land and property and water resources,

Bearing in mind the specific status of Jerusalem and in particular the need for protection and preservation of the unique spiritual and religious dimension of the Holy places in the city,

Drawing attention to the grave consequences, which the settlement policy is bound to have on any attempt to reach a comprehensive, just, and lasting peace in the Middle East.

Recalling pertinent Security Council resolutions, specifically Resolution 237 (1967), of 14 June, 1967, 252 (1968) of 21 May 1968, 267 (1969), of 3 July 1969, 271 (1969)

of 15 September 1969, and 298 (1971) of 25 September 1971, as well as the consensus statement made by the president of the Security Council on 11 November 1976,

Having invited Mr Fahd Qawasmeh, mayor of Al-Khalil (Hebron) in the occupied territory, to supply it with information pursuant to rule 39 of the provisional rules of procedure, (end of preamble and beginning of the operative paragraphs).

Commends work done by the commission in preparing the report contained in document 5/13679.

Accepts the conclusions and the recommendations contained in the above-mentioned report of the commission.

Calls upon all parties particularly the government of Israel, to cooperate with the commission.

Strongly deplores the decision of Israel to prohibit the free travel of mayor Fahd Qawasmeh in order to appear before the Security Council, and requests Israel to permit his free travel to the United Nations headquarters for that purpose.

Determines that all measures taken by Israel to change the physical character, demographic composition, institutional structure or the status of the Palestinian and other Arab territories occupied since 1967, including Jerusalem, or any part thereof, have no legal validity and that Israel's policy and practices of settling parts of its populations and new immigrants in those territories constitute a flagrant violation of the Fourth Geneva convention relative to the protection of civilian persons in time of war, and also constitute a serious obstruction to achieving a comprehensive, just and lasting peace in the Middle East.

Strongly deplores the continuation and persistence of Israel in pursuing those policies and practices and calls upon the government and people of Israel to rescind those measures, to dismantle the existing settlements and in particular to cease, on an urgent basis, the establishment, construction and planning of settlements in the Arab territories occupied since 1967, including Jerusalem.

Calls upon all states not to provide Israel with any assistance to be used specifically in connection with settlements in the occupied territories.

Requests the commission to continue to examine the situation relating to settlements in the Arab territories occupied since 1967, including Jerusalem, to investigate the serious depletion of natural resources, particularly the water resources, with a view to ensuring the protection of those important natural resources of the territories under occupation, and to keep under close scrutiny the implementation of the present resolution;

Requests the commission to report to the Security Council before 1 September, 1980, and decides to convene at the earliest possible date thereafter in order to consider the report and the full implementation of the present resolution.

The report was adopted unanimously, a great achievement, considering its language in condemning Israeli settlement without equivocation and regarding it as null and void.

When I had drawn up a draft I obtained the approval of the group of Non-Aligned states represented at the Council. The next step had been to circulate the draft to all members of the Council for their consideration. The drafts on crucial issues are sent forthwith to the capitals of the members for their perusal. Henceforth, a process of negotiations is conducted, and here is where diplomatic skills are most needed. Negotiations must be flexible enough to accommodate the views and the concerns of the parties upon whose votes the fate of a resolution hinges.

Ambassador Jim Leonard of the United States informed me that his government was willing to support the resolution, provided certain changes were made. These, as it transpired, were mainly to language rather than substance. In several paragraphs of the resolution the word 'condemn' had been used. He suggested that it be substituted by the word 'deplore'. It was not easy for a US government to condemn its closest ally, but to deplore was somewhat more palatable. I said to Ambassador Leonard that I would accept the amendment without hesitation. When I reported this change to the Non-Aligned group, Mr Tarazi of the PLO protested, but I persuaded him that the most important thing was the substance, rather than the form, and that I would not risk losing the vote of the United States over wording. The Non-Aligned group agreed.

There were other non-substantive changes to which I readily agreed. Jim Leonard, at every step, was in direct contact with Washington and when the negotiations were reaching their final phase he said to me: 'Hazem, if you agree to the deletion of the separate paragraph on Jerusalem, Washington will support the resolution.' I agreed without hesitation, and Ambassador Leonard informed Washington of Jordan's agreement.

I am sure that he must have been as surprised as his colleagues in Washington that I had agreed to this change. There was never any secret about my inextricable attachment to Jerusalem, and nothing could ever have shaken this birthplace loyalty. The final draft, with Jerusalem deleted as a separate paragraph, was transmitted to Secretary of State Cyrus Vance, a man of high character, understanding and integrity, whom we very much respected. He, in turn, as we had been told, communicated it to President Jimmy Carter, who wanted to be assured that the separate paragraph on Jerusalem, other than the one which talks about its holiness, had been deleted.

When he was told that it had been deleted, he gave instructions to support the resolution. A reader might be surprised to learn that a president of the United States has the time or interest to get involved in the nitty-gritty of a draft resolution on this issue. But the surprise will dissolve when I say that everything pertaining to the Palestine question and the Arab-Israeli conflict has a prominent place on the desk of the president. This is because of the profound internal as well as external ramifications of these issues on American politics, and this case goes to prove this fact.

No sooner had the resolution been adopted unanimously at the Security Council than a storm was unleashed against the administration by a variety of influential American Jewish organisations and the pro-Israeli lobby in Washington. The uproar was all the more vicious because of the repeated references to Jerusalem as an occupied city. For when I had agreed to the deletion of the separate paragraph on Jerusalem, it was because I had taken steps to circumvent this possibility. In almost every other paragraph referring to the occupied Arab and Palestinian territories there had been the addition: 'including Jerusalem'. It takes a Palestinian or an Israeli to recognise this fine point which, apparently, had eluded President Carter and Secretary Vance. Two days later, President Carter, whom the Palestinians respected because of his sincerity, appeared before a gathering of American Jewish leaders and meekly expressed remorse for his decision to back the resolution, promising not to do it again. Authoritative sources described what had happened regarding the resolution as 'a failure in communication'. On meeting Ambassador Young, I expressed the gratitude of my government for the United States' support of the resolution but added that it would have been more honourable if the US had opposed the resolution than to have seen the president humiliated in this way, as if he had committed a sin. President Carter lost the subsequent election to Ronald Regan. In the aftermath, one of the assistants to President Carter, Hamilton Jordan, interviewed on *CBS*, was asked for his opinion on why Carter had lost the elections. Hamilton Jordan attributed the loss to two major factors: the hostage crisis in Iran, and the United States' support for the Security Council resolution on settlements.

I have devoted considerable attention to the issue of Israeli settlements because of its 'make-or-break' impact on the overall resolution of the Palestinian-Israeli conflict. On many occasions during the Security Council debates I warned that the settlement problem would eventually torpedo any prospects for a fair and lasting solution. Today, with the four major centres of power in the world, the United States, the European Union, Russia, and the United Nations striving for a workable solution, the real obstacle is the issue of Israeli settlements which cut across any plan to create a viable, contiguous Palestine state. Geography has been so extensively abused as to convince many people, including me, that the only viable solution is a demographic one within a bi-national state, in which 5 million Palestinians would live side-by-side in peace, amity and prosperity with 5 million Israeli Jews. All kinds of constitutional hedges can be worked out to give expression to the unique character of each of these two constituents – perhaps a federal or a confederal system which gives hope and fulfilment to both peoples for a better tomorrow. A truncated and isolated Palestine is a recipe for a long-term disaster, because it is impossible to squeeze 5 million and more Palestinians into its narrow, claustrophobic confines. Openness is the answer.

Jordan, as I have mentioned earlier, has an honourable record in supporting human rights issues at the United Nations, even though at home there is still scope for improvement. But an even greater leap forward in this field was made when Crown Prince Hassan drew up a proposed 'conceptual framework' for the advancement of the issue of human rights, with instructions that it be presented to the General Assembly for debate and, hopefully, endorsement. In November 1981, the crown prince dispatched Zia Risby, a Pakistani national of considerable intellectual endowment and diplomatic skills, to New York to coordinate with my efforts towards achieving this goal. He had a thick dossier of papers on the subject, and my task was to extract the gist of them for presentation to the assembly in a coherent and digestible form. There were no striking innovations in the proposal that could be termed additions to knowledge. But it was important to bring together and streamline all the ingredients and constituents of human rights in one composite, integrated conceptual framework as a 'new international humanitarian order'. Naturally enough, this would embrace functions of the Red Cross and Red Crescent, human rights *per se* as embodied in the universal declaration of human rights, relief work, disaster assistance, and all other related humanitarian issues.

I wrote the appropriate speech and made the necessary presentation to the General Assembly, and I was thrilled to see such a positive and enthusiastic reception to the proposal from so many delegations and, in particular, Western ones. They had been enthusiastic enough to inquire about further details, as if it could be a panacea, a ready-made fix for the ills which afflict human rights. My answer was that the ideas presented were basic constituents which must evolve and be developed by the international community as a whole, and that no-one country could or should alone formulate the fundamentals and workings of the new international humanitarian order. This process was begun when the General Assembly adopted Resolution 36/136 of 14 December 1981. The following year, the assembly referred to the desirability of creating an independent body to consider the proposed order. In 1983, the Assembly took note of the establishment of an Independent Commission on International Humanitarian Issues, composed of eminent personages of world renown in the humanitarian field, or having wide experience in government and world affairs (Resolution 38/1961 of 16 December 1983).

In its final report published in 1987, it stated *inter alia*: 'Humanitarianism is a basic orientation towards the interests and welfare of people. It demands that whatever detracts from human wellbeing must be questioned, regardless of its effects on economic growth, political power or the stability of a certain order.'

In the course of its mandate between 1983 and 1987 the Commission produced a series of sectoral reports, which were later compiled and published in book form. The reports touched upon a wide range of subjects of a humanitarian nature such as famine, deforestation, desertification, street children, indigenous people, refugees, modern wars and the missing. The reports of the Commission have appeared in over 60 editions in major languages of the world. In addition, a series of TV documentaries has been produced relating to selected humanitarian issues.

In 1988, the Independent Bureau for Humanitarian Issues (IBHI) was established as the successor body to the commission. The Bureau is continuing the research and publication work initiated by the commission. It deals both with 'issues' and 'situations' requiring attention in the humanitarian field. Its reports are intended not only to help policymakers and the general public, but also to serve as the building blocks for a new international humanitarian order, as foreseen by the General Assembly of the United Nation in its original resolution.

In line with its objectives, the work of the bureau is focused on:

> Action – oriented research on humanitarian issues of concern to the international community;
> Analysis of situations leading, actually or potentially, to large-scale human suffering, for the purpose of prevention or containment of man-made disasters; and,
> Training relating to humanitarian issues, including emergency preparedness and response of nationals within and outside government structures in disaster-prone countries.

The IBHI consists of an international council, an executive committee and, a central secretariat located in the Geneva area, with liaison offices in several countries and regions, including Bosnia and Herzegovina, France, Georgia, Pakistan, and Uzbekistan.

Returning to personal reminiscences of my time at the UN, the election of Jordan in 1982 to membership of the Security Council added significantly to the load of work and responsibility, as well as to the prestige which goes with it. I had close and friendly relationships with the Secretary-

General, Dr Kurt Waldheim. He was serving the organisation with great competence and adroitness and yet, after two consecutive terms, China led a move to elect a new candidate, preferably one from the Third World. Its candidate was Selim Ahmad Selim, ambassador of Tanzania and, subsequently, secretary-general of the Organization of African Unity. Highly qualified in the ways of the UN, he had danced with joy in the hall of the General Assembly in 1972 when mainland China won the battle to replace Taiwan as the sole representative of China, notwithstanding a prolonged procedural fight in the assembly, waged by George Bush Sr, who was head of the US mission to the UN. A telling development occurred during that acrimonious debate. As manoeuvring, lobbying, and voting evolved over whether it was a procedural or a substantive issue requiring a two-thirds plurality, it had become overtly clear that the pro-China vote would win the day, and that mainland China would become the permanent member of the Security Council. I was in New York to help and advise our mission during the plenary session. The Jordanian Ambassador to the UN was Baha'uddin Touqan, an accomplished career diplomat who would carry out the government's instructions to the letter. His instructions from the government were to vote with the United States, and this was what he was determined to do. I raised with him the possibility that even the United States itself might change course, in light of the voting trends, and we could find ourselves isolated in our voting. Ambassador Touqan agreed to my suggestion that I should go to where Ambassador Bush was standing at the other corner of the assembly and explain our predicament. Mr Bush was extremely amiable and understanding and immediately answered: 'Thank you very much for your support, and as things have developed, please go ahead and vote according to what you assess to be your national interest.' I thanked Ambassador Bush, who was a friend of Ambassador Touqan, his wife Hanan, and his daughter Alia, who later married King Hussein and became queen of Jordan. I informed Ambassador Touqan of what had transpired, and we were greatly relieved not to vote against China, but just to abstain.

On the search for a new UN secretary-general, the voting and lobbying at the Security Council were becoming increasingly heated in the contest between incumbent Kurt Waldheim and his challenger, Selim Ahmad Selim. The process had gone through several rounds but had been inconclusive. And besides, there was always the possibility that China or another permanent member could veto any election result.

Consensus amongst the permanent members was a must for a decision to be adopted. As lobbying by the supporters of both candidates reached a high pitch, I received a message from Crown Prince Hassan to submit the candidacy of Saddruddin Agha Khan, UN High Commissioner for Refugees and a renowned international figure, as a candidate for the post, should the Security Council reach an impasse and fail to achieve a consensus.

I sent a letter to this effect to the president of the Security Council, and requested him not to mention it publicly until such time as the Security Council might conclude that a final impasse had been reached.

That evening I attended a reception given by David Rockefeller, chairman of Chase Manhattan Bank (today known as Chase). To my unpleasant surprise, Secretary-General Waldheim, who was attending the party, came to me and said: 'I am very disappointed and I had not expected this to come from you.' Evidently, the confidential letter to the president of the Council, nominating Saddruddin Khan, had been disclosed to him, in spite of its confidential nature. I replied that my letter to the president of the Council had made the candidacy of Saddruddin contingent on the failure of the council to come to a conclusion, and not with the aim of putting another competitor into the fray. Dr Waldheim apparently interpreted my government's move as a stab in the back, which had not been the case. Significantly, when Dr Waldheim was elected president of Austria, the United States and others boycotted him and refused to invite him to their countries because during World War II, when he was a young man in his early twenties, he had served in the German army, as though he had a choice. It was none other than a chivalrous King Hussein of Jordan who put out the red carpet for President Waldheim and received him as the honoured head of state of a friendly country and also as a sincere old friend.

Another important crisis in which Jordan, as a member of the Council, had been closely involved was the Falklands war. The late Sir Anthony Parsons, the ambassador of the United Kingdom to the UN, requested an emergency meeting of the Security Council to consider what he described as an imminent invasion of the Falkland Islands by Argentina. As is the normal practice, the Council is called to an informal meeting at an adjacent room for consultations, in light of which it may decide to meet in formal session.

Sir Anthony informed the council at its informal meeting that evening that his government had received reliable information that Argentina was planning an imminent invasion of the Falklands at dawn, and requested that steps be taken by the council to deter such an invasion. All 15 members of the council took a very serious view of the situation and authorised the president of the Council to send a warning to Argentina to refrain from such a dangerous course. At exactly the time specified by the United Kingdom, at dawn, Argentinian troops landed in the Falklands and war erupted. For weeks thereafter, the Security Council was seized with this war, as the British sent their warships and troops to dislodge the invaders.

On such occasions it is customary for every member of the Council to outline his government's views on the crisis, in the context of a general debate. Even non-members of the council may present their views, in support of one side or another. Many Latin American governments gave strong support to Argentina's military action, out of fraternal solidarity.

Jordan, with half of its territory languishing under prolonged and oppressive occupation, was in no position to be callous or indifferent towards the inadmissible acquisition of territory by force. Besides, the Security Council had given a prior warning to Argentina to desist from its planned invasion but the latter did not heed the warning. In the course of the debate, I outlined Jordan's position in no uncertain terms. I said that Argentina's claims to the Falklands were traditionally discussed in one of the General Assembly's committees which was where the issue belonged, but the use of force to acquire territory was irreconcilable with the principles and purposes of the United Nations. There could, therefore, be no question as to where Jordan stood on the war.

But the following day, as I was strolling in the delegates' lounge, I was summoned to receive an urgent telephone call from the foreign minister of Jordan. The Minister, Marwan al-

Qasim, was a good friend and colleague. He asked me about the statement which I had delivered at the Security Council the day before on the Falklands, adding that it was likely to displease public opinion in Latin America. I answered that even if this were the case we had priorities to weigh up in making our judgment, namely the inadmissibility of the acquisition of territory by force, a principle so germane in our striving to end Israeli occupation of the West Bank. When the minister persisted in his position I said that the government was the ultimate decision-maker on the issue and it would have to bear responsibility for any position it took.

This development put me on the spot. I had already stated, publicly and categorically, Jordan's opposition to the invasion. Any reversal of this position, if undisclosed before the voting was to take place, would seriously if not fatally damage Jordan's credibility, as well as my own. I, therefore, approached Sir Anthony, whose friendship as a colleague I valued, and told him that I was getting mixed signals from Amman pertaining to Jordan's position towards the conflict. I added that, as a disciplined public servant, I did not have any alternative but to vote in accordance with my government's instructions.

In the meantime, I deliberately kept myself away from the Security Council chamber, lest the president, having exhausted the list of speakers, should call for voting on the draft resolution before the final position of my government had been determined. To keep the meeting going, and to avoid premature voting, Ambassador Parsons engaged in a prolonged filibuster, explaining how the war was not over the 600,000 heads of sheep which had constituted the majority of the inhabitants of the island, but over lofty principles of international law and practice. As I was watching him on TV in one of the chambers, I felt sympathy for him as he strained to keep on speaking for almost an hour, coining words and idea over such uninspiring subjects as the fate of the sheep and the sheep farmers on the islands. (Conspiracy theories circulated that there was a lot more to the war than sheep or even a matter of principle: oil.)

Suddenly the loudspeaker in the delegates' lounge was again announcing my name and requesting that I proceed to the nearest telephone booth for an urgent call from Amman. With his familiar strong voice, King Hussein himself was at the other end to affirm that he fully supported my position at the Security Council, wondering it could be otherwise when our territories were under occupation in consequence of an act of war. And to be doubly certain that the official message had reached me, the king said that Prime Minister Mudhar Badran, who was standing next to him, wanted to assure me that that was indeed the position of the government. I thanked the king and the prime minister heartily. The conversation ended and I proceeded swiftly to the chamber of the Council. The travail of Sir Anthony in his filibuster ended forthwith, and a majority vote was recorded against the invasion.

Jordan's vote, in the event, proved to be decisive. As Ambassador Parsons described to me subsequently, his deputy leapt up and down the stairs to get to a place where safe communications could be made with London. Britain's Prime Minister Margaret Thatcher had committed herself to the Falklands war to the fullest extent and, therefore, would not tolerate this commitment being derailed by a diplomatic debacle at the Security Council. Mrs Thatcher, it turns out, got in touch with King Hussein and explained to him the gravity of the situation, and the king responded promptly and decisively. One of the dividends of this incident was that, throughout her long term in office, Mrs Thatcher maintained and cherished a warm relationship with King Hussein and with Jordan as a friendly country.

When Israel invaded Lebanon in 1982, Jordan was a member of the Security Council and I was president of the Council during October, when most of the important events, many of them ugly and gruesome, took place. As a representative of Jordan, and the Arab group, a particularly heavy responsibility devolved upon me made more pronounced by the fact that the victimised country and people did not speak with one voice. After all, Lebanon had been in the throes of a relentless civil war since 1975, a house divided against itself. Adding to the complexity was the active presence of hundreds of thousands of Palestinian refugees – restless, abandoned, confined to camps, and living in misery throughout Lebanon, including Beirut. I am not going in these remembrances to apportion blame amongst the warring parties, for all of them had responsibility one way or the other for the carnage which befell Lebanon. But it was my duty to act responsibly and with circumspection in such a delicate situation. Lebanon was extremely fortunate in having one of its outstanding and dedicated sons, Ghassan Tuweini, as ambassador to the UN. He was forthright in appraising a situation and never balked at expressing his pristine opinions, but in a most friendly way, he would present his views logically and objectively and then tell his colleagues of the Arab group to shoulder responsibility for their actions.

As for myself, I never had any difficulty in coordinating my effort with Ghassan's, whether in matters relating to the

Security Council or on other issues of concern to our countries and to our regional group.

There were occasions when, as a member and president of the Council, I took initiatives instantaneously and without elaborate consultations because the issues involved were so clear and urgent. For example, in consequence of the sustained siege of Beirut by the Israeli army and the destruction of water tanks on the roofs of buildings by incessant shelling, we received news that the citizens of Beirut were suffering from acute water shortages. I almost felt the thirst personally, as I had been familiar with a similar situation in Amman during the 1970 fighting between the army and the Palestinian armed groups. Hunger is not as serious as thirst because one can survive for weeks without food; but not without water. Furthermore, almost every home in the Arab world traditionally stores essential food items for emergencies, so the threat of starvation is remote, even during a prolonged siege.

That being the case, I submitted a draft resolution condemning Israeli bombing of water installations in Beirut and calling for a lifting of the siege of the city. In order to obviate the argument that the draft resolution was intended to relieve pressure on the Palestinian guerrilla forces, I stated that the PLO had its own means of securing water, so it was the innocent civilians of Beirut who were bearing the brunt.

The draft resolution was adopted.

The president of Lebanon, Amin Gemayel, who in September 1982 succeeded his slain brother Bashir, visited New York and all Arab ambassadors were at the airport to accord him welcome. In my capacity as president of the Security Council I had the pleasure of welcoming him when he made his presentation. Strenuous efforts were being made to get the Palestinian forces out of Lebanon, through the active mediation of Ambassador Phillip Habib of the US, and a chapter of armed Palestinian resistance in Lebanon came to an end.

But no sooner had their departure been accomplished peacefully and honourably, having boarded ships to ferry them to yet another exodus, than the horrendous genocide of Sabra and Shatila refugee camps took place, with the connivance of the Israeli forces, which were in the vicinity and watching.

It recalled to my mind the infamous atrocity at the village of Deir Yassin, on the outskirts of West Jerusalem, astride the Jerusalem-Jaffa-Tel Aviv highway in April 1948, in which up to 120 Palestinian men, women, and children were massacred in cold blood and their bodies dumped into the water wells of the village. I remember vividly that painful occasion when a handful of girls less than 10 years of age were literally thrown across the de facto demarcation line in the Musrara quarter, towards the Herod's Gate area where my brother, Anwar, chairman of the Jerusalem National Committee, lived. They were dumped across after being paraded along Jaffa Road, close to Zion Square in Jerusalem. They were in deep shock and shaking uncontrollably. Anwar took them into his care, and the National Committee provided them with food, clothing and shelter in the Old City. I cannot forget the shaken faces of those children who had witnessed a night of indescribable horror at Deir Yassin and were now orphaned. The event was so shocking that a British RAF officer with liaison duties in the building, who had visited me at my office that morning at the Daoud building in West Jerusalem, said in all seriousness that if he had had the authority he would have taken his squadron and destroyed a Jewish settlement.

Back in the fall of 1982, a security vacuum had been created in Beirut, especially in the refugee camps. Israeli tanks still surrounded the city, aided and abetted by hostile factional Lebanese forces. So the security and survival of tens of thousands of Palestinian refugees became uppermost in my mind and in the minds of many well-meaning, decent, responsible people. In the context of that grim and threatening atmosphere I took the initiative in proposing to the Security Council the dispatch of a multi-national force to protect and safeguard the Palestinian refugee camps. They consisted of Italian, French, British, and American contingents. The Italians were exemplary in carrying out their duties and the Palestinians will always be grateful to them. I do not remember the circumstances which surrounded the performance and the fate of the French forces, except to mention that they had been the target of a violent attack, in which they had suffered many dead and wounded. But the worst was to befall the American forces when a large truck loaded with heavy explosives rammed into an encampment at Beirut airport, killing 240 marines. I had made my proposal for the dispatch of multi-national forces with the best of humane intentions and almost solely for the protection of the refugees who had become vulnerable and defenceless. It had never occurred to me that it would lead to such a level of human casualties. The only wickedness in my heart, which I communicated at the time to a colleague, was the thought that perhaps American tanks would face off Israeli tanks operating in the same area, and hopefully discover the arrogance and aggressiveness displayed by the latter's' tank commanders. I do not believe anyone had anticipated the ferocity of the reaction to the presence of foreign troops on Lebanese soil. The entire landscape had been, up to then, governed by

Palestinian forces and their mainly, but not exclusively, Muslim allies on the one hand, and Lebanese Phalangist forces whose main support had come from the Maronite community, on the other.

The best-known Shiite force was still the Amal movement, and Hizbollah was still newly emerging in prominence. The suicide attack on the American base probably changed the political as well as the military balance of forces in Lebanon, and the US marines withdrew forthwith from the country.

Simultaneously with the unfolding of these events there was yet another American initiative for the solution of the problem of occupied territories. A Reagan plan had been floated which visualised a kind of autonomy for the West Bank, in association with Jordan. Like every other initiative pertaining to the question of Palestine, it had started with considerable fanfare, and hope, and the attendant publicity, only to disappear into oblivion.

But there are always collateral side effects to the main initiative, and in this particular situation they touched me. The chief of the US mission to the United Nations was Jeanne Kirkpatrick, an accomplished academician and diplomat. In the course of assuming her post, she gave an interview in which she was reported to have said that the Arab group had mastered the art of controlling the UN. She added that she would try to persuade the Arab ambassadors to, more or less, toe the line, but if they did not, then she would go over their heads. The Arab ambassadors, naturally enough, resented this dual intrusion and threat. It was haughty, immodest, insensitive, and least of all, alien to the spirit of comradeship that characterises the workings of the United Nations. The

Arab ambassadors showed their displeasure by being less than warm towards Ambassador Kirkpatrick. As time passed, relations warmed up again, but did not heal completely.

Ambassador Kirkpatrick was a neo-conservative and would have been ideal serving at the United Nations during the George W Bush administration. But this was not the case in the early 1980s. Never before 11 September 2001 had the Arab world been collectively rounded up, put into the dock, and stigmatised with the phenomenon of terrorism. Needless to say, only a tribal frame of mind would incriminate an entire nation of 300 million overwhelmingly decent citizens and their fraternal brethren in the far wider Islamic world with the abominable and criminal acts of a handful of individuals, whose very existence no-one had ever heard of before the New York and Washington bombings.

But returning to 1982, the nature of my assignment and my own sense of commitment, responsibility, and integrity, required me to immerse myself fully in the pursuit of my work, particularly at the Security Council, guided only by my sense of right and wrong. This meant taking stands and pursuing arguments that were not always palatable to certain policy-makers in Washington, particularly amongst those who have not grasped the profundity of the Palestinian question. The Jordanian Embassy in Washington was the *conduit* through which complaints were made against my stands and requests filed to have me removed. This was done carefully and discreetly, knowing full well that King Hussein had confidence in me and would not, in any event, tolerate interference in his own choices, except for some overriding reasons.

The Reagan Plan must have been the ruse which swayed the king to agree to my relocation. I received a letter from the foreign minister of the day Marwan al-Qassem, informing me of the government's decision to relocate me from New York. When I returned to Amman, the highest people in the know confirmed to me that my transfer had been made at the prodding of the US government, directly and through our embassy in Washington.

But as a matter of fact the request dovetailed with my own desire to return home after seven full years of hard work for the cause which I cherished from my childhood in Jerusalem and throughout the other phases of my long career. But this did not mean that the end of my stay in New York had been totally to my heart's liking. The United Nations is one of the most challenging duties, not only to career diplomats but also to leaders of nations at all levels of government. It is the world forum *par excellence*. I was involved in it in a number of roles that I have described, and finally as a permanent representative. But, as the veteran Ambassador of Spain to the UN, Hainnies de Pinnies told me on my arrival back in 1976: 'There is no such thing as a permanent delegate.'

It is never permanent. I have seen throughout the decades some of the best Arab brains exerting themselves in the service of their nations' causes. Dr Charles Malek, my professor of philosophy at the AUB and a co-chairman of the committee which drew up the Universal Declaration of Human Rights, in league with Eleanor Roosevelt, whom my wife and I had the pleasure of meeting at Hyde Park in 1951 as part of a student group; Farid Zeineddin, a versatile speaker; Ahmad al-Shuqairi, a highly gifted orator who used to stay up at night, at the Barclay Hotel in New York where he lived, writing long speeches on Palestine; and Fayez Sayegh, a top level debater whom, it had been said, even Aba Eban would evade challenging. At the special political committee, which annually would debate the problem of the Palestinian refugees, I had taken over from the British the task of making the first and major presentation, detailing facts and figures, as well as giving the political dimension of the issue and its ramifications. The debate would continue Monday through Friday, with one speaker after another contributing to it, until noon on Friday, the last day of the debate.

Dr Fayez Sayegh would give an oration without even a paper in his hands, synthesising all the plethora of details into a coherent brainstorming theme on behalf of the Palestinian refugees, of whom he was one. Leaving the hall for lunch at the end of the session, the US representative at the meeting remarked to me: 'What a big gun you have in Dr Sayegh'. And who can overlook or forget the spectacular presence and performance of Ambassador Jamil Barudi in almost every committee of the General Assembly? He was a frail figure but with a formidable mind, a stout heart and soul who knew all the issues pertaining to the United Nations, and was undaunted in expressing his views about them. He was nicknamed Mr United Nations, and identified intimately with its causes, not only as a political assembly but also as an organisation with thousands of employees who had inherent rights to be safeguarded. He participated on one occasion with one of their public protests and insisted on having his meals in their restaurant instead of the delegates' dining hall. He told me once that he was married to two wives, and when I indicated my surprise (him being a Christian) he looked up to me and said: 'My second wife is the United Nations.'

The podiums of the United Nations also witnessed the contributions of some of the foremost Arab statesmen, foreign ministers and luminaries, including: Faris al-Khouri, a former prime minister of Syria who struggled skilfully at the Security Council in the mid-1940s to achieve the withdrawal of French and British forces from his country; Dr Mahmoud Fawzi, the acknowledged *doyen* of Egyptian diplomats who led the efforts at the General Assembly for the withdrawal of French and British forces from the Suez Canal; Dr Fadel Jamali, prominent foreign minister of Iraq before the 1958 revolution in Iraq which overthrew the monarchy; Munji Slim, an eminent foreign minister of Tunisia who distinguished himself at the UN; Abdel Munim al-Rifai, a former prime minister of Jordan and a highly accomplished diplomat; Abdul Aziz Bouteflika, president of Algeria and a former president of the General Assembly; Mahmoud Riyadh, Ismat Abdul Majid and Amr Musa, three foreign ministers of Egypt who distinguished themselves in the work of the UN as heads of their country's missions; and last but not least Clovis Maqsoud, former head of the Arab League in the United States, a highly articulate brainstormer.

This is not a compendium of names associated with the work of the UN; I mentioned them only to emphasise that whatever successes or failures may have been recorded – and the Arab world has had both – the outcome was not the result of a lack of talent, or lack of effort. At any rate, these diplomats performed better than their military counterparts, none of whom shone brightly in the diplomatic-military encounters of the past 50 years, although some achieved infamy in unconstitutional seizures of power and in misgovernment when they had succeeded in doing so.

For a first time visitor, New York may seem daunting, wild, unfriendly, noisy, and disorderly. This was my impression and that of my wife when we landed in the Big Apple in 1951 on our way to Princeton where I had enrolled. The hotel was near a railway station, with all the noise and hustle and bustle that goes with it. Fire engines tore through the streets, conveying the impression that it was a city on fire. The ambulances were loud enough to wake the dead. I was nonplussed by even the sheer commotion of New Yorkers rushing to and from work, or a bus driver who replied sternly to my friendly 'good morning' to him.

With hindsight, my first impressions were superficial and unrepresentative of the New York which I came to know and admire in later years. New York dwarfs by far any other city in dynamism, and in the variety and quality of life. Reading *The New York Times* at 6am every morning over coffee was, in itself, enriching, and the 400 or so pages of the paper and its magazine supplements reviewing the week's important events, were sufficient to consume the stillness and long hours of a New York Sunday morning. The cultural life of New York is enormously rewarding: the museums, the theatres, libraries, the round-the-clock art exhibitions and auctions, the philharmonic performances and music libraries, the publishing houses; the Waldorf Astoria, the Plaza, the Pierre and numerous other hotels where the wheels of life never stop. Some restaurants in New York are legendary, and outclass their counterparts in their indigenous countries of origin, whether French, Japanese, Chinese, Mexican or Indian. Restaurants that come to my mind include Petit Marmite at 866 UN Plaza, the building that houses the Jordan Mission, Hime of Japan, the Indian Shezan, and numerous Italian and Chinese restaurants. The Oscar of the Waldorf Astoria was a favourite for a quick meal, as was the Maxwell Plum for good hamburgers, and Tavern on the Green at Central Park. The Bear Mountain in upstate New York also made a most enjoyable outing. Restaurants in New York are innumerable because they are where everybody goes for lunch. In our part of the world luncheons are at home, and people go out to restaurants only on special and infrequent occasion. The two differing habits represent two different ways of life, or two different stages of social engineering and development.

Regrettably, there are no Arab restaurants of high quality, despite the large waves of immigration in the late 19th and 20th centuries. The offspring of the early immigrants must have become immersed in the American melting pot to the extent that the *shish kebab* had become indistinguishable from the hamburger, and peanut butter a substitute for *ful* and *hummus*. I know that good Arab dishes, particularly those cooked and served in homes, have won the hearts of numerous American citizens who have visited, and continue to visit the Middle East. But preparing good Arab dishes is laborious and time-consuming, and even in modern Arab homes this process has become rare because it is ill attuned to the tempo of modern life.

New York is so multi-racial and impersonal as to preclude, or at least minimise, the feeling of estrangement and alienation. With the exception of tourists, who usually swarm through the city in great numbers, and whom one can identify by their necks protruding towards the sky, fathoming the elevations of the forest of skyscrapers, the hallmark of Manhattan, everyone is a citizen against whom no-one can discriminate except at his own peril. This may not have been the case 50 years ago, but it is, by and large, today.

Central Park is the pride and jewel of New York, affording space, greenery and relaxation, contrasting with the confinement and congestion of the skyscraper city. Near to my residence, between Lexington and Park, I often made long walks in the park, sometimes riding the swings, of the kind I had enjoyed in my childhood at the children's playgrounds which Mrs Vester of the American Colony Hotel had founded in Saaddiyah quarter, in the Old City of Jerusalem.

We had been warned, as diplomats, not to stray too far towards the west of New York for fear of being mugged. During my seven years of residence in New York, I was fortunate in being spared the scare, or even the injury, of mugging, even though the residence of my predecessor had been the target of an assault in 1973. Fortunately, neither Ambassador nor Mrs Laila Sharaf were in the residence at the time. But the offender put a long knife to the throat of the embassy guard and forced him to hand over the $150 that was in his pocket. I went with the police to the scene of the incident on behalf of the ambassador who was in California, in the company of Crown Prince Hassan. Ambassadors had been advised unofficially to carry at all times around $150 in cash so that, if mugged, they could hand over the cash to the attacker and say, with a feigned smile and apology, that they wished they had more to give.

Muggers are desperate and act impulsively, as well as compulsively, as often as not to obtain money with which to satisfy their insatiable lust and penchant for the drug of their liking. A mugger is a victim of manipulative traffickers and needs to be cured and rehabilitated more urgently than being thrown into jail, only to resurface with greater venom and longing. Washington Square in Greenwich Village was rampant with such addicts during my sojourn, and it is a great pity that the exhilarating and enjoyable atmosphere there, with its artists and musicians, should be so infected.

An urban megapolis with close to 10 million inhabitants can never be security-proof, but there are intimate neighbourhoods, nonetheless, in which people live and communicate closely together and lead normal lives. They represent the vast majority of people. Deviations and crime are the exception, although their occurrence attracts attention.

My transfer this time did not entail any family hardships. My eldest daughter, Laila, had already finished her university education at the American University of Cairo and was happily married to her cousin, Zaki. Haitham had graduated from Washington and Jefferson University, and after a brief period of training at Chase Manhattan Bank, was working with a bank in Amman. Lina had just graduated from the University of New York with a Master's degree, and Khaled, the youngest, had graduated from Columbia University, and later pursued graduate studies at Princeton University.

I finished odds and ends in New York and prepared myself for departure on New Year's Eve. I cannot claim that I did not feel a heavy heart at departure, because over the seven long years I had enjoyed my work at the UN, tiring and nerve-wracking as it may oftentimes had been. I had developed a liking for life in New York, resonant with fond memories and experiences. But for every beginning there is an end, as is the case with life itself. And even the good things in life, if continuous and sustained, suffer from the workings of the law of diminishing returns. They lose their novelty and become routine, making one aspire for change, for better or worse. Another chapter in my life had been closed, with a new one ready to open.

CHAPTER 16

RETURN

I looked forward to returning to Amman to resume my activities on national soil after almost a decade and a half of living abroad. A royal decree had been issued appointing me to the Upper House of Parliament – the equivalent to the Senate in the US, save that membership in the Upper House in Jordan is by selection not election. The term of service is four years, renewable at the pleasure of the king, but with the advice of the prime minister and other counsellors. I served two terms, ending in 1989.

Membership in the Upper House is more than a sinecure office, and the qualification of an eligible senator, as stipulated in the constitution, is to have served the kingdom in the higher echelons of government, including as prime minister, minister, diplomat, military commander, writer or anyone else noted for his or her meritorious service in public life.

Amongst its other legislative functions, it acts as a countervailing power, checking legislation passed by the elected Lower House of Parliament. The presumption is that this exclusive body, because of the high quality and experience of its members, is endowed with legislative expertise which could, if the need arose, counterbalance any excesses or deficiencies in the legislative processes of the Lower House. Every piece of legislation must be scrutinised and passed by the two houses and if a draft law passed by the lower house is turned down by the Upper House, then a joint meeting of the two houses is convened, and its vote is final.

On many occasions, differences are not on substance but on formulation or some other procedural dimension, in which case the lower house accepts the alteration or amendments with good grace. But differences on substantive issues can be heated and challenging.

During my terms of service, only the Upper House was functioning. The tenure of the elected parliament, representing the two regions of the kingdom, the West Bank including Arab Jerusalem, and the East Bank, with Amman as the capital of both, had expired in the mid-1970s. Patching-up, filling vacancies, and repeated extensions, had run their course, and new elections could not be held because of the occupation of the West Bank in June 1967. King Hussein appointed an advisory council to substitute temporarily for an elected parliament. While this was high-powered in its composition, it could not be a credible substitute for an elected parliament. It served its purpose for a while, and was then dissolved.

When I took my seat in the Upper House in January 1983, its jurisdiction was much curtailed because no legislation could be enacted, in the absence of the Lower House. Our energies, therefore, were focused on other public functions at home, and no less importantly, representing Jordan at the annual meetings of the Inter-Parliamentary Union (IPU) and other international functions. The union had accepted our accreditation as the 'Jordan group', in consideration of the *force majeure*, in consequence of the occupation of half the kingdom, and the sheer impossibility of holding elections under the circumstances.

The plenary meetings of the IPU, in various capitals of the world, were extremely simulating. I attended many of these meetings, either as a member of the Jordanian group, if the group was led by the speaker of the Upper House, or as head of the delegation if it was not.

I attended one such meeting in Helsinki, Finland, and was highly impressed by the fact that there was not one policeman on the streets because none was needed. But as we were taking a walk in one of those streets we observed, to our surprise, a lone policeman guarding an embassy. We were told, to our dismay, that it was the Libyan Embassy. Could an Arab embassy again be a lone misfit in such serene surroundings, we wondered.

I also attended a couple of conferences in Geneva, as beautiful as ever, which I had known as a non-resident ambassador. I was then leader of the delegation to an IPU meeting in Lima, Togo. The hotel accommodation was spartan and barely two-star. But our delegation was lodged in tourist bungalows on the seashore of the Atlantic Ocean of West Africa. To us in Jordan, landlocked except for a short strip at Aqaba on the Red Sea, abutting an ocean for the week of the conference was a treat, watching the white crests of the waves breaking rhythmically and unendingly over each other.

I also led the Jordan parliamentary group to the annual meeting of the IPU in Buenos Aires. I had visited Buenos Aires as foreign minister in 1962, as part of my Latin American tour to advocate the Palestinian cause. Buenos Aires had impressed me as one of the best-planned cities in the world, like Paris in its orderliness and beauty. The river Plate was unlike any other river which I had seen before. It is so expansive that one does not see its opposite bank, as one does even of large rivers like the Nile. I asked the Argentinian diplomat, who was accompanying me on the visit whether the Plate was truly a river and not part of the sea, and he assured me that it was and its water was sweet.

There is a large and influential Syrian-Lebanese community in Argentina, and the Syrian ambassador invited their leaders to a special gathering at the embassy to hear a statement from me on the question of Palestine. Attending the gathering was the Syrian military attaché Colonel Amin al-Hafez who, a mere two years later, became head of state. I also attended IPU meetings in Bangkok, Guatemala City and Budapest.

Typically at an IPU conference there is a general debate on the political, economic and social situation of the world. Each delegation has a first and a second speaker, and there is a very strict time limit afforded to each, in the range of five-to-seven minutes. A speaker who exceeds those limits is abruptly cut off, which makes many speakers rush their deliveries in order to cram in as much as they can. Also participating in those meetings are non-governmental organisations, representing wide-ranging interests and concerns, such as the environment, women's and children's rights, and human rights, to mention only a few.

The main items each year reflect the international community's focus on a particular issue that may be in vogue, and there is generally a confluence between the concerns voiced at the United Nations and those chosen as items for discussion at inter-parliamentary conferences. The activities of both are interactive and mutually reinforcing, notwithstanding that each belongs to autonomous and separate domains.

A highlight in my participation in the work of the IPU came in 1988 when I attended the centenary celebrations in London. It was a deserving tribute to have chosen London for this historic occasion, acknowledging the House of Commons as the undisputed mother of parliaments. The celebrations included a grand gala at Westminster, attended by Queen Elizabeth, Prime Minister Margaret Thatcher, important personages from various walks of life, and the parliamentarians themselves, members of the IPU.

The United Kingdom, unlike almost all other countries of the world, does not have a written constitution, but an evolving system of laws and customs developed over centuries. It consists of various statutes enacted by parliament, established practices and important law cases. The key principle is the rule of law and not of men, where every citizen is subject to the laws of the land, and the unrestricted supremacy of parliament. In the past, the House of Lords shared power with the House of Commons, but such powers as had been shared, have since been whittled-down, particularly since the reforms of 1911, to symbolic functions.

The process of transferring power from the monarch to the people began in the 13th century when King John was forced to restrict his power by signing the *Magna Carta*. This was the beginning of the devolution of power and by no means the end. As one who has studied English history at school and beyond, I am familiar with the fate of English kings who, at times, have been tyrannical, arbitrary, ruthless, and plain foolish: King George III who lost the colonies of North America, or King Henry VIII, with his numerous wives, and the split that he caused in the English church to accommodate his worldly needs.

I am not trying to simplify the interpretation of important milestones in the history of the country which, deservedly, prides itself as being the fountain of modern parliamentary democracy. But I mentioned the episodes above to show that the attainment of truly credible and established democracy was not a simple affair, but an uphill and costly struggle over generations, if not centuries. During the grand gala at Westminster, I saw paintings of seemingly impressive personages hung on the walls of the grand hall. I asked a member of the House of Commons who was standing beside me who those gentlemen were. His answer explained eloquently the problems involved in establishing democracy. He said: 'These are the pictures of the gentlemen who were beheaded in the Tower of London.'

This is a lesson that must be understood by those who are preaching the cause of democracy, as though it were a ready-made, easy-to-swallow panacea for good governance, unmindful of the struggles, strivings and sacrifices that are necessary before it can triumph. From our experiences in the Arab world over the past 50 years, we can deduce that democracy, once described by Winston Churchill as the worst form of government apart from all the others that had been tried, is not simply the drawing-up of a pristine constitution, with appropriate mechanisms for elections and other paraphernalia of a democratic system. Most of the Arab countries lived under the most liberal and progressive constitutions in the early part of the last century, copied almost literally from European constitutions and civil laws. But these were either overthrown by military coup d'états, or otherwise manipulated and shorn of their real substance.

Democracy, as a form of government, is the allocation of power, rights and obligations by peaceful means: who gets what, when and how, by the rule of law. Despots achieve these goals by the use of violence, organised state violence. Democracies operate by means of peaceful pursuits, bargaining, compromises and judicial processes. The success of democracy requires, above all, a moderate temperament, tolerance and the readiness to accept peaceful change and, if necessary, defeat. By and large, the march of democracy in the Arab world is on-going and, I dare to hope, unstoppable. But it will take time, not the centuries of its evolution in the United Kingdom, but many decades nonetheless.

In 1986, I joined once again the executive branch of the government, in addition to being a member of the Upper House. It was a cabinet formed by Prime Minister Zeid al-Rifai, his second term of office, the first having been in the mid-1970s. He is a personal friend and colleague, and is very able. My assignment was minister in charge of prime ministry affairs, which is the focal point for all other ministries. I had served with Zeid's father, Samir al-Rifai, as minister for foreign affairs in 1963, in a short-lived cabinet because parliament withheld confidence in it as a result of internal political machinations. The former Prime Minister Samir al-Rifai, veteran statesman with great experience, belonged to an older generation, possibly a decade and a half older than me; his son, Zeid, is a decade and a half younger.

In 1963, I was entrusted, by Samir Pasha, along with two other colleagues, Nasuh al-Taher and Dr Khalil el-Salem, with writing the speech from the throne, the equivalent of the State of the Union address and here, once more, after a quarter of a century, I had been entrusted by his son with writing the policy statement, on the basis of which a cabinet would seek the Lower House's vote of confidence. With the material made available to me, I could state that Jordan had travelled far in its social and economic development. Over a period of 20 years it had developed an infrastructure second to none in the region. Electric power, running water, and a highly developed and extensive road system covered almost 100 percent of the country. This was in addition to the establishment of a multitude of universities, colleges and technical institutes, and the provision of medical and social services for the entire country. Literacy extended to nearly 90 percent of the population and soon illiteracy was expected to be a thing of the past.

It is on such solid foundation, in all walks of development and growth, that Jordan today, under the leadership of King Abdullah II ibn al-Hussein, is embarked on an ambitious programme which aims at no less than catching up with the developed world in the age of information and its concomitant technological advances. There is every indication and hope that great strides will have been achieved towards this daring goal within the next 10 years.

Concurrent efforts are being made to consolidate the workings of democracy, in various sectors and strata of society, including freedom of the press and speech. It is a bumpy road and there are ups and downs along the way, generated by considerations of national security, juxtaposed against the yearnings for unrestricted freedoms. Recently this dilemma came to the fore when a Jordanian family, whose son had carried out a suicide attack in Iraq, accepted, in the traditional way, the condolences of the citizens of Salt, his town. A newspaper carried the item under the headline: 'Family celebrates the martyrdom of its son in an operation in which almost 200 Iraqis were killed and many scores wounded'. The Iraqi government was not at all pleased to hear the killing of such a high number of its citizens by a suicide bomber described as an act of martyrdom. It lashed out against Jordan, withdrew its ambassador from Amman, and temporarily closed the common border. How much value should be attached to freedom, on the one hand, and considerations of national interest on the other? The crisis has since been settled at the highest levels, but the episode remains a lesson to be heeded.

After a year of service in the cabinet, I decided that it was time to pay attention to my own interest, having dedicated my entire career to public service. I chose to resign and return to private life. I had already passed the legal age of retirement and I reckoned private life could be as rich and stimulating as public life, provided one had the will, the energy, and the commitment to make it so.

The most prudent attitude to retirement is a refusal to acknowledge it as an abandonment of active life and to branch out with activities and pursuits which keep one's mind and body fully engaged. The tempo may be somewhat slower as years go by, but not the mind or spirit which represents the moving force in human existence. Although deeply immersed in the past, even nostalgic, I have always found my solace in the future, the unfathomable, undefined, and promising future, which connotes continuity and defies the finite and the mortal.

Adopting this attitude is not an escape from mortality but an active encounter with it to offset its debilitating impact. Whenever I found myself unable to carry out some favourite project, for reasons beyond my control, I always consoled myself with the certainty that some day in the future I would carry it out, and I meant what I had said within my innermost soul. It is the future that kindles the flicker of life and sustains it. Those who give up on life upon retirement, at the relatively young age of 60 or 65 and accept retirement as a fate ordained and unchallenged end up counting the days before doomsday.

That makes doomsday all the more daunting, all the more imminent and inevitable. But as long as one's heart throbs with life one should make full use of it, without negativism or constraints. I am writing these remembrances in my eighties, and yet I do not feel that I am carrying the burden of so many cumulative years. I go almost every afternoon, or early evening, to the Royal Automobile Club in Amman, a 10-minute drive from my residence. It has an excellent health club, a half-size Olympic swimming pool, a spa, tennis courts (although I do not play tennis, once my forte, anymore), a buffet and cafeteria, and everything else that one aspires to have, including qualified physiotherapists. The subscription fees are reasonable and affordable, yet the club is restricted to its members to avoid being deluged by outside crowds.

This optimistic and positive outlook on life is perhaps inborn and genetic, but it could also be largely nurtured within the norms and mores of human societies. In our own Arab Islamic heritage, for example, I have been inspired by two sayings of the Prophet Muhammad on how to strike a balance between worldly and other-worldly affairs, the mortal and the eternal. One of them states that if the end of the world were nigh and you had a palm shoot in your hand you should go ahead and plant it. The other saying ordains: 'Work for your world as if you were to live forever, and work for the thereafter as if you were to die tomorrow,' i.e. live virtuously.

These are more than simply preachings advocating the work ethic: they are urging one to sustain life, regardless of how formidable the challenge may be, what sacrifices may be demanded, and how ephemeral life is. Life has a self-sustaining logic and pulsation of its own. And for it to be sustained, physically as well as mentally, one must curb and discipline one's elemental instincts. The word 'moderation' is, perhaps, the key to wellbeing, in food, drink, work, and overall modes of behaviour. Temperance in acting and reacting to events can induce catharsis, free of excessive joy or inordinate and crushing sorrow. Envy should, likewise, be diminished, because the envious can never be envious enough to achieve satiation. Invidious comparisons are the surest avenues to unhappiness, and the greater the comparisons, the greater the unhappiness. There is a considerable difference between negative envy and healthy competitiveness which seeks to excel and overtake, but not to watch, brood, sulk, and otherwise render life miserable. Faith, profound spiritual animation rather than mundane rituals, could be conducive to happy living, as are, I assume, such Eastern philosophies as yoga. Worry must be constrained or endured with circumspection. It is a mechanism to alert against unsavoury events which seem to be impending, but should never acquire a life of its own which could be self-consuming. Can such qualities of temperance, coolness, positiveness, goodness, optimism be imbued or inculcated? I wonder. But I know they are the prerequisite for healthy life and longevity, other physical conditions being equal.

All along but more imperatively in advanced age, the intake of food and drink must be sparing in quantity and selective in quality. I venture to use the much-used term 'Mediterranean' menus to emphasise the importance of fruit, vegetables and olive oil, and a generally fat-free diet. I always have on the table a plate of freshly sliced tomatoes with olive oil dressing, or mixed salads. I have no lust for meat, particularly junk food meat, and all other food injurious to good health. But all these health conscious modes of life, no matter how meticulously observed, could never provide full protection against a deadly disease. Three of my brothers have suffered from the ravaging disease of cancer, without having lived prodigal or wasteful lives. There is no escape from fate and God's will in His ultimate judgment. But here again, the laws of nature are consonant with God's laws which ordain that humans should not lead themselves down destructive paths. Fate or luck and a healthy code of behaviour are mutually inclusive, and none of them should be discarded as non-existent or irrelevant.

My term of service in the Upper House ended in 1989, and I had all the spare time I needed for my private life. In 1994, the National War College, which has appropriately changed its name to the National Defence College, asked me to teach a course on international relations, and I readily obliged. The student body includes bright staff officers from other Arab countries, particularly from the Gulf States. For five consecutive years I declined to accept financial remuneration for my teaching, not because I was floating on money but out of a sense of national duty, having accumulated wide experience, including from decision-making meetings with world leaders during my years serving the nation. The curriculum of each semester course was basically derived from the one I studied at the Woodrow Wilson School of Public and International Affairs at Princeton University in 1951, updated to take into account new concepts and theories, and the impact of certain events in the intervening half century. The Harold and Margaret Sprout collection of studies in their textbook *Elements of National Power* took pride of place as the point of departure in international relations. And so were theories on national interest which is also pivotal. International law and moral imperatives were not ignored either as fundamental constituents. Social and economic dimensions were likewise portrayed as the ingredients in nation-building. Discussions on current issues were invariably lively and absorbing. At the end of each semester, the commander of the college and his senior assistant would invite me to lunch at the college, in the course of which a shield would be presented with appropriate words for the occasion. I have a collection of five such plaques bearing the college's emblem which have become a part of my rich collection of medals awarded to me by heads of state in the course of my service. Some of the awards are ceremonial, while others are more personal, more specifically appreciative of my contributions to various fields of human endeavour.

Apart from academia, we Jerusalemites in Amman and other parts of Jordan, numbering close to a quarter of a million, with their progeny, felt an urge in 1990 to get together after decades of dispersal, in the aftermath of 1948 and 1967. This urge became more pronounced and gathered greater momentum after the return from Kuwait of an entire community of Palestinians, in the range of half a million people, the great majority of whom were Jordanian citizens from the East and the West Bank. Many of them had been active in Palestinian affairs during their long sojourn in Kuwait and wished to continue their pursuits in Jordan. These activities had included 'Jerusalem Day', in memory of Salahuddin's liberation of Jerusalem in 1187, led by Dr Subhi Ghosheh, a Jerusalemite physician and activist.

In 1990, a society called the Jerusalem Forum came into being and elected Dr Musa al-Husseini to be its chairman. Subsequently, I was elected chairman for two consecutive terms and after a three-year *interregnum*, was re-elected again in 2005, and made honorary chairman for life. The forum is a non-political cultural association which invites prominent historians, politicians and civic leaders to give lectures on Jerusalem and the Palestine question in general. It is an 'ingathering' of the exiles who meet at regular intervals to exchange memories of their former Jerusalem homes, as well as to talk about their careers and achievements since the uprooting of their families 50 years ago. It is truly cathartic to exchange such remembrances and rich experiences acquired across the globe, from Australia to the United States, and from Europe to the East. The Israelis claim to be a nation of immigrants, and here are their Palestinian victims outdoing them in terms of migration and metamorphosis.

But the Jerusalem Forum has been doing something more. It has been assisting, through the modest donations of its members and friends, in carrying out some good deeds in Jerusalem: the repair of selected historic but dilapidated buildings in the Old City, and the provision of financial assistance to university students in Jerusalem and its environs. These contributions are certainly modest when compared with those of *al-Taawun* (The Welfare Organization), an association which includes in its membership scores of Palestinian bankers, millionaires, and business people, under the chairmanship of Abdul Majid Shoman, founder and chairman of one of the largest banks in the Middle East, the Arab Bank, with reserves amounting to over $30 billion.

The Jerusalem Forum, with a younger and more ambitious board elected recently, is brainstorming to explore greater avenues of service to its beloved Jerusalem. But the forum, in league with other Jerusalem societies representing Silwan, Lifta, Ein Karem, Kolonia, Malha and other quarters or environs of Jerusalem, are unwaveringly committed to a platform of eventual return to their homes and homeland, from which they had either fled or had been forced to flee in the chaos and mayhem which followed the disintegration of the British mandatory government. Their activities are designed to keep alive in their hearts the city of their forefathers.

My other interest in life, years before I even thought of retiring, was my farm in the Jordan Valley. In recent years, as I explained previously, this has suffered painful degradation, in consequence of the drought afflicting our part of the world. My farm, as well as others, was dependent on underground, renewable wells, fed each year by rainfall over the range of mountains overlooking the valley and elsewhere. With diminished replenishment to offset the drought, uncontrolled and illegal drilling of wells, and the River Jordan and its tributaries starved and diverted unilaterally by Israel in the mid-1960s to other water basins. Water, the life-line of agriculture, has become a scarce commodity. To obtain water one has to drill to deeper aquifers. Also, the government is giving priority to domestic, industrial and touristic usages at the expense of agriculture. I developed an emotional attachment to the farm over more than four decades, during which I had come to know the bounty of even individual trees, producing 30 or 40 crates of the most delicious Jaffa and Washington oranges, tangerines, grapefruit and lemons. Seeing those trees wither for lack of adequate water was agonising and emotionally draining for me, and yet I could not do much about it. Expenditure on farms is never-ending, and with diminished income on account of the degraded produce, in quality and quantity, the project became a heavy, if not unbearable, burden. I remembered Professor Jacob Viner's assertion in his seminars on international trade at Princeton that the terms of trade were invariably against the producers of raw materials and in favour of manufactured goods. The prices of fruit and vegetables over the years, and particularly over the past decade, have dipped to frightening levels. Over-production and open markets have taken a heavy toll, and in our part of the world, unlike the United States or Europe, there are no farm price supports of any kind. So, at my own instigation, a heavy moving machine was hired to fell almost 80 percent of the trees, nurtured with loving care over four decades. If some adversary had wrought such wistful havoc I certainly would have sued him to the ends of the earth. But here I had no-one to blame but myself, but still suffered torment. And with my optimistic instinct, I console myself with the thought that sometime in the near future I shall refill it with thousands of the best date producing palm trees.

Meantime, Amman has continued to grow, and is no longer the quiet city which I came to know in the mid-1950s. The first circle, which was its outer boundary in Jabal Amman, now extends to an eighth circle, with bulging and ever-expanding off-shoots to the west, east, north and south.

I was serving in Wasfi Tal's cabinet in the early 1960s when traffic lights were installed for the first time, creating both a novelty and a nuisance. Back then there some 15,000 cars on the streets. Today, Amman's streets are filled with something like 750,000 cars.

I have lectured extensively over the past decade, on a variety of issues, foremost of which was Jerusalem, past, present and future. Another major topic has been comparative culture and civilisation, particularly in light of the worldwide dialogue on the so-called 'clash of civilisations', which I feel strongly is an exaggerated misnomer. Jerusalem has always been the focal point in my speaking or writing activities, and two such lectures stand out as uniquely expressing my viewpoints. One is entitled: 'Contemporary Jerusalem, the Jerusalem I knew'. This is the Jerusalem, whole and indivisible, old and new, Arab and Jewish, Christian and Muslim, with all communities living side-by-side in relative amity, territorial integrity and prosperity as the capital of Palestine under British mandatory government between 1918 and 1948. There are remembrances which only a few could call up because of the inexorable passage of time. There are insights which might prompt efforts towards restoring Jerusalem to its former self as the symbol of peace, inter-faith tolerance and moral purpose, as you will learn in the final chapter.

The other topic, a 'Dialogue of Civilisations' also aspires to bridge the gap which is perceptibly and imperceptibly widening between various areas of culture and civilisation. Exactly 50 years ago I made an academic distinction between culture and civilisation, and analysed it my book *The Ideas of Arab Nationalism*. This is a useful guide to evaluating the apparent differences between various areas of consensus, but which are presently presumed to be intrinsic, pre-ordained and therefore, insurmountable. Some still remember Rudyard Kipling's poem, at the height of British imperial expansion, in which he wrote: 'East is East and West is West, and never the twain shall meet'.

I firmly believe that civilisation, embodying the material instruments and components of life and culture which express the value systems, norms and mores, are universally interactive and inclusive. The difference is one of degree rather than of kind, even within individual societies. In approaching the subject of comparative civilisations, I thought that the best avenue for my purpose was to gauge, assess and compare Arab and Islamic civilisation and culture with that of the West, through reading my own educational map, and the accumulated influences which have shaped my being, spiritually, emotionally, intellectually and in every other formative sense. It is a map of parallel orientations, often overlapping, intermingling and interacting.

CHAPTER 17

CONTEMPORARY JERUSALEM: THE JERUSALEM I KNEW

The Jerusalem I shall be talking about was a unified, indivisible city before its dismemberment by the cataclysmic events of 1948. Almost the whole of the walled Old City, and most of new Jerusalem, in addition to the outskirts and nearby townships, were predominantly Arab-built, Arab-owned and Arab-inhabited, even though some of these quarters carried non-Arab names, such as the German Colony in Baqaa, the Greek Colony, the Italian hospital area, French Hill, and the American Colony. The American Colony is still a prestigious hotel which boasts of world celebrities who have frequented it since the early years of the last century. It is a collection of impressive Jerusalem mansions, built in style and owned by the Husseini, Nashashibi and Nusseibeh families and eventually sold to a group of American-Swedish missionaries, of whom I knew the Larsons and the renowned Mrs Vester. In her younger years, she was reputed to have been a beauty, and several of the older Jerusalem *effendi* class were said to have been amongst her admirers.

The Russian Compound, in the middle of West Jerusalem, is today an Israeli interrogation centre. It used to house the law courts. How much I loved attending some of those trials with Arab, British, and Jewish judges, attorneys, and defence lawyers, all wearing wigs and attired in black robes, which gave a unique aura of respect and awe. I remember a certain Mr Hogan, an extremely accomplished attorney general, fluently presenting his legal arguments, the way you see trials presented today in films or TV shows. He later became chief justice of Hong Kong. Musa al-Alami, next in line as assistant attorney general, became a distinguished and highly respected Palestinian leader. I am proud of his friendship, and served on the board of trustees of *al-Mashrou al-Inshai*, the agricultural reconstruction project in the Jericho area. This provided accommodation and education for generations of Palestinian orphans, and Musa al-Alami was the project's dedicated chairman.

Practising in those law courts also were equally distinguished Palestinian and Jewish lawyers of whom I specifically remember: Henry Kattan; Judge Mani, who taught jurisprudence at the Jerusalem Law School; Anwar Nusseibeh, judge and lawyer; Anton Attallah who served at the district court; Majid Abdul Hadi of the supreme court; Awni Abdul Hadi, lawyer and statesman; Abdul Latif Salah, also a Palestinian leader, and his son, attorney Walid Salah; Umar Saleh Bargouthi, who taught *al-Majallah* (Ottoman Civil Law) at the Jerusalem Law School where I studied in 1943-48; Sheikh Hussam Uddin Jarallah, who taught us Islamic Shari'a Law; and Michael Qattran, court registrar. Palestinians will also always remember Chief Justice Sir William Fitzgerald, who chided his government in 1936 for destroying old Jaffa city, under the pretext of town planning. The real intention had been to help the authorities combat the Palestinian rebellion which had just broken out and lasted until 1939 when World War II began. In his judgment, Fitzgerald shamed the British Palestine government for not having the courage to acknowledge its real intentions; but, alas, the demolition had already taken place. Despite all the unforgivable sins of the British mandatory government in Palestine, the British judiciary stood out as being proud and impeccable, resistant to pressures or foul practices.

One of my most frequent destinations growing up in Jerusalem was St Julian Road leading to the imposing YMCA and the equally imposing King David Hotel. To this day it has not been out-shone by any other hotel in the city, despite the huge number of such facilities built over the years in both East and West Jerusalem. Somehow the King David remains in a class of its own when it comes to grandeur. This is, I suppose, because it had originally been built to serve the aristocratic elite, the only ones who could afford to travel in the first half of the 20th century. Equally imposing is the towering YMCA, about which I wrote earlier.

Just off St Julian Road and close to the Mamilla thoroughfare is the Shamaa quarter which was a mixed Arab-Jewish market place, and in which the first Arab-Jewish violence was ignited for a few days in 1947, in reaction to the UN partition plan. I was informed by eyewitnesses on the spot that British security forces on the scene had been indifferent and ineffectual in the face of this ominous development, even though the forces were still at their peak before their gradual dismantling in the months ahead.

Also on the Jaffa Road leading to Zion Square was where the Zion Cinema stood, the first cinema house in

Jerusalem. One of the first films to be shown was an Arabic film entitled *Wardat al-Hubb al-Safi* (The Rose of Pure Love) in which the celebrated Egyptian star singer and composer, Muhammad Abdul Wahab, played the central role. I remember vividly crowds of women, most of whom in the early 1930s were still veiled and wearing the *milayas* (long black robes), walking briskly towards the cinema. They were excited at the prospect of watching a talking film in Arabic for the first time in their lives. None came by car or bus, because these were a rarity, and walking was the order of the day. It would be inconceivable today to see such big Arab crowds wandering at ease in the heart of the Jewish quarters, without as much as a raised eyebrow in surprise or protest. The two peoples were still living side-by-side in amity and peace, notwithstanding their diametrically opposed political platforms.

All these, and many others, were Arab quarters, meticulously demarcated by Chief Justice Fitzgerald, and endorsed by UN Resolution 181 in 1947.

This was the greater contemporary Jerusalem which I had known up to 1948. Its growth had been speedy and spectacular after 1925, extending beyond the municipal boundaries which had existed during the British mandate, to the villages of Abu Dis and Eizariya in the east, Lifta, Rumeima, Kolonia, Battir, Malha, Deir Yassin and Ein Karem to the west; Shufat and Issawiya to the north, and Bethlehem, Beit Jala, Beit Sahour, Sur Bahir, Beit Safafa and Artas to the south. These districts encircle Jerusalem like a bracelet, consecrating on the ground its human, geographical, agricultural and economic depth, in perfect and complementary harmony.

The UN allocated tens of millions of dollars for the establishment of the proposed international regime for

Jerusalem and promulgated a basic law to govern its workings. The administrative demarcations were based entirely on the demographic and geographic distributions existing on the ground between Arabs and Jews. The basic law also provided for the abrogation of the section pertaining to the concessions and privileges granted to the European powers by the Ottoman Empire in the years of its decline.

In describing the above, I am not trying to belittle, less still to deny, the heavy Jewish presence in Jerusalem and its environs, highlighted by quarters such as Rahavia, Telpioth, Mikor Haim, Mea Shearim, Mutza and others, mainly in the central as well as the western parts of the city. Indeed, the people of Jerusalem complained that the mandatory administration had included, in Jerusalem proper, adjacent Jewish suburbs while denying the same rights to similar Palestinian suburbs, resulting in numerical advantages to the Jews of Jerusalem *vis-à-vis* the Arabs.

The Jewish presence in Jerusalem had grown significantly since the latter part of the 19th century when the British Jewish philanthropist, Sir Moses Montefiore, had established the Jewish quarter named after him, astride the road between Jaffa Gate and the government printing press. The land had belonged to the Duzdar family of Jerusalem, and prior to the rise of the Zionist movement, the people of Jerusalem had had no inhibitions regarding a sale or grant to the Jews, who were regarded as an integral part of the Palestinian people. Indeed, the biggest Jewish cemetery on the Mount of Olives in East Jerusalem was leased to the Jewish community by the Islamic *Waqf* (religious endowment foundation) Department in the latter part of the 19th century for a period of 100 years.

When violence broke out in 1947-48, Montefiore, as well as adjacent quarters, came under constant crossfire, and I always made a point of driving alongside a British or a Jordanian army vehicle to reduce the chances of being caught in this fire. But my office at the *Daoud* building, which housed international journalists as well as the government information office, was extremely vulnerable and often was caught in the crossfire. I used to call it the daily afternoon tea party. On the roof of this tall building – the tallest in the area – was a British sergeant who evidently enjoyed participating in these exchanges with his Bren machine gun, even though the building had not been a target for either the Arabs or the Jews. I complained to the British commanding officer and informed him that by joining the fray the sergeant was turning us into a target. I showed him the bullets which had pierced the windows of my office and lodged in the walls. That very same day, I saw British troops carrying their seriously wounded comrade down the stairs on a stretcher. I felt sorry for him and wished him speedy recovery but could not help thinking that he had brought it on himself.

Jewish immigration ceased during World War I, but resumed at full speed during the British mandate. By the 1940s, the number of Jews in greater Jerusalem had become equal to that of Arabs, in the range of 100,000 of each. The Municipal Council of Jerusalem was constituted of 12 members, six Arabs and six Jews, with an Arab as the Mayor. Palestinian leaders Ragheb Nashashibi and Dr Hussein Fakhri Khalidi were among those were elected to this prestigious post at different intervals until the beginning of the 1940s when the Jews, claiming that they had numerically superseded the Arabs, demanded the mayoralty. The Palestinian Arabs rejected this demand, on the ground that even if the Jews had achieved numerical superiority, which they disputed on grounds of unfair gerrymandering to which I referred earlier, the mayoralty of Jerusalem should be in Arab hands, being the capital of Palestine and because of its sanctity in the Arab and Islamic worlds. The question remained unresolved until the end of the mandate in 1948, when the Arabs and the Jews established separate municipalities.

The expansion of Jerusalem had precedents in the city's long history. In ancient times, the walls were said to have extended beyond the present ones around the Old City, and excavations by the Israeli authorities, have latterly unearthed relics of a wall in the heart of *Musrara* quarter. Mujir al-Din al-Hanbali, the authoritative historian of Jerusalem, writing 500 years ago, in his classic *Al Uns al-Jalil fi Tarikh al-Quds wa'l-Khalil* on page 59 observed:

> 'In the outskirts of noble Jerusalem from every corner are to be found groves containing a variety of fruits, including grapes, figs, apples and others. The best location is known as Baqaa, in the outskirts of noble Jerusalem (*al-Quds al-Sharif*) from the west towards the *qibla*, a *waqf* endowment from Sultan Salah al-Din, for the benefit of the *Khanaqah* seminary for Sufis (mystics)'.

The historian adds:
> 'In Baqaa and adjacent areas are palaces built in perfect order and their owners, each year live in them during the summer, several months, and spend plenty of money'.

The historian gives further details on the quarters of west Jerusalem and their utilisation. On page 127 he writes: 'Judge Sharaf al-Din Issa ibn Sheikh as-Shuyukh Jamal al-Din Ghanim al-Khazraji, the Judge of Jerusalem and the Sheikh of *Salahiya Khanaqah*, was the one who leased the lands of Baqaa in sacred Jerusalem, in the endowment *waqf* of *Salahiya Khanaqah* (seminary) in the year 793 AH [1392 AD], and it was transformed into groves, and its revenues increased to the benefit of the endowment, and people became attracted to it, and its utilization increased.'

It is not out of place to recognise here – and this might surprise some, even within the family – that the Bani Ghanim al-Khazraji family, which played such a leading role in Jerusalem, and in Palestine in general, from the Ayyubid and Mamluk eras up to the beginning of the Ottoman era (early 16th century), is the forefather of the present Nusseibeh family. The Khazraj, who came to Jerusalem with the Caliph Umar at the helm of the Arab Islamic conquest; gave the first governorate of Palestine to Ubadah ibn al-Samit al-Khazraji, a companion of the Prophet, by order of Caliph Umar. But the family took refuge in the village of Bureen, near Nablus, when the Crusaders conquered Jerusalem in 1087 and massacred most of its inhabitants. The historian of Jerusalem Mujir al-Din al-Hanbali, gives the following biography of the founder of Bani Ghanim on page 146 as follows:

'The leading Sheikh and authority King Ghanim ibn Ali ibn Husain al-Ansari al-Khazraji al-Maqdisi, born in the village of Bureen near Nablus, in the year 562 *Hijri*. Sultan Salah al-Din Yusuf ibn Ayyub, entrusted him with the Sheikhdom of the *Salahiya Khanaqah*, named after him in Jerusalem, to be under his supervision. I saw Salah al-Din's signature and the handwriting of the Sultan on it. When I had read it I thanked God for his blessings and bounty. His biography has lapsed because of ancient history and time long past. He was the first to administer the *Khanaqah*, and lived in Jerusalem since that date. His offspring were well-known and famous, and I shall mention what I can of their names, God willing'.

Sultan Salahuddin granted not only the *Khanaqah* to Bani Ghanim but, more importantly, the custody of the Church of the Holy Sepulchre, whose gate, up to this day, must be opened at dawn by a member of the Nusseibeh family, at present cousin Wajeeh, and closed by him in the evening. The practice has become so firmly established over the centuries that even during curfews imposed by the Israelis during the past four decades, for one reason or another, a search would be undertaken to fetch him wherever he might be. A member of the Nusseibeh family, again Wajeeh, on Holy Saturday, the day preceding Easter, is amongst the solemn procession of bishops and priests, in their gorgeous robes, carrying silk and gold embroidered banners and chanting their beautiful litany, while circling three times round the Sepulchre. A member of the Nusseibeh family descends into the inner and outer circle of the Rotunda, and a priest is chosen each year to be 'the bishop of the holy fire'. Everyone in the crowd carries a torch or a candle to be lighted. And after a moment of silence, a voice from within the sepulchre proclaims that the miraculous holy fire has been kindled. A Nusseibeh down below puts his seal upon the event every year, and the fire, amidst cries of thanksgiving, is distributed to the rejoicing crowds.

These services and observances are Eastern in origin, and the Syrian Christians of the land, the indigenous people as far back as the 9th century, believed that an angel of God was appointed to light the lamps over the Sepulchre of Christ every Easter eve. Westerners do not subscribe to this observance, but Easterners draw comfort and hope from it. Moreover, the people of Jerusalem, Bethlehem, and Nazareth regard the Easter pilgrimage as an annual financial bonanza, with numerous pilgrims coming from Russia, Greece, Cyprus, Egypt, and other countries of the Eastern Churches.

Sultan Salahuddin also granted the Bani Ghanim, now the Nusseibehs, al-Lubban al-Sharqi village, along with 50,000 dunums of fertile land on the plain between Jerusalem and Nablus. The family received *ushr* (tithes) on the produce of the area under all governments up to 1967.

It would be remiss of me at this point if I did not make reference to a very important recent discovery, with close connections to the family. I am referring to the approximately 900 Islamic documents – the *Haram* collection – discovered, almost accidentally, in August 1974 and October 1976 in the Islamic museum located within the precincts of Haram al-Sharif by the curator Amal Abul-Hajj. Situated in a vaulted hall built by the Crusaders, just west of the Aqsa Mosque, the museum had been closed for renovations and repairs, and the curator's curiosity had been aroused by the fact that some of the display cases contained locked drawers. When unlocked, one of them turned out to be stuffed with 354 documents, written on paper and parchment of various sizes. Abul-Hajj later discovered an even larger group of documents from the same period in another locker. Amal Abul-Hajj and Linda S. Northrop cooperated in publishing *A collection of medieval Arabic documents in the Islamic Museum at the Haram al-Sharif*, in *Arabica* 25, (1979). Subsequently, Donald P Little made a catalogue of the documents, with a very incisive analysis of them.

According to Little, the documents, the largest ever such discovery of the Mamluk era, were the private library of chief justice of Jerusalem Sharafuddin Abu al-Ruh Isa ibn Sheikh al-Shuyukh Jamal-al-Din Abul Jud Ghanim al-Ansari al-Khazraji al-Shafii, and Sheikh al-Khanaqah al-Salahiya. The documents reveal that he had served as acting judge of Nablus. He also held significant non-judicial positions in Jerusalem, including another institution founded by Salahuddin, namely the al-Maristan al-Salahi hospital, where in 1393-94 AD he was *nazir* (superintendent) of the endowment which financed it. Northrop concludes the comments as follows:

> 'Finally, a number of documents dated 1388-94 AD which refer to him as Nazir al-Awqaf al-Mabrura, i.e. supervisor of the blessed endowments of Jerusalem, show that he had duties and responsibilities in administering endowments, beyond the two specific institutions mentioned above. Only with this realization can the nature of the *Haram* documents be understood, that is if my hypothesis that they represent, to a great extent, the remains of records belonging to and collected by Judge Sharafuddin al-Khazraji is correct.'

I shall not go any further in discussing the Nusseibeh-Bani Ghanim metamorphosis, except to remark that it is disorienting and perplexing to have to endure a change of name, even though it occurred seven centuries ago. Many other old Jerusalem and Palestine families have had similar changes of names: el-Deiri is now Khalidi; Bani Jamaa became al-Khateeb; al-Alam is now al-Alami; al-Hasqafi became Jarallah; and Hanbal Jaafari is today Hashem of Nablus, just to mention a few.

Going back to the new Jerusalem in which I lived, worked and played, I can state without hesitation that its quarters, such as upper and lower Baqaa, Qatamon, Talbiya, and others were and are among the cleanest and most beautiful residential quarters in the world. They contained, predominantly, houses built with engraved white and red stones from the famous quarries of Jerusalem, Bethlehem and Hebron, as well as the crystal clear white stone of Jamaa in the Nablus district. The stately pine trees adorning its streets have become even more beautiful with the passage of years.

My aunt, Zuhra, owned a house in Ratisbon quarter, close to the Eden Cinema (which I used to frequent), from which she received a handsome rent up to 1948. In 1950, she was 80 years old and asked me in all innocence: 'How is it that the tenant of my house has not paid his rent for two years? Is this reasonable? Is this possible? In the past, she used to send me with her long-time maid, Muhammadiya, to fetch her cheque.' I answered, feigning ignorance, that she had nothing to worry about, and that I would arrange payment to be made soonest.

That was 60 years ago and, not a cent has been paid to her or any other Jerusalemite, the tens of thousands of Jerusalemites who built, owned, lived in, or leased their private properties in West Jerusalem. These properties were built with their hard-earned toil and savings, and it is incomprehensible to them that others should be living in them, without, at least, paying rent.

Which provision of human rights could allow such flagrant illegality, such unredeemed injustice over 50 years? And yet every November the world celebrates the anniversary of the Universal Declaration of Human Rights, which includes the sanctity of life, private property and the plethora of rights and duties enumerated therein. And by what code of justice are these quarters regarded as Israeli and non-negotiable in any discussion on a final status? The aftermath of the war of 1948 left to the people of Jerusalem a few sparse quarters, outside of the walled Old City, mainly Sheikh Jarrah and the

Herod's Gate quarters. But even this parsimonious remnant is being coveted by Israel for incorporation into the 'eternal and united capital of Israel', and by corollary denied to the Palestinian people.

If Israel, indeed, wants a united Jerusalem, I for one, would be all for it, as would every other Jerusalemite. But it must be a unity of equals and not of occupiers and occupied, of the free and not the chained, of first class and not second class citizens, apartheid style. This chapter was closed in South Africa, and no-one in the world would accept its resuscitation in whatever form. Let us reunite Jerusalem, East and West, which is the most natural thing to do, but under a regime of joint sovereignty, equality, human rights and freedoms.

The contemporary expansion of Jerusalem outside the walls of the Old City began in the second half of the 19th century when it once again became a focal point of the Western world after a break of several centuries. Mary Eliza Rogers, sister of the British vice-consul in Jerusalem and consul in Haifa, wrote a book more than 150 years ago entitled *Domestic Life in Palestine* which I enjoyed very much. An astute and incisive observer of land, people and nature, a talented writer, she describes how Jerusalem in 1855, consisted only of the walled Old City. She narrates how its gates – seven of them – would be closed at 10pm every night and reopened at dawn, by personal order from the pasha, the governor.

William Bartlett, in his books *Jerusalem Revisited* and *Walks about Jerusalem*, published in the middle of the 19th century, gave a vivid, comprehensive description of the Old City's streets and alleys, churches, mosques, and synagogues, which almost matches that of the Jerusalem historian Mujir al-Din al-Hanbali some 400 years earlier.

For me, it is always fascinating and breathtaking to revisit old Jerusalem. A few dozen metres from the Holy Sepulchre is a relatively modest mosque, the Mosque of Umar, where the caliph performed his prayers 1,400 years ago after accepting the keys of the city from Patriarch Sophronius. He declined the invitation of the patriarch to say his prayers within the precincts of the church, lest future generations of Muslims took that as a precedent to break the covenant which he had made with Sophronius to respect the sanctity and inviolability of this church. The mosque was renovated a few years ago, and in the process layers of even older constructions were uncovered.

Adjacent to the Holy Sepulchre is the *Salahiya Khanaqah* for Sufis to which I have already made reference. It was presented to Salahuddin by the Greek Orthodox patriarch who, along with his fellow Orthodox compatriots, had been expelled from Jerusalem by the Latin Kingdom rulers. He made this award in appreciation of his church's reinstatement by Salahuddin when the latter recaptured the city. The two premises the Holy Sepulchre and the *Khanaqah*, are so contiguous as to have led to a dispute a few years ago over ownership of a wall in a tiny room used by a priest as a bedroom. I was a member of a mission sent to Jerusalem in 1998 to adjudicate the dispute. The mission succeeded in resolving the dispute peacefully and amicably.

Walking the streets of Jerusalem, you come across *Khassaki Sultan*, a philanthropic foundation which offers, on a daily basis, hot wheat soup *(freekeh)* to the poor of the city, as well as to its visitors and pilgrims. It is both delicious and nourishing, and many Jerusalem families have been known occasionally to avail themselves of a helping. There is a similar establishment in Hebron which up to this day serves the poor and the needy.

Khassaki Sultan, the donor, was the Russian wife of the Ottoman sultan five centuries ago who set up abundant endowments for the foundation's upkeep on a sustained basis.

The city was once endowed with many public baths – known in the West as Turkish baths. Brides used to be prepared for their weddings during three days of attention at these baths by women who were beauty experts. Removal of superfluous hair with an adhesive plaster of strong gum rendered the skin both bright and polished. The bride usually invited her friends to accompany her to the public bath before the wedding day, and all of them generously applied soap and henna (the local dye from the crushed leaves of the henna tree or *lawsonia*), as well as *kohl* (sulphide of antimony) to highlight the eyebrows.

Over the three days, refreshments and coffee were served as the bride was led through different passages, gradually increasing in temperature, with fountains overflowing over marble floors to a jet of hot water, and by slow degrees to more moderate temperatures. Up to the middle of the 20th century such baths were still in operation, not only for washing, but also for traditional ceremonies. With private baths in every home, public baths have become superfluous.

There are also many *zawiyas* (retreats) for religious meditation, studies and practices: an Indian retreat, a Maghrebi retreat and many others from various countries, following the practice of a multitude of Sufi schools (orders), such as al-Mawlawiyya, al-Naqsahbandiyya, al-Gilaniyya, and others. These are scattered around the various quarters of the Old City, but by far the greatest concentration of schools, both religious and secular, are clustered in and around the Haram al-Sharif sanctuary. The Aqsa Mosque and the Dome of the Rock themselves provide a forum for religious instruction, and any visitor, except during prayer time, will see different congregations clustered around learned men reading and interpreting the texts. Since the latter part of the Bahri Mamluk era, the four main law schools of Islam – Hanafi, Shafii, Maliki and Hanbali – have been accepted in Palestine on equal terms. Each has its *qadis* (judges) administering justice. During the Ayyubid era, the Shafii school was predominant, during the Ottoman Empire, the Hanafi school. Without delving into the intricacies and niceties of jurisprudence, I can state without hesitation that whatever differences exist are in degree and not in kind. Some are more liberal than others in interpreting Shari' a law, and particularly on matters relating to personal status, and there are minute differences in rituals. But, basically, they are in confluence. This applies to the Shiite Jaafari mainstream, but not to the multitude of extreme sects which are regarded as dissenters from Islam.

    I need not enumerate the monasteries and churches which are so prominent on the landscape and in the architecture of the Old City. They are ancient and stately. The Church of the Holy Sepulchre is 1,700 years old, even though it has been afflicted by fires – one was in 1812 – earthquakes and other disasters. The Aqsa Mosque and the Dome of the Rock are approximately 1,300 years old or more. They have miraculously withstood the vicissitudes of time, and their unequalled beauty must have persuaded the conquering Crusaders, nine centuries ago, to spare them and to convert them into churches. The Old City itself sits on layers of older buildings, shops, tunnels and waterways which could be unearthed without too much difficulty. One retired Jordanian officer told me that he had actually walked beneath the Old City from end to end, from Damascus Gate to Jaffa Gate, without any obstacle. I have no way of verifying his claim, but I am inclined to believe it.

Jerusalem is bewitching in the beauty of its architecture and its historical harmony. A few years ago, I accompanied my brother, Muhammad, who lives in Jerusalem, on a visit to the new municipality premises near Jaffa Road and the Russian Compound to pursue the completion of the offices and shopping centre which the family owns in Salahuddin Street and has remained unfinished since 1967. I was shown a circular balcony from which one captures the whole panorama of Jerusalem, new and old, East and West. And as I was admiring this magnificent view my mind instantly travelled back to Rome. The latter is the larger city, more sprawling and metropolitan, more stately, and has unique treasures belonging to all eras, with St Peter's Square at the centre and the River Tiber traversing it. After all, it was the capital of an empire, in which Jerusalem was the capital of a province.

But, when all is said and done, Jerusalem to me, with all its modesty, seemed equal in grandeur, beauty and ancientness. Is it not the cradle of all the monotheistic faiths, their focal point? But why should one indulge in invidious comparisons and compare the incomparable. I may be partial when I state that, to me, and in my eyes, there is no place more beautiful than Jerusalem. Its heritage goes back to the Canaanites, Hebrews, Romans, Umayyads, Abbasids, Fatimids, Ayyubids, Mamluks, and Ottomans.

True enough, it had not been their political capital, and there are prerequisites for choosing a political capital. But in the case of Jerusalem, its de-politicisation was designed to spare it the vicissitudes of mundane conflicts, although unfortunately, without much success. Israeli ambassadors at the United Nations have incessantly tried to denigrate its pivotal importance to us by claiming that it had never been the capital of those large Arab and Islamic conglomerates. My answer was that while Mecca was never a capital this fact has never detracted from its prime spiritual status in Islam. Muslims believe and insist that both Mecca and Jerusalem shall forever be spiritual rather than worldly capitals.

But Jerusalem has always been the provincial capital for the Palestinian people within the larger conglomerates, and was not, as Israel claims, solely King David's capital some 3,000 years ago. Palestine as a province had been largely self-governing only because of the difficulties of communication and transportation. The governor was named *Naib al-Hukm*, and a chief justice was the equivalent of a governor, in all matters, temporal and religious.

As an integral part of the Abrahamic faith, Islam has always regarded David, Solomon and other Judaic prophets with the greatest veneration. Indeed, Islam regards them as its own, and Islam itself is a continuum and a completion of one and the same message. This is ecumenism in its universal manifestation. The Islamic Hebron sanctuary (*Haram al-Ibrahimi al-Sharif*), which supposedly houses the sepulchres of Abraham and his immediate seed, male and female, is only second to Jerusalem's sanctuary in sacredness in the sight of Muslims. The tomb of King David on Mount Zion in Jerusalem is venerated by Muslims as the *Nabi Daoud* (Prophet David) Mosque, and one of the renowned Jerusalem families, the Dajanis, have been its custodian for centuries. It is not, therefore, out of bigotry or exclusiveness that we object to declared Israeli designs against the Aqsa Mosque and the Dome of the Rock.

The Israeli authorities demolished the Maghrebi and other Arab quarters west of the Aqsa Mosque in order to widen the area of the Wailing Wall. Not until the 16th century did Jews request to say their prayers at the Western Wall of the Haram al-Sharif. This happened when a Jewish doctor expelled from Andalusia along with the Muslims took refuge in Turkey and convinced the authorities there to grant the Jews the right to pray in a small area at the Western Wall. The request was innocuous enough, without any thought that one day it could develop into an aggressive design against one of Islam's holiest sites. And besides, there are highly religious Jews who regard the mere act of climbing Mount Moriah (the Temple Mount, to the Jews) to be a sacrilegious act, pending the advent of the true Messiah. A senior official of the *Waqf* Department told me that after Israel had occupied Jerusalem in 1967, the Israeli minister of the interior visited the department. He was invited to visit the holy sanctuary but declined on religious grounds. When the Messiah does come, he will surely have the vision to solve the problem amicably and to the satisfaction of all.

A few years ago Israel, and more specifically the municipality of Jerusalem, celebrated the 3,000th anniversary of King David's city. This would not have been so controversial and open to challenge if it had not been so blatantly exclusive, and tainted by a desire to deny the Palestinian Arabs' existence in or association with Jerusalem. Scholars and historians in Amman felt that such denial should not be left unanswered. Under the patronage of *Aal al-Bait* Institute for Islamic Thought, a prestigious semi-governmental establishment whose president was Dr Nasser Eddine al-Asad, Jordanian,

Arab and international scholars, well versed in the history of the Holy Land, were invited to make their contribution. Needless to say, they all substantiated what had already been acknowledged across the ages and in the Old Testament itself, namely that the Jebusites, a branch of the Canaanites, were the founders of the city of Jerusalem which they named *Uru Salem*.

In contradistinction to Israel's slogan of 'Jerusalem 3,000', the scholars in Amman coined their own: 'Jerusalem 5,000'. The then Mayor of Jerusalem, Ehud Olmert, clearly unable to deny this fact, declared that what mattered were the significant years, meaning the Jewish era; upon which Jordanian scholars reminded the mayor that Israel's nemesis, the Canaanites, were the ones who gave to the world its most important invention: the alphabet.

Let me leave those historical disputations where they belong, with the historians, and emphasise that whether we go back 3,000 or 5,000 years, the uninterrupted inhabitants of the Holy Land were the indigenous Palestinian people, whereas the Jews, after their expulsion by the Romans 2,000 years ago, ceased to exist in there. International law is unequivocal in emphasising that the sovereign rights over any land belong to the indigenous people who have had a sustained existence on the land, regardless of conquests, foreign rule and other adversities. Scores of nations over the ages conquered Palestine and subjected its people to foreign rule; but Palestine remained for its indigenous people, together with others who opted to integrate and merge with them. It is commonly acknowledged that the people of Greater Syria, including Palestine, are an amalgam of many races, and there are families whose roots go back to the time of the European Crusaders and other conquerors.

The new quarters of Jerusalem began to spring up in the second half of the 19th century. There were incipient and modest beginnings, and for a more detailed study I would refer those interested to a valuable book published in 1999 and entitled *Jerusalem 1948*. The editor of the study is Salim Tamari, under the sponsorship of the Institute of Jerusalem Studies and BADIL Resource Centre for Palestinian Residency and Refugee Rights. I must confess that when I started reading the study, and specifically the introduction of the editor under the heading 'The Phantom City', my stomach was churned up, not because of any surprises contained therein but because it evoked in me a profound feeling of sorrow as I read about the fate of a city in which I had spent so many happy years of my life, and which I only left on 15 May 1948, two hours after the departure of the British high commissioner. I left clean, beautiful, well-built, well-furnished homes and a highly advanced citizenry in those quarters, and overnight, the city was ransacked, the homes left desolate.

But a much earlier and authoritative source was again Mary Rogers, an eyewitness writing more than 150 years ago. European families, especially those with children, living in the Old City, she narrates, would spend all the summer months from June to September in tents set up on the outskirts of the city, a mile away. Men would go to work in the Old City in the morning and return to their families in the camps before sunset. At that early stage in the slow emergence of New Jerusalem, we begin hearing names of European consuls and missionaries who became well-known in the early part of the 20th century, as did the schools set up by the foreigners.

Here are some examples: Bishop Samuel Gobat, a Lutheran, established an English school on Mount Zion; St George's School on Nablus Road, established by Anglicans in 1899, from which generations of Palestinian students graduated, including many of my close relatives; the German Schneller Technical School; the Terra Sancta School; the French Frères School and scores of others. There were similar influxes into Syria and Lebanon, represented by such famed institutions as the American Protestant College in Beirut (renamed the American University of Beirut) which contributed immeasurably to the Arab awakening in the last century. The names Bliss and Dodge, families associated with the founding of the AUB, are known and respected in the eastern part of the Arab world.

The last of the Crusades ended in the 13th century, and for close to six centuries there was an almost complete break in European relations with the peoples of the East, with the exception of formal contacts with the Ottoman Empire, to which I shall make brief reference later. European interest and exertions shifted to the newly-discovered world across the Atlantic, and with drastic changes in the trade routes via the Cape of Good Hope. So a visitor like German Priest Felix Fabri to the Holy Land in the 15th century was a rare event. One senses the bewilderment, loneliness and estrangement he felt while on that brave visit, eloquently recording his observations in two published volumes. Sailing to the Holy Land was in itself fraught with danger, aside from the many other dangers overland.

Thus those early European influxes were pioneering in every sense, opening the way to a resumption of human contacts after centuries of separation. A British consul in

Jerusalem, James Finn, was the first, according to Rogers, to build a stone house in Talbiya quarter, which in the 1930s and 40s was the most fashionable Christian Arab quarter outside the Old City, along with Qatamon, and upper and lower Baqaa. It had been a thriving, sophisticated and cohesive community of Arab Christians, numerically roughly on a par with their Arab Muslim compatriots, and living side-by-side in neighbourly amity and friendship. I knew many of those families and had close friendships with them. I shall give here a cross-sectional spectrum of them, to show how such a public-spirited, peace-loving and civilised community was decimated overnight, and its members dispersed around the globe, with a conspiracy of silence over their fate and that of their Muslim compatriots in greater Jerusalem. As mentioned earlier, since Israel's conquest of East Jerusalem in June 1967 there has been a further and much accelerated diminution of the Arab Christian presence.

Let me mention some of those great Christian families and distinguished individuals. I had a close friendship with the Tannous family, and their home in Talbiya was one of the most elegant. Suleiman Tannous was a highly successful businessman and representative of General Motors in Palestine and Jordan; his son George was my room-mate at AUB. Then there was Dolly, his charming wife, Fuad, his brother, and his wife Tania. Dr Izzat Tannous, a venerable doctor, was for many years a recognised representative of Palestine at the United Nations. One of the senior members of the Farraj family, Yacoub Farraj, was deputy mayor of united Jerusalem in the 1930s, and Fuad Farraj was a cabinet colleague in the 1960s. The Jamal family, Teddy and Eddy, ran a thriving business. I remember, too, the family of the late Edward Said, the outstanding author and linguist, who wrote, among his numerous other works, *Out of Place*, a most readable autobiography. I remember very well Bulos Saeed's library and stationary store at Bab al-Khalil, which was the central shopping centre for Arabs and Jews in the 1930s. Anton Attallah, as I mentioned earlier, was a distinguished judge and later foreign minister of Jordan, while Munir Attallah was a leading businessman in Jordan, married to the charming Odette. A member of the Attallah family, I am told, had been a patriarch of the Orthodox Church 500 years ago, before it was taken over by the Greek hierarchy under the Ottoman regime. Then there was the Senunu family, one of whose sons had served as chief-of-staff in President George Bush Sr's White House. From the Hanania family, Anastass Hanania was a judge who later served as Jordan's minister of finance and ambassador to London, and his son Dr Daoud Hanania, former head of the King Hussein Medical City, was a pioneer in open-heart surgery in the Arab world. The Deeb family, under the British mandate, had the Dead Sea concession for extracting salt. Gabi and Raymon Deeb were tennis champions. My rivalry with Raymon on the tennis courts of the Jerusalem YMCA was intense. The Palestine tennis champion for three consecutive years was Roland Mayo, although I managed to beat him once in a semi-final. As for the Sakakini family, its head, Khalil, was one of the foremost educationalists in Jerusalem and his books are still being taught at schools. I also knew his son Sari and his daughter Hala, in the celebrated socialite circle of Katy Antonius, who did so much for the cause of Palestine. Emil Ghouri, secretary-general of the Arab Higher Committee, represented Palestine during the debate on partition in 1947. Dr Sami Khouri was a highly accomplished surgeon and a close friend. Born in Nablus, he was brought up in Jerusalem, attending St George's School. He later graduated from the AUB and served as chief surgeon at the Augusta Victoria Hospital on the Mount of Olives. Shafeeq Mansour was head of the boys' department at the YMCA, where I was one of 100 founding members. Henry Qattan was a distinguished jurist who authored several books on the question of Palestine from the vantage point of international law. Then there was the Majaj family, with Dr Amin Majaj, who served as mayor of Jerusalem in the aftermath of unity with Jordan in 1949-50. Yacoub Juri served as UN resident representative to Iraq, the Caribbean and other countries. Yusuf Beidas was a brilliant man who, immediately after the catastrophe *(Nakba)* of 1948, established Intra Bank, one of the foremost in the Middle East in the 1950s and early 60s. Hostile forces in Lebanon conspired to bring down the bank in 1966, notwithstanding its considerable assets which by far outweighed its liabilities. There had been a run on the bank which caused a cash shortage, and the Central Bank allowed Intra to go under. The Halabi family were in the pharmaceutical business, and I remember distinctly as a child the Anton Halabi pharmacy at *Bab al-Amud* (Damascus Gate), one of the entrances to the Old City. And Issa Nakhleh, a distinguished lawyer, who represented Palestine for many years at the UN, authored a unique compendium on the Palestine disaster, akin to an encyclopaedia.

This community of diverse skills and achievements was uprooted on 15 May 1948 by a war machine which walked over their militarily naked quarters, and defenceless citizenry. Each one of them had to seek a future in other lands and begin life anew.

The construction activities outside the Old City in the latter part of the 19th century were necessary because conditions within the walls had become uncomfortably congested. So, families with means started building huge houses, literally mansions, to accommodate the relatively large family units which were the norm. I lived in one of those palatial residences in the early 1930s in *Bab al-Zahira* (Herod's Gate) quarter. My father built two such mansions early in the 20th century, each one consisting of 20-30 rooms, surrounded by tall pine trees. The quarter was so quiet and tranquil that the only noise one would hear was the rustle of leaves on a windy day. The buildings were eventually leased to several enterprises, one of which was the Danziger Jewish Hospital another was the Tamrin government school with Talat as-Saifi as headmaster. The upper floor of one of the buildings was the residence of the renowned Ahmad Sameh Khalidi, leading educationalist, historian and director of the Arab College. His son, Professor Walid Khalidi of Harvard University and the AUB, and his sister, Sulafa, were my good friends and neighbours, and we used to play together in our childhood.

In 1898, Kaiser Wilhelm II laid the cornerstone for a church and hospice on the Mount of Olives. It was named after his wife, Augusta Victoria, and was opened in 1907. It is now an Arab hospital.

The latter part of the 19th century also witnessed an influx of European families of various nationalities, British, French, German, Russian, Austrian, Greek, etc. They were primarily church people of different denominations, mainly missionaries, pilgrims and educationalists. This inflow ended centuries of separation from the outside world, stemming from hardships encountered in reaching Palestine and other countries of the Orient, and the difficulties of settling there because of language barriers and adapting to the life and traditions of its people. I have already mentioned the estrangement which Father Fabri felt during his visits to the Holy Land. Gradually these visitations became more normal and acceptable, and a process of change began. I still remember as a child spending a winter vacation in Jericho and watching with curiosity as Russian Orthodox priests, tall in stature and with long beards, visited the monastery on *Jabal Qruntul* (the Mount of Temptation) overlooking the whole panorama of the Jordan Valley, the Dead Sea, and further east the Jordanian heights. It was a challenge to me as a child to climb the narrow, winding pathways leading up to the summit. There, I inscribed my name beside numerous other inscriptions by pilgrims, wayfarers and simple climbers like me.

The Old City consisted, as it still does today, of three residential constellations: the Muslim quarter, the Christian quarter and the Jewish quarter. But there is cohesiveness and intermingling between these quarters, with the main covered thoroughfare running from the north at Damascus Gate to the south at Bab el-Khalil, where the ancient citadel abuts the main square, named after Caliph Umar.

The Europeans were, by and large, clustered in and adjacent to the Christian quarter, with close proximity to the Holy Sepulchre and other Christian churches and monasteries (Latin, Lutheran, Armenian, Orthodox, and Coptic), as well as foreign consulates. The northeast and the west comprise most of the Muslim quarters, such as Bab Hutta, Bab al-Silsila, Bab al-Wad and other sub-quarters and alleys. These quarters traverse the Via Dolorosa, close to Rawdha College (renamed *al-Umariyya*) right opposite the French school for girls, *Madrasat Sahyoun* (Zion School), one of the best girls' schools in Jerusalem, and from which my two young sisters, Sama and Hala, graduated.

Jerusalem houses are stone-built and stout, with self-supporting roof arches and deep walls as insulation against heat in the summer and biting cold in winter. Piled onto deep elevated recesses would be mattresses, pillows and warm *lihafs* (covers) ready for guests and visiting relatives. It was only natural to have such facilities in the past, with extra rooms specifically earmarked as guest bedrooms, because of the absence of hotels. This tradition of housing guests and relatives has all but disappeared today.

Since the closing part of the 19th century and early 20th, furniture in Jerusalem homes adopted a mixture of Western as well as Eastern patterns. I saw such mixed influences in my own house, coexisting in workable harmony. Every house in Jerusalem, particularly in the Old City, had a large cistern beneath a part of it to collect rain water during the rainy months of winter, by and large from September to the end of April. Collecting water this way is a deeply entrenched tradition from long ago, deeply engraved in the mind and consciousness of the people. The reason is obvious. There are no rivers or large springs in or near Jerusalem, and if the water supply from elsewhere were to be cut, then life in the city would be choked. This would particularly be the case in years of drought, and worse still in wartime. In the aftermath of the 1948 war, the water supply to East Jerusalem was totally cut off by Israel's occupation of the major source of water for Jerusalem at Ras al-'Ain in the central plain of Palestine, between Ramleh and Lydda. We suffered shortages until an alternative source was developed from a spring to the northeast of Ramallah. It was a big day, a day of celebration, when King Hussein inaugurated the utilisation and piping of this new source of water to Jerusalem.

Up to the second part of the 19th century, aside from a short route from Jerusalem to Bethlehem, there were no proper tracks to enable the use of horse-drawn carriages, in contrast to the case in Europe and America. Travel in Palestine had to be on horseback or on donkeys, for the rich as well as for the poor, the high and the lowly. It may sound amusing, but it is a fact that, whether he was a governor, a consul of Her Britannic Majesty, or a humble postman, he had to travel on a beast of burden, enduring, for example, a 12-hour ride between Jerusalem and Jaffa, or Nablus in the north. Carriages were only introduced in the 1920s and 30s, to be supplanted soon afterwards by buses and scores of automobiles, vying slowly and shyly with carriages. I lived through this transition. I remember when my father used to return from the municipality, where he was a council member, by a horse-drawn carriage to our house in Sheikh Jarrah. They were similar to the carriages hired by tourists in New York, near the Plaza Hotel, at Fifth Avenue. I am still at a loss to explain how in the 1930s the horses drawing the carriages in Jerusalem were fitted with specials sacks to contain horse manure, while in New York, 50 years later, there was no such provision, with the result that manure was allowed to pollute the streets of this city of cities.

Buses were introduced in the early 1930s, a welcome novelty. There were three major bus routes: No. 33, from Sheikh Jarrah to Jaffa Gate and Mamilla Road; No. 9, from the Hebrew University and Hadassah Hospital on Mount Scopus to Jewish quarters in the west; and Nos. 6 and 4, from Jaffa Gate to the new quarters of Jerusalem at lower and upper Baqaa, the Germany Colony, the Nammari quarter and Qatamon.

It was amusing to watch the *effendi* aristocracy of Arab Jerusalem, attired during summer in well-pressed white or off-white silk suits, with polished shining shoes and silk ties, taking their seats in the bus. The fare was five *fils*, the equivalent of 1 cent. Once settled in their seats, a public conversation would ensue, on every variety of topics, from politics to cooking, until the bus reached a stop to allow passengers to embark or disembark. When a newcomer boarded and attempted to pay the fare to the bus driver, a chorus of voices would start, requesting the driver not to take the fare from the new passenger. In the then relatively small Jerusalem, everyone knew everyone else, and it was an act of accepted generosity to pay the fare of the newcomer. A heated discussion would follow as to who was the first to have declared the offer to pay the fare of the newcomer. The bus, of course, would in the meantime remain at a standstill, and after a period of suspense, agreement would be reached that the driver himself (his name was Haz) would arbitrate as to who of the disputants had made the offer first. He would announce his decision, the winner would pay the fare and the bus would resume its journey.

Needless to say, apart from what was deemed proper generosity, those elders were quite intrusive and not at all prepared to mind their own business. They had been accustomed to exercising authority, whether at work, in retirement or, especially, at home. It was a male-dominated society where the father reigned supreme and everyone else in the house was reverently at his beck and call. How else could the head of a house maintain discipline, with 10 children or more of various ages running around wildly. Being accustomed to giving orders, this *effendi* class would give themselves the liberty to castigate a young passenger if, when he boarded the bus, they observed that perhaps he had not polished his shoes, that there was a stain on his clothes, or even that his hair was dishevelled. And the young passenger would take his castigation without a murmur of protest. Such was the intensity of in-built discipline in the early 20th century years. At present, in many capitals of the Western world, the elderly, renamed senior citizens would be happy if the youth would only leave them in peace.

Sometimes I would catch the No. 9 bus which passed to the west side of my house, whenever the 33 failed to arrive on time. Placed at the front of the bus next to the driver were two small tin boxes. Every Jewish passenger who boarded the bus would deposit, in addition to the fare, a lump of sugar in one box and half a *piaster* in the other. I forget what the purpose was, but I was highly impressed by these collective donations, trivial as they may have been. Money, of course, was extremely tight in those days, tied as it was to the gold standard, and in a relatively poor and undeveloped country. But these donations expressed commitment to the Zionist cause, while the Arabs of Palestine, being still the overwhelming majority, were complacent, and largely impervious to the dangers that were lurking ahead, in the not-too-distant future.

The telephone was introduced to Jerusalem in the late 1920s. I know that we had a telephone installed at the house by 1927 which, incidentally, became known as the year of the earthquake that struck Jerusalem and other parts of Palestine, particularly Nablus, where extensive damage was caused. The telephone numbers were in the hundreds, indicating the scarcity of telephone services in those early years.

Jerusalem, in those days, also had many schools and colleges, private, governmental and foreign. Almost every

European country had a school, and my first schooling was a Swedish kindergarten in the Musrara quarter. The British mandatory government established two high-level secondary schools, the Arab College and the Rashidiyya School. It may sound somewhat strange, but it is true all the same, that at the Arab College the curricula included the teaching of Latin and Greek, on the same pattern as English public schools. Palestine had two highly qualified directors of education: Mr Humphrey Bowman, who recommended to my father sending me and my brother, Mahmoud, to Victoria College in Alexandria; the second was Mr Jerome Farrell, a classicist and a highly learned scholar. He was a disciplinarian and a perfectionist, who would not accept second-rate performance. He would recite important literary works by heart and with gusto.

But when the mandate ended there were only four government secondary schools in the whole of Palestine. The philosophy guiding the system was to educate the elite, a limited number of civil servants, to help run the machinery of government, but no more. Those academically less endowed were expected to acquire vocational skills and work their way into the private sector. Education was based on class orientation, which had been the case in Britain itself.

Sports began creeping into the life of society in the late 1920s. My cousin, Ibrahim, established the first football club in 1927. Its initial location was under a tree in the Herod's Gate quarter and was named the Arab Club. It took a while to arrange the money to lease premises for the club, renamed the Ahli Club. There were, subsequently, competing clubs in Jerusalem, as well as in other cities and towns of Palestine. In Jerusalem, the hottest competition was against the Rawdha College-based club. There was also the Orthodox Club, and eventually a Dajani Club.

I have not included in my listing the YMCA Club and the Civil Service Club which were set up later. The breeding grounds for talented soccer players were the schools, each of which had a team of its own. St George's School near my house had an excellent football team, trained by Mr Buyajjian, Mr Maatouk and Shukri Harami.

Other clubs in Palestine included the Islamic Club of Jaffa, the Orthodox Club of Jaffa, and the *Shabab al-Arab* (Arab Youth) of Haifa. Competition was very intense, and on many occasions would end up in fights involving fists, sticks and stones, with the fans of each club joining in. The home teams always had the upper hand because of their numerical superiority, but the victimised club would make a point of taking its revenge on the aggressor club when it came back to its own city for the return match. Regulations against mob violence, which the international football authorities have introduced, did not exist then. Tragically, all the teams that I mentioned above closed in the aftermath of 1948. They vanished, together with their country.

If study and sports were two prominent features of the life of Jerusalem, political, national and religious activities also took pride of place. As capital of mandated Palestine, it was the headquarters of all the national movements in the land. These began with the Executive Committee in the 1920s and early 30s, the Islamic-Christian Coalition, the successive Arab Higher Committees, and last but not least, the Higher Islamic Council under the leadership of the Grand Mufti of Jerusalem. These institutions were the legitimate representatives of the Palestinian people, in all matters affecting the fate of Palestine, for good or ill.

Likewise, the Jewish Agency had its headquarters in King George Street in Jerusalem, as did other Jewish institutions related to education, health and sports. Up to the early 1930s, Palestinian clubs played against Jewish clubs, without inhibitions or restraint. I remember a match between the Arab Club and the Maccabee team, on a football field near St Hadriya Street. The football field is no longer there, having given way to buildings on the Israeli side.

The British mandatory government, naturally, had its headquarters in Jerusalem. The high commissioner's residence was at Jabal al-Mukaber, with a panoramic view of Jerusalem. It had been built in an oriental style, with arched colonnades and roofs. With the end of the British mandate on 15 May 1948, the premises found itself in no man's land, and under the Armistice Agreement signed by Jordan and Israel on 3 April 1949 it was taken over by UNTSO. To this day the building has remained in UN hands, pending a final settlement. I went to this palatial building in 1955 when I was head of the Jordanian delegation to the Mixed Armistice Commission, and my wife and I were invited to lunch there by General William Burns, chief of UNTSO.

The secretariat of the government (the equivalent of the prime minister's office) was housed in several buildings, the grandest of which was a German-owned building adjacent to the Damascus Gate. The ownership of the building had changed hands more than once since World War I, in consequence of war sequestrations. At present it accommodates the German Schmidt's School for girls, which moved from West to East Jerusalem.

One of the major Muslim national-religious annual festivals was that of *Nabi Musa* (the festival of the Prophet Moses). The festival coincided with Christianity's weeklong celebration of Easter. The peace treaty concluded between Salahuddin and Richard the Lion Heart in 1191 guaranteed free access for European pilgrims to visit the Holy Sepulchre and other religious sites during Easter. But fearing a surprise attack by Europeans assembled in great numbers against Jerusalem during the festivities, Salahuddin instituted a series of festivals throughout Palestine, the most important being *Nabi Musa* in Jerusalem and *Nabi Rubin* in the coastal areas.

On Friday, crowds of people from the city of Nablus and its surrounding areas used to come to Jerusalem and disembark right in front of the historic mosque in Sheikh Jarrah, 100 metres from the family house. They would perform acts of swordsmanship, and hold contests involving swords and shields. All the while they raised national-religious banners, sang nationalist songs and danced the *dabka*. They then proceeded on foot towards the Haram al-Sharif, where they would unfurl their banners, say their prayers and get ready to merge with similar crowds from the city of Hebron and its environs. On Sunday, crowds from Jerusalem, Nablus and Hebron would gather near Jaffa Gate for a grand march, in which tens of thousands would participate. The festivities reached a peak after noon prayers when the crowds would travel to the *Maqam Nabi Musa* (the Prophet Moses' mausoleum), mid-way between Jerusalem and Jericho. There are special *awqaf* to defray the expenses of hosting such large crowds. One of the features of those festivities was the parading on horseback of children whose circumcision was timed to coincide with the festivities. Parents were proud and happy to see their children so paraded. I was circumcised, along with my younger brothers, Mahmoud, Hisham and Ahmad, at a special celebration at our home, to which my father invited around 15 notables of Jerusalem, including the headmaster of Rawdha College, Sheikh Muhammad al-Saleh, an awe-inspiring figure. The act of circumcision was perpetrated by a barber who specialised in this field. We were paraded into our salon, dressed in beautiful off-white silk garments. Although I was given no anaesthetic whatsoever, because I was in the presence of such an imposing audience I endured the pain without a murmur. Mahmoud was less inhibited and screamed at the top of his voice, not only cursing the barber's father, but also his father's father.

These festivities, which once brought joy and pride to young and old, men, women, and children, were suspended in the aftermath of the great rebellion of 1936-39 and again during World War II. During the unity years with Jordan, attempts were made to resurrect these festivities, but to no avail. What a pity that a traditional, ages-old festival should just fade away.

On of the most durable of my childhood memories is of being at Rawdha College on a particular day in 1931. Islamic leaders from all over the world assembled to consider what they regarded as a threat to the Aqsa Mosque, following the disturbances over the Buraq-Wailing Wall. They included bearded and highly revered *Mawlana* Shawkat Ali, leader of India's large Muslim population, before its partition and the establishment of Pakistan and Bangladesh. We witnessed with curiosity and awe such an assembly of leaders and dignitaries, but without realising what the conference was all about.

In 1933, Jerusalem was the scene of violent demonstrations by large crowds led by Musa Kazem Pasha al-Husseini, head of the Palestine Executive Committee and members of the committee against the Balfour Declaration which had promised the establishment of a Jewish national home in Palestine. The demonstration turned violent when a Jerusalemite on top of the wall of the Old City, at New Gate opposite the French Hospital, dropped a brick that instantly killed a British constable on horseback. In the fray, many were injured and my father was in the forefront of the demonstration. He returned home at noon, sweating and visibly shaken. He was already over 60 years of age. A similar but even more violent demonstration took place the next day in the city of Jaffa where running battles broke out between Palestinian demonstrators and British security forces, both using sticks and batons to drive back the other.

I have referred in passing to the earliest restoration of links between Europe and Palestine, at the formal level of the Ottoman state and the major powers of Europe. But at the commercial level, relations had evidently continued uninterrupted, though on a relatively small scale. At the interstate level, France was the first to establish a consulate in Jerusalem, in 1621, and its primary purpose was to oversee Catholic interests pertaining to the holy places. The consulate enjoyed the protection of the relevant provisions stipulated in the agreement on concessions between France and the Ottoman state. Austria followed suit in 1642 and Poland 1676.

In 1840, the British consul obtained from Muhammad Ali Pasha, governor of Egypt and his son Ibrahim Pasha, his viceroy in Palestine and Syria, agreement to permit the Jews to pave the narrow space in front of the Wailing Wall. But a

Jerusalem consultative council rejected the plan and it was subsequently abandoned.

In 1808, a big fire destroyed the wooden roof of the Church of the Holy Sepulchre. Intense competition flared up between the Western and the Greek Orthodox Church to gain the award for repairing the church. The Greeks had been favoured in the administration and the governance of the Ottoman state, as Greece was still a part of the Ottoman Empire, and their influence enabled them to win the contract. The Westerners later claimed that the repairs undertaken by the Greek Church had altered the original design of the roof of the church, as it had existed since the Crusades.

Western writers also accused the Ottomans of misrule and corruption in the latter decades of the empire. While their criticisms were partly justifiable, they were also, more often than not, bigoted and ill-intentioned. They were consciously and unconsciously influenced by the legacy of the Crusades, accentuated by the Ottoman incursions into the Balkans which, at one point, brought them to the doorstep of Vienna. The literature of the 19th century brims with such adverse sentiments, not only against the Ottomans but also against Muslims, and Islam as a faith.

It was little wonder, then, that when General Allenby, commander-in-chief of Allied forces, entered Jerusalem in 1917 and received its keys from the Arab mayor of the city he famously declared: 'The Crusades have now ended.' This utterance was made despite the fact that the Arabs had allied themselves with the British against their co-religionists the Turks.

Several British historians have expressed doubts as to the authenticity of the utterance, attributing its origin to a cartoon in *Punch* magazine. It is difficult to verify or disparage the authenticity of the statement. But in recent years a cousin of mine, Ahmad Fuad Nusseibeh, related to me quite inadvertently a version which he had heard from his father, Fuad, an officer who had served in the Ottoman army, who in turn, had heard it directly from his father, Abdul Latif. His father had been standing at the entrance to the Church of the Holy Sepulchre to receive General Allenby and his entourage. After touring the church, Allenby asked Abdul Latif for the keys, and when he received them turned and said: 'Now the Crusades have ended.' He then returned the keys to Abdul Latif and said: 'Now I return to you the keys, but this time they are not from Umar or Salahuddin, but from Allenby'. When my cousin narrated this story to me, I sent a letter to this effect to the London *Times*, but it was never published.

I have no reason to doubt the veracity of this event, as my cousin related it to me. Besides, Abdul Latif would have been there as a matter of course to receive the victorious general on this historic occasion. Moreover, it had been an occasion for theatrics, according to eyewitnesses. Victory can be sweet and heady wine. Nonetheless, the British declared their intention to maintain the *status quo* pertaining to the holy places, and they kept their promise until the day they left Palestine.

General Henri Gouraud, commander-in-chief of French forces, expressed similar sentiments when he captured Damascus in July 1920. Standing before Salahuddin's tomb, he declared: 'Now we have returned, O Salahuddin.' As a soldier, he would have been better advised to have stood in reverence before a man who was as great in triumph as he was in magnanimity towards his adversaries and in his strict observance of human rights and the norms and ethics of war.

Returning to the 21st century let me summarise my thoughts on recent events in Jerusalem. It has suffered more than any other city. The whole of West Jerusalem was occupied in 1948 and East Jerusalem suffered the same fate in 1967. On the first occasion, the citizens, totally unarmed and vulnerable, left the city without a bullet being fired. In 1967, a battle raged between two armies, and when the dust had settled, the population of the city, or at least a large part of it, remained, confident that they were entitled, according to the Fourth Geneva Convention of 1949, to protection. But the convention was virtually ignored, and Israel has carried out a massive colonisation programme, in which 20 towns and settlement centres have been created, encircling East Jerusalem. These towns and settlements have been dubbed the new walls of Jerusalem. The settlement programme has been carried out on Palestinian-owned land, as well as on state domains, which are the communal property of the citizens of the occupied area. Both are equally unlawful and implemented against the categorical provisions of international law and relevant conventions, Security Council resolutions and, not least, a definitive ruling by the International Court of Justice in 2004, which declared such Israeli action as null and void. Later the Israelis constructed the notorious wall of separation, which devoured additional Palestinian lands and made ordinary life impossible.

Israel deliberately created, with bricks and mortar, a new *fait accompli* on the ground, in flagrant disregard of the rest of the world, let alone, the inalienable rights of the Palestinian people. The properties of the Palestinians are meticulously recorded with the United Nations, house by house, and inch by inch. The British government kept detailed records and made them available to the United Nations when they left Palestine. Sami Hadawi, a senior Palestinian officer at the lands department of Palestine during the mandate did excellent work with the Conciliation Commission, and on his own, to update and revamp the available records, he used to visit me in my office at the Jordan mission to the UN in New York, seeking assistance from my government to further pursue his worthy work. He later retired to Canada.

Palestinian properties are worth hundreds of billions in current currency values. Israel has been attempting to whittle down, if not liquidate altogether, these rights and properties in two ways: first, to claim that the maintenance of such properties by the so-called custodian of absentee owners costs in excess of the rentals received, which could not be a credible claim unless the rents accruing were nominal. Maintenance costs should never exceed 10-15 percent. Second, the Israelis insist on linking the rights of Palestinian refugees for compensation with the question of Jewish properties in Arab states. This is an untenable linkage and should be discarded forthwith.

The Palestinians recognise the rights of Jewish immigrants to Israel to seek and obtain recompense for properties which they left behind in Arab states, much as they insist on restoring their own properties in Palestine. But it would be the height of irony if, by some misguided logic, they were called upon to pay compensation to those who had displaced them when they left the Arab states – voluntarily – and came to live in Arab homes, properties and farms in Palestine. The Palestinian people are not custodians of the Arab states, and if any compensation were to be paid, it should be paid to the Palestinian people who have been grievously victimised by those Arab states that allowed, facilitated, or even colluded in the emigration of their own Jewish citizens to Palestine, to supplant the Palestinian people in their homeland.

In 1998, all the societies representing Jerusalem and the surrounding towns and villages held a conference, which I chaired, at the Society for the Defence of Jerusalem. All the delegates were unanimous in declaring that their own choice was repatriation to their cities, towns and villages, from which they had been expelled. They rejected financial remuneration as an alternative to an inalienable right, consecrated by international law and UN resolutions, as well as the Universal Declaration of Human Rights. They added, in a proclamation, copies of which were signed and circulated to the United Nations and to all states, big and small, that repatriation was a personal as well as a national right and, therefore, no authority, Palestinian or otherwise, was authorised to forsake this sacred right.

In this chapter, I have recounted some, but not all, of my memories of Jerusalem, the important, the trivial, the happy, and the sad, as the human story of a person born and reared in the city, but whose final destiny and destination was ordained to be beyond its hallowed soil. When the end comes, my remains, will not nurture the soil which generations of my forefathers have nourished for 14 centuries. But my spirit will, forever, hover above this sacred land until the promised Day of Resurrection in God's unfathomable time.

CHAPTER 18

Who Am I?
A Question of Identity

The last theme I want to explore as I approach the end of my book is the relationship between East and West. My definition of East for this purpose is the Arab and Muslim worlds, and does not include the civilisations of the Far East, Hindu, Buddhist, and others, great as they are or may have been.

I hold the view that what is known today as Western civilisation is fundamentally world civilisation, which had its cradle and origins in the Near East, broadly speaking in the lands of natural Syria, Mesopotamia, and the Nile Valley, the Syriac-Canaanite civilisation about which Toynbee spoke in lavish terms, basing his judgment on the solid foundations of archaeology, substantiated subsequently by discoveries in Northern Syria in the mid-1970s.

The Syriac-Canaanite civilisation has three great feats to its credit: it invented the alphabet; it discovered the Atlantic; and it arrived at a particular conception of God, which is common to the three monotheistic faiths: Judaism, Christianity and Islam.

The other civilisation in this Near Eastern triangle was Sumerian, whose achievements in law, religion, and life are universally acknowledged, as are those of its contemporary, the ancient Egyptian civilisation with its monumental achievements, not least of which had been its belief in God, the creator of the universe, These civilisations had their genesis in the Arabian peninsula, the birth place of the Semitic peoples, whose waves of migration into the fertile crescent over tens of thousands of years were impelled by the gradual desiccation of the peninsula and climatic changes which had transformed the region from a green land into a barren desert.

What is the relationship between East and West? One way for me to assess and compare the Arab-Islamic civilisation with that of the West is through reading my educational map and the accumulated influences which shaped me, emotionally, spiritually, intellectually and in every other formative sense. It is a map of parallel orientations, often overlapping, intermingling and interacting. The flow of ideas is an imperceptible process. Although the Islamic era is said to have given way to the modern one from the 19th century onwards, there is no implication that Islamic influences ceased to be equally important. It is taken as a new era because the Islamic way of life had petrified during the preceding millennium, and in the 18th century started to open up to a plurality of influences, with a significant trend away from the old and toward a new synthesis. Professors H.A.R Gibb and H. Bowen in their book *Islamic Society and the West*, described well that process beginning in the 18th century.

It must be noted that within the amalgam of East and West there are two great areas of human experience and activity: culture and civilisation. The first refers to values, styles, emotional attachments, and intellectual pursuits; the second denotes utilitarian material instruments and basic technology. It is not possible, for example, to prove or disprove the thesis that Western culture is superior to other cultures. Civilisation, however, is measurable according to efficiency standards. Electric energy is manifestly more efficient than human or animal muscle.

The borderline between technology, social organisation and culture is not easy to delimit because it is constantly changing. Nevertheless, such a distinction is basically sound, while cognizant of the phenomenon of cultural lag. This means that when changes occur in the material culture, i.e. civilisation, they stimulate changes in the non-material culture, which sociologists characterise as the adaptive culture but often with a time lag, thus giving rise to disequilibrium and maladjustment within changing societies.

Within these parameters, I shall begin outlining my cultural road map, first in its Eastern dimension and then its Western one. At Rawdha College, in the late 1920s and early 30s, we were made to learn part of the Quran *(Juz' Amma)* by heart at an early stage of our elementary schooling.

The sayings of the Prophet Muhammad also had an important impact on religious awareness and on morals and mores. My maternal grandfather, Jawdat Nashashibi, was highly observant of his religious performances and would invite my younger brothers, sisters and myself to his house once a month to sing together the praises of the Prophet Muhammad, in chants composed by illustrious poets and singers across the ages. The closest parallel in Christianity was the hymn singing in chapel every morning at the AUB before going to class. My grandfather would also expect us to say our daily prayers on time, at the nearest mosque in the neighbourhood.

The fast of Ramadhan had a particular social and religious aura, and would be observed with traditions and festivities bequeathed from one generation to another. The traditional *Mussahir*, beating his drum and intoning the sleepers to wake up for breakfast, before sunrise and the start of fasting, was to me thrilling, notwithstanding the inconvenience of interrupting one's sleep, particularly in the cold of winter.

Correct and polite behaviour was always demanded and observed, both at home and at school. Respect for parents and elders was as important as that for teachers. We were taught a saying which read: 'Whoever has taught me a letter, I shall be his slave.' Aside from smoking in the presence of my father being considered disrespectful, even laughing loudly or acting childishly are anathema in the scale of values of Jerusalemites over centuries, as one discerns from history books.

Such attitudes were so extreme as to earn Jerusalemites the opprobrium of *mkabbass* (stiffness) by those in less structured towns and cities. This could well be attributable to the religiosity of the city. Under the British mandate, nightclubs or similar places of entertainment were strictly forbidden within the municipal boundaries of the city. At present, the secular elements amongst the Israeli residents of Jerusalem are exiting the city in significant numbers, fleeing the constraints imposed by ultra-religious Jews.

Rawdha College was a bastion of Arab nationalism which peaked during and after World War I and the dismantling of the Ottoman Empire. Hitherto, the term Arab had been submerged by the Islamic identity and used to denote the bedouin sectors of the population. The citizens generally were identified as Ottoman. Immigrants to America from Syria and Palestine were categorised as Turks or Syrians, rather than Arabs.

Arab nationalism was just emerging as the national identity of the Arab-speaking world, extending from Morocco to the Gulf. It was so robust and invigorating that the punishment imposed on us as children was undeniably chauvinistic. Depending on the extent of our misbehaviour, we had to write 50-100 times the sentence: 'The Arabs are the most noble of nations; he who doubts my statement would be committing a blasphemy.' This had been so deeply inculcated in my mind that when I went to Victoria College in Alexandria I became embroiled in fist fights with some Egyptian students, particularly one belonging to the ruling Khedive Albanian dynasty, who refused to acknowledge his Arab identity, despite the fact that he was Egyptian and Egypt was the heartland and leader of the Arab world. Arabism, however, came finally into its own, after the 1952 Egyptian revolution that brought Gamal Abdul Nasser to power.

But, notwithstanding its Arab-Islamic affiliation and credentials, Rawdha College aspired to inculcate in its students the penchant to learn and identify with contemporary civilisation, while appreciating our intellectual and religious heritage.

As I mentioned earlier, the Quran was paramount in its powerful and inimitable language and revelations. Then came the life story of the Prophet, as narrated in several volumes by Ibn Hisham, who was the closest historian, time-wise, to the era of the Prophet and the emergence of the Islamic community and state in Medina. The sayings of the Prophet run into the tens of thousands. But only around 10,000 have been judged as genuine, through a scientific and intricate chain of attributions *(isnad)*, a science of its own.

Learning poetry was a quintessential part of the Arabic curriculum at school, and we recited the choicest Arabic poetry at school and on public occasions. The celebrated odes, the *Muallaqat* or 'suspended poems' were the legacy of the *Jahiliyya* (the period of ignorance), the few centuries before Islam. It is now generally agreed that the term 'ignorance' as used in the Quran and by Muslim historians does not mean 'ignorance' as much as wildness, and that its antithesis is not *ilm* (knowledge) but rather *hilm* (temperance).

At school we used to engage in a competition called *al-Mahbuka*. The contestant had to take the last letter in the verse of his opponent and begin a new verse with the same letter. On one occasion, the letter 'n' came back to me seven times and I was hard put to begin an eighth verse starting with 'n'. The poetic duel was taking place at a certificate award ceremony, attended by the Grand Mufti of Jerusalem, Haj Amin al-Husseini and many dignitaries from various parts of Palestine, including my father. In this dire moment of challenge I looked across the hall to the wall opposite the podium where I thought I had found my salvation. The inscription on the wall contained the motto of the school and, it started and ended with an (n). The following is a rough translation from Arabic:

> We are free and proud
> Seeking life in dignity
> The Rawdha of learning is the nucleus
> For men of faithfulness and fidelity

I read the verses loudly and clearly, and the gathering, evidently impressed by the spontaneity, clapped enthusiastically. But, alas, the referee disqualified this recitation as reading and not memorising and I lost the contest.

We also learned at school that the Arabic-Islamic heritage includes great philosophers and thinkers who developed, articulated and transmitted Greek philosophy into Europe. Foremost amongst them was Avicenna (Ibn Sina), whose books on medicine, in addition to philosophy, continued to be taught at European universities until the late 18th century. Also Averroes and al-Farabi who, in addition to philosophy, laid down the basic tenets of classical music. Arab Muslim scholars are also credited with the invention and application of the empirical method in their scientific pursuits, and some have claimed that the motivation was the attempt to convert certain metals into gold. Whether true or not, the empirical method is the foundation of modern scientific and technological research.

In literature, the Arab heritage is a compendium of great scholars and poets, foremost of whom was al-Mutanabbi (whose poems were the most popular, the most consonant with the Arab psyche). At our philosophy classes at the AUB in 1941, Dr Charles Malik would make invidious comparisons between Western luminaries like Shakespeare, Dante, and Goethe, and Arab poets, claiming that the latter were no match for the former. The entire class would stand up in revolt at this conclusion. While conceding that great Arab poets never used the genre of plays to convey their thoughts, as Western poets did, they were no less successful in giving expression to the profound human traits and experiences.

The canon of Arab poetry is monumental, but it is not easily translatable into other languages.

The contemporary Arab Renaissance, we learned, produced great thinkers, poets, and men and women of literature. Jamal al-Din al-Afghani, the voluminous Islamic activist, Muhammad Abduh, a pillar of modern Islamic reform, Rashid Rida, publisher of the renowned *Al-Manar* journal, and Taha Hussein, who created great controversy in Egypt in the early 20th century with by his book *Al-Shir al-Jahili* (The Poetry of the Jahiliyya Epoch), to name but a few. Then there were Ahmad Zaki and Ahmad Hassan al-Zayyat, publishers of the weekly literary magazine *Al-Risala*, which my generation used to read from beginning to end because of the literary brilliance of its writers and the most elegant and eloquent classical Arabic. It is not nostalgia that prompts me to say that the Arab world today, even though many times more numerous and more literate than during that age, cannot produce a magazine of its status. Even if it did, it would not sustain the kind of loyalty which *Al-Risala* enjoyed amongst the elites of the Arab world. Outstanding poets included Ahmad Shawqi, crowned by his contemporaries as the prince of poets, Jibran Khalil Jibran, who achieved fame in the United States, Hafiz Ibrahim, Mahmoud Taha, al-Rasafi, al-Jawahiri, Mikhail Naimeh, Saeed Aqel, author of the Syrian national anthem, Ibrahim Touqan, author of the most popular Arab national song *Mawtini*. As students at the AUB, we would chant this for hours on end in demonstrations against the Vichy French or the British, or even in protest against the raising of the price of bread.

Abdul Munim al-Rifai composed the Jordanian royal anthem and many poems in support of Palestinian *intifadas* (uprisings) and rebellions. Celebrating the Palestinian revolution against the British mandatory government in Palestine, Abdul Karim al-Karmi wrote a particularly poignant poem in 1936, which we, as teenagers, used to recite. It describes Government House on Jabal al-Mukaber, residence of the British high commissioner, where 14 centuries earlier the Caliph Umar dismounted from his horse to enter Jerusalem on foot to receive its instruments of surrender. The following is a rough translation of Karmi's first two verses:

> Jebel al-Mukkabber, our lance shall not bend
> Until we have destroyed the Bastille built above you
> Jebel al-Mukkabber your slumber has over-extended
> Get up to hear the Hallelujahs and the God is Great.

The Arab Islamic heritage contains a copious amount of works on international law, including law of the seas and maritime trade and the rule of civil law. The founding theorists on the latter had made a distinction between the *Dar al-Adl* (abode of justice) and the *Dar al-Baghyi wal Jawr* (abode of tyranny and oppression). The former is a country where a legitimate ruler or caliph possessed of all the necessary qualification is installed. Obedience to him is mandatory, so long as he remains faithful to the law. The abode of tyranny is a country where government had been seized by the strongest party without regard to the legal provisions governing the office of the caliph. Obedience to government in this abode is not obligatory and should be limited to the absolute minimum required by the exigencies of the situation.

International law and the laws of war and peace in the Arab Islamic heritage dovetail with Roman law, which is the foundation of contemporary international law. Hugo Grotius, writing in the 17th century, is regarded as the founder of codified international law. But Arab Muslim scholars, foremost of whom was Imam al-Shaibani, preceded him by several centuries in works on international law governing situations of war and peace. Shaibani's basic distinction was between the 'abode of peace' and the 'abode of war', consequent upon external aggression, and from this are derived his theories on the 'just war' and the 'unjust war'.

I do not wish to go any further in making comparisons; I shall, therefore, turn to some of the pillars of Western civilisation, as I perceive them to be from my cultural map.

It goes without saying that one of the main bastions of contemporary Western civilisation is the religious heritage of the Holy Scriptures, as the Quran is in the case of the Islamic heritage. Indeed, art, painting, sculpture, and classical music were born and flourished in the bosom of the church. The Christian heritage which had its sustenance from the Old and new Testaments also had great thinkers who expounded the Christian faith, foremost of whom was St Augustine, in his *City of God*, and St Thomas Aquinas in his *Summa Theologica*. But it is equally true that modern Western civilisation would not have achieved such astonishing heights, but for an inexorable process of secularisation over many centuries. The Reformation, the 30-Year War between Catholics and Protestants, which ended in deadlock and thereby contributed to religious co-existence; the Age of Reason, the Enlightenment, the age of social and economic progress following the Industrial Revolution, and so on.

I began my own readings of the modern era with Francis Bacon who, writing in the 17th century expounded his vision of human enlightenment. I also read the works of René Descartes, known as the Father of Modern Philosophy, of Machiavelli, author of *The Prince* in which the end justifies the means, and of Voltaire, advocate of social reform and critic of Catholic Church dogma. My reading then included the works other major writers such as Montesquieu and Rousseau – and Locke the great proponent of freedom who believed that human nature was characterised by reasoned tolerance. Prominent, too, in the long list of notable Western writers that I encountered in my early life was John Stuart Mill. In his book, *On Liberty*, he defended the right of dissent, as no less important than that of liberty. In his brilliant analysis, Mill argued that without dissent there would have been no Christ in his rebellion against the malpractices of the Jewish society of his times, nor Muhammad who rebelled against the norms and mores of intemperate Arab society. But, I must admit that the Islamic heritage gives much greater weight to the community's general will *(Ahl al-Sunna w al-Jamaa)* than to dissenters who are, by and large, frowned upon.

I also consumed the works of the great poets like Chaucer, Shakespeare, Milton, Gray, Coleridge, Goethe, Byron, and Dante. The latter was influenced by the Islamic heritage as depicted in the Prophet's nocturnal journey to Jerusalem and his ascension to the heavens to witness God's creation. But Dante was less than kind to that heritage, by placing Islamic personages in various degraded degrees of his inferno.

Of the novels I read during my formative years, the ones that stand out in my memory were by Tolstoy, Dostoevsky, Charles Dickens, Thomas Hardy, D. H. Lawrence, and Hemingway.

I wish to emphasize that in the brief glance above at some of the Eastern and Western influences on my education and the subsequent years of my life was never intended to be anything like comprehensive. After all, this is a memoir, an autobiography, a living memory and not an exercise in controlled research of the kind needed for my book on *Ideas of Arab Nationalism*, published some half a century ago. But I feel I have cited a sufficient number of influences to be able to say that the genesis of Eastern and Western cultures seems to have been identical in many ways. They parted ways when Arab Islamic culture atrophied many centuries ago, while Western culture continued its march unceasingly up to the present day. Western culture is not simply the invention of a machine, a robot or a rocket. It is a cumulative civilisation which has been gathering momentum since the Industrial Revolution, backed by a profound intellectual and moral heritage, which is the moving spirit behind achievements and progress. To give but one example, the legalisation of a social-economic concept in the 19th century, namely 'limited liability', has contributed immeasurably to the growth of modern corporate capitalism in Europe, America, and Japan, while restrictive and misguided limitations, masquerading in the name of the Arab-Islamic heritage, could unnecessarily retard progress towards catching up with the advanced world.

There is nothing in the Islamic heritage which would curtail, less still forbid, the most far-reaching transformations. Analogy, interpretation and consensus, which the Indian-born Pakistani philosopher and poet Muhammad Iqbal called 'the principle of movement in Islam', plus common interest *(al-Masalih al-Mursalah)* and consensus, closely akin to the general will, are instruments which make possible the most far-reaching transformations, provided they are carried out by learned and enlightened religious scholars.

We should all, Easterners and Westerners, be striving to build bridges between our societies, especially in this modern world of globalisation and instantaneous communication. Yet, alas, and particularly in the aftermath of the horrendous crime of 9/11, there has re-emerged a pathological surge of Islamophobia in the Western world in general, and in the United States in particular. It is as though the 1.5 billion adherents of the Islamic faith, throughout the five continents of the world, had committed that heinous crime with collective guilt of unprecedented proportions. Indeed, the very foundations and pillars of the Islamic faith were overnight metamorphosed into accessories to the crime.

The Islamic spiritual, doctrinal, political, social, artistic, scientific, and juridical legacy of 15 centuries was reduced with the stroke of a pen into a few, totally out-of-context excerpts. So-called experts on Islam contrived to distort the Islamic heritage, turning it into crass stereotypes in order to associate the Islamic faith with innate belligerency. References in the Quran to the internecine tribal fighting in the Arabian Peninsula 15 centuries ago – a normal happening in the rise of every human movement in history – were transmuted and transplanted as a call to arms against the West. But in reality it was a war against recalcitrant tribes, led by none other than the Prophet's own Quraysh tribe.

Interventions were discreetly made with Muslim governments, urging them to change certain texts in the Quran and to delete all references to such terms as the misunderstood word, *Jihad* (struggle), even though its most important connotation and function in the Islamic faith is the struggle against one's greed, selfishness and evil doings in general.

The Prophet, after the victory over the Muslims' adversaries, addressed his supporters, saying: 'You have emerged from the smaller *Jihad* [meaning warfare] into the larger *Jihad* [the struggle over one's self].'

The recrudescence of attitudes prevalent during the relatively limited wars of the Middle Ages, which carried the misnomer of 'Crusades', after a break of 800 years augurs badly for the peace, tranquillity and prosperity of the globalised world of the 21st century.

The 'we' and 'they' attitudes are admittedly embedded aspects of human existence. There are always different forms of the same thing, and the differences sometimes encounter each other head on. But such interaction should be in the pursuit of a more elevated and worthier existence, which does not seem to be the case in the current confrontational stance between the Islamic world and the West.

Anyone surveying the landscape of the aforementioned relationships would instantly see at least half a dozen Arab and Islamic countries being pulverised, or targeted for pulverisation, on the basis of a plethora of excuses and justifications, lacking mostly in substantive contents. One sees conflicts in Afghanistan, Iraq, Palestine, Sudan, and Somalia, and with no end in sight. Pakistan could soon be added to the list. No wonder the masses of the sprawling Muslim world are convinced that under the slogan of combating terror, we are being torn asunder by a new Crusade, regardless of any assertions to the contrary.

It is not ideology that needs to be reconciled, nor is it a fundamental theological dichotomy that afflicts such relationships. The issue is more mundane, one of conflicts that have bedevilled such relationships over the past 100 years. The 9/11 episode, horrendous, incredible, and I might add, mysterious as it was may have legitimised – indeed energised – the latent and blind forces of hostility towards the Islamic world, oblivious to all other friendly dimensions, relationships and interactions that exist in all fields of life.

It would be futile to consider what might have been wiser counsel in response to 9/11. An aggressed superpower, on its own turf, and challenged to the core by that aggression, would naturally be expected to unleash gargantuan forces against the perpetrators of the crime and their accessories. But the question that challenges the mind, and is far-reaching in its consequences upon the present and the future, is what the implications will be for the choice of the wrong target for rightful retribution.

It is inconceivable that a simple peasant, in the dreary mountains of Afghanistan or the shoddy slums of Iraq could have contrived and executed one of the most sophisticated urban crimes of modern times. And yet, seven years after 9/11, those helpless people are being bombarded by 'smart', 2,000 pound missiles that kill and wound innocent civilians, with the assailants calling such murder 'collateral damage'.

The destructive war against Iraq, a sovereign independent state, under manifestly false pretences can in no way be related to 9/11, under any criterion. And yet, it is a country which has been dismembered, impoverished, and virtually destroyed, as a society and a state.

The human cost is highlighted by more than 1 million people killed, and 4-5 million others forced to become refugees. Is this a democracy that people, any people, would aspire to? And over and above the overall carnage has been the sowing of the seeds of hatred and alienation amongst members of a hitherto cohesive society, notwithstanding its brutal regime, masquerading under devious sectarian divisions and institutionalised in the constitution.

Throughout the many years of my ambassadorial career, it never even occurred to me to ask any of my Iraqi counterparts about his sectarian affiliation, and yet, in the post-invasion period, it has become the basis of apportionment across the entire spectrum of government and non-governmental activities, corrosively undermining society's social solidarity and cohesion. The United States suffered and overcame, albeit painfully, the ravages of its own civil war in the mid-19th century. It should, therefore, be the last country to foment one in Iraq and elsewhere.

A far more effective way of the United States responding to the 9/11 atrocities, and one that would have been less costly and more in tune with international justice, would have been a joint intelligence and security operation. In the manner of the anti-mafia campaign in Italy, this operation could have apprehended and punished those implicated with the 14 alleged perpetrators of the crime and their associates.

These were young educated urban people who, we are told, hatched their conspiracy in the comfort and quiet of an apartment in Germany, and not in some cave in the wilds of Afghanistan. Usama bin Laden aside, the remnants of the Jihadis in Afghanistan had been trained and armed by the United States to fight the Soviet army there in the 1980s, which they did with momentous success. But it was not those Jihadis, frequently shown in the media exercising and doing military training, who conspired, or could have conspired to bring about the hellfire of 9/11. Even so, many of the fighters from Afghanistan have landed up in the unspeakable Guantanamo Bay concentration camp.

The entire thrust of the United States' retribution was out of focus, understandably emotional, but decidedly unwise. And it appears to be leading nowhere. We have witnessed seven years of colossal and ineffectual effort, to capture, at best, a phantom, at a cost which has brought the United States and much of the world along with it to the brink of economic disaster, akin to the Great Depression of 1929.

As if this were not enough, the United States seems to be slipping gradually, into the quicksands of adjacent Pakistan, a proud Muslim country of 160 million people, in its contrived war against the phantom of Islamist terrorism, and in the process is destabilising a nuclear-armed country and egging it on to a disastrous civil conflict. After all, the people inhabiting the border areas of Pakistan and Afghanistan are bound together by the same racial and religious affinities, and do not support fighting an internecine conflict which they regard as unjust not their own war.

The open-ended campaign against the Islamic world is ideologically misguided and strategically misconstrued. It is also endless, for it has no achievable goal. Dressing it up with the intellectual aura of a clash of civilisations adds nothing to its credibility. It amounts to shadow boxing and is decidedly counter-productive.

I have taken part in a number of interfaith conferences and seminars, in various parts of the world over recent years, and have always come to the same conclusion: that I am preaching to the converted. The rabbi, the bishop and the Sheikh are deeply steeped in the same Abrahamic tradition, and at least as far as the Muslims are concerned, they recognise, revere and feel a profound sense of affinity to the two other religions which pre-dated their own as *Ahl al-Kitab* (people of the book, namely the scriptures). Their task is a joint one of keeping their respective adherents within the faith, and of upholding the validity and relevance of their common faith in an age of astounding scientific discoveries, boundless intellectual doubt, scepticism, and sheer indifference.

Parochial partisan zealotry should be out of place, because it is anchored to false pretences and is greatly damaging to world harmony. The advocates of war against the Islamic world should look elsewhere for an adversary, if that was their aim, on the basis of a real, rather than a misconceived conflict of ideology or interest, as a *raison d'être*. The present orientation of this endless, unrealisable war against so-called Islamist terror is misguided, but could be a self-fulfilling prophesy, if sustained.

Moreover, and equally damaging is the fact that Islamophobia has ricocheted to inflict grievous harm upon Western societies themselves, in the form of a substantial curtailment of civil liberties.

As the reader will know by now, I lived in America for many years and some of the most precious of its attributes to me were its freedom, openness and libertarianism. How much those cherished goals have been compromised is difficult to gauge, but landing at any airport in the United States, or Europe for that matter, instantly reveals signs of this. The millions of cameras watching one creates the atmosphere of George Orwell's dreaded *1984*.

Is this confrontational trend irreversible? It most certainly is reversible, provided the contentious issues are courageously and objectively resolved, on the basis of fairness, legitimacy and mutual respect. As a student at the AUB in the early 1940s, among people at large in the Arab world the

United States was by far the most popular country on the globe – the 1919 League of Nations' King-Crane Commission plebiscite of the people of Syria, confirmed this fact – thanks to a handful of men and women of goodwill.

The Bliss, Dodge and other missionary families came to the Near East to serve and educate, not to extirpate and subjugate. They did not need a Sixth Fleet to protect them or their country's interests. Today, the embassies of the United States in much of the world sit as isolated redoubts and impenetrable citadels, remote from the peoples to whose countries they are accredited.

The pioneering Americans advocated the principles of freedom, democracy and self-determination, and their advocacy was a source of genuine inspiration to generations of the rising leaderships of the Arab world, because they were genuine and friendly voices. Similar calls by US leaders of late, by contrast, have sounded hollow and insincere.

As I stated earlier in the chapter, Western and Arab-Islamic civilisations are legatees of the same cultural and spiritual roots. I have lived and worked among great men and women in both civilisations. Any cleavages are the result of different stages of development which are bound, over time, to coalesce. In two decades, the West, along with the rest of the world, will be dealing with an Arab world of 0.5 billion people. This exponential demographic growth will be accompanied by far-reaching qualitative human transformations, representing a great leap into the advanced world.

This will enable the Arabs to integrate more effectively with the mainstream of universal civilisation, of which they constitute an integral part. At this point, the much vaunted clash of East and West will have become a foregone memory.

Index

A

Aal al-Bait Institute 407
Abdul Hadi
  Awni 131, 390
  Hisham 316
  Majid 390
Abdul Jabbar, Ahmad 302
Abdul Majid, Ismat 263-4, 365
Abdul Wahab, Muhammad 306, 392
Abu Dayyeh, Ibrahim 64
Abu Dis 336, 392
Abu Gharbieh, Bahjat 64-5
Abu Ghosh 11, 317
Abu Quir 47
Abul-Hajj, Amal 398
Ahli Club 54, 420
Al-Amiri, Muhammad Adeeb 57, 72, 208
Al-Asad, Nasser Eddine 407
Al-Difa 55, 169
Al-Husseini
  Abdul Qader 64
  Adnan 118
  Amin, Captain 208
  Haj Amin 136, 436
  Hind 203
  Ishaq Musa 80
  Munif 136
  Musa 384
  Musa Kazem Pasha 44, 425
Al-Khawli, Hassan Sabri 253, 269
Al-Khazraji, Bani Ghanim tribe 395-8
Al Nahayan, Sheikh Zayed bin Sultan, Ruler of Abu Dhabi and President of the UAE 205, 246, 302
Al-Rifai
  Abdul Munim 196, 207, 213, 245, 311-2, 365, 438
  Samir 147, 280, 377
  Zeid 259-60, 269-70, 281, 377
Al-Sabah
  Sabah Ahmad 263, 311
  Sabah Salem 277
Al-Salem, Abdullah 70, 76
Al-Shafii, al-Khazraji 398-9
Al-Shati refugee camp 212
Al-Yamani, Zaki 302
Albright, Madeleine 244
Algeria 164, 171, 191, 285, 308, 311-2, 365
Algiers 174, 310, 312
Allenby Bridge 104, 209
Allenby, Edmund 285, 426-7
Amer, Abdul Hakim 194, 247
American Academy of Learned Societies 86
American Colony Hotel 61-2, 103, 143, 203, 368, 389
American Consulate in East Jerusalem 317
American Protestant College in Beirut 410
American University of Beirut, see AUB
American University of Cairo 369
Anabtawi, Adnan 304
Antonius, George 133
Antonius, Katy 133, 412
Aqsa 8, 13, 24, 42-3, 197, 199-200, 334, 398, 404, 407, 424
Arab Bank 385
Arab Club 54, 156, 420, 422
Arab College 10, 47, 335, 414, 420
Arab Defence Council 144
Arab Gulf 92, 189, 285
Arab Higher Committee 69, 131, 136, 412, 421
Arab League 94, 134, 149-50, 157, 224, 263, 312, 365
Arab Revolt 92
Armistice Agreement 73, 102, 194, 203, 335, 422
Artas 392
As-Samu, village of 144, 192-3
Assad, Farid 73
Attallah, Anton 151-2, 206, 390, 412
Attallah, Munir 412
Ataturk 284, 286-7, 289
AUB (American University of Beirut)

451

10, 51, 84, 87, 90, 93-4, 206, 302, 315, 363, 410-11, 413-14, 433, 437-8, 448
Augusta Victoria Hospital 108, 413
Austin, Warren 60

B

Babylonians 27, 43
Badran, Mudhar 269, 321, 356
Baghdad Pact 129, 181
Bandung 170-1
Bartlett, William 401
Barudi, Jamil 364
Beer Sheba 111, 148
Beit Jala 159, 392
Beit Safafa 392
Beit Sahour 159, 392
Ben-Gurion, David 62, 74, 131, 309
Benvenisti, Meron 143
Bernadotte, Folke 240-2
Bhutto, Zulfiqar Ali 170
Bir Zeit University 335
Bouteflika, Abdul Aziz 164, 311, 365
Bowen 432
Brewster, Charles 103
British Consulate in Jerusalem 242
Broadcasting Station 58, 69-72, 81
Bulos, Naseeb 242
Bunch, Ralph 73
Buraq-Wailing Wall 424
Burns
    Findley 197
    General Edseem 103
    General Williams 422
Bush, George Sr 351, 412
Bushnaq, Abdul Rahman 80

C

Camp David Accords 334
Canaanites 26-7, 405, 408, 431
Caradon, Lord 213-14
Cardinal Cassarolli 296-7
Carnegie Endowment for International Peace 137
Carter, President 116, 345-7
Chase Manhattan Bank 155, 352, 369
Chief Justice Sir William Fitzgerald 34, 390-2
Chou En-lai 170-1
Churchill, Winston 284, 376

Clinton, President 116
Cohen, Amnon 30, 105, 285
Columbia University 369
Common Arab Defence Treaty 196
Copts 199
Cornell University Press 85, 249
Count Bernadotte 241-2
Couve de Murville, Maurice 171

D

Dajani
    Ali 121
    Hassan Sidki 131
    Hussam 84
    Najmuddine 124, 127
    Salwa 292
    Subhi 292
Dajani Club 421
Dajanis 406
Damascus Gate 10, 199, 405, 413, 415, 422
Danziger Jewish Hospital 414
Daoud
    Brigadier Muhammad 270, 273-5
    Captain Muhammad 102
De Gaulle, Charles 172-3, 293
Deeb
    Gabi 412
    Raymon 412
Deir Yassin 65, 211, 359, 392
Development Board, Jordan 70, 119, 123-5, 127, 149, 153, 173
Dirlam, Joel 125
Dodge, Bayard 87
Dover College 315
Downing Street 290
Droble, Matityahu 338
Duzdar family 393

E

Eban, Aba 363
Eddine, Nasser 407
Eden Cinema 400
Eisenhower, President Dwight D 149, 164
Eisenhower Doctrine 119
Eisenhower Foundation 211
Elysée Palace 290
Erhard, Chancellor Ludwig 128
Eshkol settlement 249

F

F-4 American jet 122, 176
Faisal, King of Saudi Arabia 131, 140, 274, 302
Falkland Islands 353-6
Farouk, King 151, 268
Farraj, Fuad 411
Fatah 141-2, 267
Fatimids 43, 405
Fawzi, Mahmoud 365
Fawzi, Muhammad 194 251
Finn, James 411
Finney, Tom 53
Firestone Library 86
Food and Agricultural Organization (FAO) 304
Ford Foundation 125
Forestall, James 168, 256
Fourth Geneva Convention 106, 206, 342, 428
French Frères School 410
French Hospital 425
Friends College in Ramallah 82

G

Gandhi, Mahatma 81
Gemayel, Amine 358
German Colony 389
German Priest Felix Fabri 410
German Schmidt's School 422
German Schneller Technical School 410
Ghosheh, Subhi 384
Ghouri, Emil 412
Golan Heights 191, 209, 213
    Occupied 262
Gore, Albert, Sr 109
Gouraud, Henri 427
Government House, Jerusalem 118, 335, 439
Grand Mufti of Jerusalem 422, 436
Gromyko, Andrei 178, 328

H

Habib, Phillip 359
Hadawi, Sami 429
Haganah 55, 63
Hague Convention 206
Haifa 46, 131, 136, 307, 337, 401, 421
Hanania
    Anastass 412
    Daoud 412
Hashem, Ibrahim 118
Hashem, Ihsan 72
Hassan, Crown Prince 175-7, 328, 339, 348, 352, 368
Hebrew University on Mount Scopus 60, 200, 334
Heller, Walter 125
Herod's Gate, Jerusalem 7, 32, 36, 64, 75, 359, 401, 414, 420
Higher Executive Committee 44
Higher Islamic Council 421
Hilliard, John 125
Hitti, Dr Phillip 87, 100
Hoffman, Paul 126
Holy Sepulchre 9, 17, 23, 143, 197, 199, 298, 397, 402, 404, 415, 423, 426-7
House of Lords 375
House of Representatives 126
Hussein, King of Jordan 104, 113, 116, 118, 120, 126-7, 134, 136, 140-2, 144-5, 149, 151, 153, 167, 170, 172-3, 175, 177, 181-4, 208-9, 212, 240, 243, 249, 251-4, 260, 268, 274, 276, 281, 296, 303, 313, 321, 352-3, 356-7, 362, 372, 378, 412, 416
Hussein bin Nasser, Sherif 142, 173, 176

I

IBHI (Independent Bureau for Humanitarian Issues) 350
Idriss, King of Libya 252-4
Ijha, Najib 157-8
Imam Yahya 70
Inter-Parliamentary Union, *see* IPU
International Bank for Reconstruction and Development 177
International Court of Justice 428
International Labour Organization (ILO) 331
IPU (Inter-Parliamentary Union) 332, 372-5
Irgun Zvai Leumi 54
Israeli Knesset 333
Issa, Judge Sharaf al-Din 395

J

Jaffa Gate 33, 199, 393, 405, 417, 423
Jaffa Road 33, 58, 359, 391, 405

Jamali, Fadel 365
Jarring, Gunnar 239-40, 242, 245
Jefferson University 369
Jewish Agency 55, 63, 338, 422
John, King 375
Johnston, Eric 148-9
Jordan-Israeli Mixed Armistice Commission 322
Jordanian House of Representatives 136
Jose, Colonel Alex 56
Jumaa, Saad 195-6

K

Karameh 107
Kardous, Abdullah 111
Kattan, Henry 390
Kennedy, John F 137, 168
Khan, Sir Zafrullah 164
Khouri, Iskandar 80
Khouri, Sami 412
Kimche, John 55
King Abdullah I of Jordan 71, 80, 107, 130, 298
King Abdullah II of Jordan 378
King David Hotel 13-14, 54, 62, 318, 391
King Hussein Bridge *see* Allenby Bridge
Kirkpatrick, Jeanne 361-2
Kissinger, Henry 256, 259-60, 265-6

L

Labouisse, Mr Henry R. 108-9
Lash, Brigadier Norman 241
League of Nations 7, 32, 50, 90, 330-1, 449
Leonard, Jim 340, 344-5
Levy and Tubin, Professors 89
Lewis, Bernard 285
Lincoln, Abraham 89

M

Macomber, William 169
Macy, Ward 125
Magnes, Judah 60
Majali, Dr Abdul Salam 278
Malek, Charles 363
Mandela, Nelson 81
Mansour, Khaled 264
Maqsoud, Clovis 365

Marshal Plan 126
Marshall, George 168
Mayo, Roland 412
McDougall, William 41, 276
Mea Shearim 19, 59, 393
Meir, Golda 26, 62
Menderes, Adnan 288
Middle East Peace Conference 333
Montefiore, Sir Moses 393-4
Montgomery, Field Marshall 46
Muhtadi, Fayez 58
Murad, Abdul Rahman 136
Musa, Amr 365

N

Nabi Daoud 406
Nabulsi, Suleiman 177, 207
Najah College 46
Najjar, Abdul Qader 93
nakba 77, 413
Naqrashi, Mahmoud 131
Nashashibi
  Azmi 72, 170
  Fattouma (Fatima) 8
  Isaaf 80
  Jawdat 316, 433
Nasser, Gamal Abdul 95, 120, 130, 137, 139, 142, 145, 148, 170, 173, 176, 194, 196, 200, 246-52, 254-6, 268-9, 274-5, 277, 279, 407, 435
National Defence College 382
Negev 111, 148, 168
Nehru 170, 181-2
Nevi Yacoub 56-7, 118
Nimeiri, President Jaafar of Sudan 271, 276, 279
Nixon, Richard 254, 256, 264
Non-Aligned Movement 181, 264
Northrop, Linda S. 398-9
Noufal, Sayyid 312
Nusseibeh
  Ahmad 104, 107, 198, 24, 433
  Anwar 8, 51, 63-6, 82-3, 104-5, 143, 203, 205, 261, 359, 390
    Bani Ghanim metamorphosis 399
    Farm in Jordan Valley 121, 127, 316-17, 319, 322, 385-6, 429
  Haitham 108, 262, 369
  Hala 104, 205, 415
  Hassan 8, 66
  Hisham 104, 106, 115, 143, 424, 433

Sharaf, Laila 323, 368
Sharaf, Sami 272
Sharon, Ariel 264
Sheikh Jarrah 7, 14, 36, 111, 133, 249, 400, 417, 423
Sherif Hussein of Mecca 92
Shihabi, Samir 289
Shihabi, Taher 241
Shihadeh, Aziz 73
Shoman, Abdul Majid 385
Shupra 185
Snavely, William 125
Soltau, Roger 90
Sprout, Professor Harold 89
Stephenson, Adlai 164
Stern Gang 53, 240
Straits of Tiran 192-5, 198
Stuart Mill, John 80, 441
Suez Canal 148, 260, 262, 365
Suez Canal War 117, 119
Sunna, Sami 304

T

Taha, Sami 131
Tal, Wasfi 126, 130, 134-5, 140, 144, 146, 153, 195-6, 278, 387
Talhouni, Bahjat 210
Tamari, Salim 409
Tannous, George 411
Tannous, Izzat 136, 411
Tarawneh, Ahmad 274
Tarout, Raphael 159
Taylor, Philip 125
Telpioth 393
Terra Sancta School 410
Thatcher, Margaret 356-7, 375
Thomas, Victor S. 99
Touqan, Baha'uddin 351-2
Toynbee, Arnold J 27, 294, 431
Tuqan, Ahmad 208-9, 243-4
Tuweini, Ghassan 357

U

UNEF (United Nations Emergency Force) 193-4
UNESCO (United Nations Educational, Scientific and Cultural Organisation) 109-10
Unified Arab Command 191-3
United Arab Emirates 205, 246, 302

United Arab Republic 117, 119, 139, 147
United Nation Relief and Works Agency, see UNRWA
United Nations' King-Crane Commission 449
University of Jerusalem in Abu Dis 336
UNRWA (United Nation Relief and Works Agency) 67-8, 108-12, 322
UNSCOP (United Nations Special Commission on Palestine) 59
UNTSO (United Nations Truce Supervision Organization) 103, 271, 335, 422
Uthman, Amin 131

V

Vance, Cyrus 345
Victoria College 10, 47, 92, 245-6, 420, 435

W

Wahbeh, Hafiz 289
Wailing Wall 13, 40-1, 407, 424-5
Walker, Hugh 125
Wallace, Dean 89
Weizman, Ezer 105
Wissam al-Jumhurriya, Egyptian medal 278

Y

YMCA 13-4, 21, 53-4, 62, 291, 412-3, 421
Young, Andrew 340

Z

Zaben, Akkash 184-5
Zeineddin, Farid 363
Ziyadeh, Farhat 100, 165
Zuaiter, Akram 179, 208, 314

Khaled 6, 280, 315, 369
Laila 87, 101, 108, 205, 280, 321, 369
Lina 112, 280, 315, 369
Mahmoud 14, 47, 104, 420, 424, 433
Muhammad 129, 143, 314, 405, 433
Qadar Taher (Masri) 82, 86, 108, 201, 244, 254, 277, 305
Sama 104, 204, 415
Wajeeh 397
Zaki 205, 321, 369
Zaki Abdul Rahim 7-8, 10, 32-3, 44, 47, 61-2, 69, 71, 160, 210, 284, 316, 414, 417, 420, 424-5, 434, 436
Ziba 104

O

October War 259, 302, 310
Olmert, Ehud 408
Organization of African Unity 351
Oslo Agreement 243
Oval Office 151, 206

P

Pachachi, Adnan 117, 208
Palestine Broadcasting Service 10, 52, 57, 59, 241
Palestine Electric Company 61
Palestine Executive Committee 425
Palestine Hotel 151
Palestine Information Office 80
Palestine Liberation Organisation 46, 73
Palestine National Council 141
Palestinian Red Crescent Society 211
Papal See 211
Parsons, Sir Anthony 353, 355-6
Partial Test Ban Treaty 176, 178, 180
Patriarch Sophronius 402
Paul VI, Pope 296
Peres, Shimon 62
Perse School in Cambridge 10, 51
Philistines 27-9
PLO Chairman Ahmad al-Shuqairi 75, 136, 140-1, 146, 153, 171, 200, 363
PLO Chairman Yasser Arafat 141, 271
Plum, Maxwell 366
Pompidou, Georges 173
Princeton University 84, 86-7, 89, 91, 99-100, 165, 197, 366, 369, 383, 386
Prophet Muhammad 13, 93, 380, 433

Q

Qadhafi, Colonel Mu'ammar 252
Qattan, Henry 413
Qattan, Khalil 159
Qawasmeh, Fahd 343
Quaker School 82
Queen Elizabeth 375

R

Ramadhan 11, 33, 434
Ramallah 22, 56-8, 67, 69, 75, 82, 165, 205, 241, 335, 416
Ramleh 69-70, 103, 416
Ras al-Tin Palace 268-9
Rashidiyya School 420
Rawdha College 10, 12, 21, 46, 92, 415, 421, 424, 433-5
Reagan Plan 361-2
Reed, Ralph 92
Riyadh, General Abdul Munim 145
Riyadh, Mahmoud 150, 244, 365
Rock, Edmond 295-6
Rockefeller, David 155, 352
Rogers, William 254
Rogers Plan 242, 254-8, 269
Royal Fiscal Commission 125
Rumolo, General Carlos P. 325
Rusk, Dean 163, 166-9
Russian Compound 59, 390, 405
Rutenberg, Pinchas 61

S

Sabra and Shatila refugee camps 359
Sadat, Anwar 130, 277
Said, Edward 411
Sakakini, Khalil 80, 412
Salah, Abdul Latif 390
Salah, Abdullah 174-6, 208, 259
Salah, Yahya 304
Salahiya Khanaqah for Sufis 9, 395-6, 402
Sauma, Edward 304
Sayegh, Fayez 363-4
Scranton, Governor William 256-7
Shafii, Hussein 145
Shahbandar, Dr Abdul Rahman 131
Shalev, General Aryeh 105
Sharaf, Abdul Hamid 34, 170, 258-9, 261-2, 310, 321-2